# Conversations with Vladimir Nabokov

Literary Conversations Series
*Monika Gehlawat*
*General Editor*

# Conversations
# with Vladimir Nabokov

Edited by Robert Golla

University Press of Mississippi   *Jackson*

www.upress.state.ms.us

The University Press of Mississippi is a member
of the Association of American University Presses.

First printing 2017

∞

Library of Congress Cataloging-in-Publication Data

Names: Nabokov, Vladimir Vladimirovich, 1899–1977. | Golla, Robert, editor.
Title: Conversations with Vladimir Nabokov / edited by Robert Golla.
Description: Jackson : University Press of Mississippi, 2017. | Series:
     Literary conversations series | Includes index.
Identifiers: LCCN 2016045902 (print) | LCCN 2017004767 (ebook) | ISBN
     9781496810953 (hardback) | ISBN 9781496810960 (epub single) | ISBN
     9781496810977 (epub institutional) | ISBN 9781496810984 ( pdf single) |
     ISBN 9781496810991 (pdf institutional)
Subjects: LCSH: Nabokov, Vladimir Vladimirovich, 1899–1977—Interviews. |
     Authors, American—20th century—Interviews. | Authors, Russian—20th
     century—Interviews. | BISAC: BIOGRAPHY & AUTOBIOGRAPHY / Literary. |
     LITERARY CRITICISM / American / General. | LITERARY CRITICISM / Russian &
     Former Soviet Union.
Classification: LCC PG3476.N3 Z46 2017 (print) | LCC PG3476.N3 (ebook) | DDC
     813/.54 [B]—dc23
LC record available at https://lccn.loc.gov/2016045902

British Library Cataloging-in-Publication Data available

# Books by Vladimir Nabokov

*Stikhi* [*Poems*]. St. Petersburg: self-published, 1916.

*Al'manakh: Dva puti* [*Almanac: Two Paths*]. With Andrei Balashov. St. Petersburg: self-published, 1918.

*Colas Breugnon.* (VN, Trans.) Berlin: Slovo, 1922.

*Grozd'* [*The Cluster*]. Berlin: Gamaiun, 1922.

*Gornii put'* [*The Empyrean Path*]. Berlin: Grani, 1923.

*Alice in Wonderland.* (VN, Trans) Berlin: Gamaiun, 1923.

*Mashen'ka* [*Mary*]. Berlin: Slovo, 1926.

*Korol' dama valet* [*King, Queen, Knave*]. Berlin: Slovo, 1928.

*Vozvrashchenie Chorba* [*The Return of Chorb*]. Berlin: Slovo, 1929.

*Zashchita Luzhina* [*The Luzhin Defense*]. Berlin: Slovo, 1930.

*Podvig* [*Glory*]. Sovremennye zapiski: Paris, 1932.

*Kamera obskura* [*Camera Obscura*]. Sovremennye zapiski & Parabola: Paris, 1933.

*Otchaianie* [*Despair*]. Berlin: Petropolis, 1936.

*Laughter in the Dark.* Indianapolis: Bobbs-Merrill, 1938.

*Sogliadatai* [*The Eye*]. Berlin: Russkie zapiski, 1938.

*Priglashenie na kazn* [*Invitation to a Beheading*]. Paris: Dom Knigi, 1938.

*The Real Life of Sebastian Knight.* New York: New Directions, 1941.

*Nikolai Gogol.* New York: New Directions, 1944.

*Three Russian Poets: Selections from Pushkin, Lermontov and Tyutchev.* (VN, Trans.) New York: New Directions, 1945.

*Bend Sinister.* New York: Henry Holt, 1947.

*Nine Stories.* New York: New Directions, 1947.

*Conclusive Evidence.* New York: Harper & Brothers, 1951.

*Dar* [*The Gift*]. New York: Chekhov Publishing House, 1952.

*Stikhotvoreniia:1929–1951* [*Poems: 1929–1951*]. Paris: Rifma, 1952.

*Lolita.* Paris: The Olympia Press, 1955.

*Vesna v Fial'te* [*Spring in Fialta*]. New York: Chekhov Publishing House, 1956.

*Pnin.* Garden City, NY: Doubleday, 1957.

*A Hero of Our Time.* (VN and Dmitri Nabokov, Trans.) Garden City, NY: Doubleday, 1958.

*Nabokov's Dozen.* Garden City, NY: Doubleday, 1958.

*Poems.* Garden City, NY: Doubleday, 1959.

*The Song of Igor's Campaign.* (VN, Trans.) New York: Vintage, 1960.

*Pale Fire.* New York: G.P. Putnam's Sons, 1962.

*Notes on Prosody.* New York: Bollingen Foundation, 1963.

*Eugene Onegin.* (VN, Trans.) New York: Bollingen Foundation, 1964.

*The Waltz Invention.* New York. Phaedra, 1966.

*Nabokov's Quartet*. New York: Phaedra, 1966.

*Speak, Memory*. New York: G.P. Putnam's Sons, 1967.

*Nabokov's Congeries*. New York: The Viking Press, 1968.

*Ada or Ardor: A Family Chronicle*. New York: McGraw-Hill, 1969.

*Poems and Problems*. New York: McGraw-Hill, 1971.

*Transparent Things*. New York: McGraw-Hill, 1972.

*A Russian Beauty and Other Stories*. New York: McGraw-Hill, 1973.

*Strong Opinions*. New York: McGraw-Hill, 1973.

*Lolita: A Screenplay*. New York: McGraw-Hill, 1974.

*Look at the Harlequins!*. New York: McGraw-Hill, 1974.

*Tyrants Destroyed and Other Stories*. New York: McGraw-Hill, 1975.

*Details of a Sunset and Other Stories*. New York: McGraw-Hill, 1976.

*The Nabokov-Wilson Letters: Correspondence Between Vladimir Nabokov and Edmund Wilson 1940–1971*. New York: Harper & Row, 1979.

*Stikhi* [*Poems*]. Ann Arbor: Ardis, 1979.

*Lectures on Literature*. New York: Harcourt Brace Jovanovich / Bruccoli Clark, 1980.

*Lectures on Ulysses*. Bloomfield Hills, MI: Bruccoli Clark, 1980.

*Lectures on Russian Literature*. New York: Harcourt Brace Jovanovich / Bruccoli Clark, 1981.

*Lectures on Don Quixote*. New York: Harcourt Brace Jovanovich / Bruccoli Clark, 1983.

*The Man from the USSR and Other Plays*. New York: Harcourt Brace Jovanovich / Bruccoli Clark, 1984.

*Perepiska s sestroy* [*Letters to His Sister*]. Ann Arbor: Ardis, 1985.

*The Enchanter*. New York: G.P Putnam's Sons, 1986.

*Carrousel*. Aartswoud, Netherlands: Spectatorpers, 1987.

*Vladimir Nabokov: Selected Letters: 1940–1977*. New York: Harcourt Brace Jovanovich / Bruccoli Clark Layman, 1989.

*Krug* [*The Circle*]. Leningrad: Khudozhestvennaia Literatura, 1990.

*P'esy* [*Plays*]. Moscow, Iskusstvo, 1990.

*The Stories of Vladimir Nabokov*. New York: Alfred A. Knopf, 1995.

*Nabokov's Butterflies: Unpublished and Uncollected Writings*. Boston: Beacon Press, 2000.

*Dear Bunny, Dear Volodya: The Nabokov-Wilson Letters, 1940–1971*. Berkeley: University of California Press, 2001.

*Verses and Versions: Three Centuries of Russian Poetry Selected and Translated by Vladimir Nabokov*. New York: Harcourt, 2008.

*The Original of Laura*. New York: Alfred A. Knopf, 2009.

*Selected Poems*. New York: Alfred A. Knopf, 2012.

*The Tragedy of Mister Morn*. London: Penguin Books Ltd, 2012.

*Letters to Véra*. London: Penguin Books Ltd, 2014.

# Contents

Introduction   x

Chronology   xiv

The Author of *Lolita*—an Unhurried View   3
   *Martha MacGregor / 1958*

Author of *Lolita* Airs Views on Censorship, Role of Artist   8
   *Gladys Kessler / 1958*

Vladimir Nabokov and Lionel Trilling Discuss *Lolita*   10
   *Pierre Berton / 1958*

What Hath *Lolita* Wrought?   16
   *Edward E. Van Dyne / 1958*

My Child *Lolita*   18
   *Alan Nordstrom / 1959*

An Absence of Wood Nymphs   21
   *Robert H. Boyle / 1959*

The Author of *Lolita*   27
   *Neil Hickey / 1959*

Nabokov   30
   *John Coleman / 1959*

Vladimir Nabokov Discusses *Lolita*   34
   *Kerry Ellard / 1959*

After *Lolita*: A Conversation with Vladimir Nabokov—with Digressions 41
  *John G. Hayman / 1959*

The Man Who Scandalized the World 47
  *Helen Lawrenson / 1960*

V. Nabokov Unresting 59
  *Phyllis Meras / 1962*

Vladimir Nabokov on his Life and Work 62
  *Peter Duval Smith / 1962*

Playboy Interview: Vladimir Nabokov 70
  *Alvin Toffler / 1964*

On the Banks of Lake Léman: Mr. Nabokov Reflects on *Lolita* and *Onegin* 90
  *Douglas M. Davis / 1964*

USA: The Novel—Vladimir Nabokov 94
  *Robert Hughes / 1965*

Nabokov 100
  *Penelope Gilliatt / 1966*

The Artist in Pursuit of Butterflies 110
  *Herbert Gold / 1967*

An Interview with Vladimir Nabokov 120
  *Alfred Appel Jr. / 1967*

Vladimir Nabokov: The Art of Fiction XL 143
  *Herbert Gold / 1967*

"To be Kind, to be Proud, to be Fearless"—Vladimir Nabokov in Conversation with James Mossman 155
  *James Mossman / 1969*

Nabokov: A Portrait   161
  *Alfred Appel Jr. / 1971*

Understanding Vladimir Nabokov—A Red Autumn Leaf is a Red Autumn
Leaf, Not a Deflowered Nymphet   180
  *Alan Levy / 1971*

An Interview with Vladimir Nabokov   195
  *Mati Laansoo / 1973*

Checking in with Vladimir Nabokov   200
  *Gerald Clarke / 1975*

Vladimir Nabokov on the Loose   212
  *Hugh A. Mulligan / 1977*

A Blush of Color—Nabokov in Montreux   220
  *Robert Robinson / 1977*

VN—RIP   225
  *William F. Buckley Jr. / 1977*

Index   229

# Introduction

"To have another language," Charlemagne said, "is to possess a second soul." When contemplating the life and work of Vladimir Nabokov, who was trilingual from childhood, the quotation becomes not only poetic but suddenly very plausible. Nabokov was a Russian-American polymath. He was a translator, poet, entomologist, professor of literature, composer of chess problems, deviser of crossword puzzles, and acclaimed by critics throughout the world as one of the twentieth century's master prose writers. In a career that spanned over six decades, he developed the luminous and enigmatic style that advanced the boundaries of modern literature more than any author since James Joyce. He produced dozens of iconic works, including *Invitation to a Beheading*, *The Gift*, *Bend Sinister*, *Pnin*, *Lolita*, *Pale Fire*, and *Ada*. Though upon debut many regarded these novels as scandalous or pornographic, they have since become monuments in the Western canon.

Despite the international readership that Nabokov attracted after the publication of *Lolita* in 1955, and which he sustained with groundbreaking works in the two decades that followed, he did not write for social utility or literary immortality. As he explained to the BBC's Peter Duval Smith in 1962, he wrote "for the sake of the pleasure, for the sake of the difficulty. I have no social purpose, no moral message; I've no general ideas to exploit but I like composing riddles and I like finding elegant solutions to those riddles that I have composed myself." During an interview in 1965 with Robert Hughes for National Educational Television, unaired and published here for the first time, Nabokov encapsulated his joy in writing as the "thrill of diabolical pleasure in discovering that you have somehow cheated creation by creating something yourself."

The scores of journalists who made the pilgrimage to interview Nabokov found that the extraordinarily high standard of quality he demanded of his own writing extended to any journalistic venture in which he consented to participate. He was uniquely conscious of his public image and granted interviews, with very few exceptions, on the condition that they not be extemporaneous. When asked by Robert Robinson why he had taken this approach, he answered, "The tape of my unprepared speech differs from my written prose as much as the worm differs from the perfect insect—or, as I once put it, I think like a genius, I write like a distinguished author, and I speak like a child." To that end, Nabokov required interviewers to mail him a list of their questions. He would write out his answers, having altered or deleted any question that did not meet with his approval. His beloved wife Véra then typed the document in its entirety and scheduled a date when the journalist could collect the "interview" and meet with Nabokov. These meetings tended to be brief encounters, generally over drinks or dinner, where the journalist could ask for clarification or amplification of the written responses. He allowed them because they provided the semblance of spontaneity and gave color to the interview. Any follow-up enquiries or requests for modifications were conducted via mail. This elaborate ritual was how Nabokov cultivated his public image and protected his literary reputation for more than half a century.

The twenty-eight interviews in this volume span nineteen years, from the American publication of *Lolita* in 1958 to Nabokov's death in Switzerland in 1977. They have been carefully selected to represent the artistic high points in his life and were drawn from numerous print and broadcast appearances over the course of his storied career. On display is a detailed portrait of the life of Vladimir Nabokov: from his early years in Russia, captured with such haunting resonance in his autobiography, *Speak, Memory*, to his education at Cambridge, a meager existence as a young author in the capitals of Europe, and the decision in 1940 to emigrate to the United States which changed the entire course of his life.

Nabokov parried questions in a number of interviews on both his early Russian-language novels and his lauded English-language works, giving particular emphasis to his formal experimentation with structure, dialogue, locale, and the integration of themes into a narrative. A fascination with the illusive nature of memory and time pervades his *oeuvre*, and he discoursed with considerable eloquence on the literary techniques he had developed to navigate themes often left to the sciences. He addressed the mystery of creativity and the limitations of imagination without scientific perspective. "Imagination without knowledge leads no farther than the backyard of primitive art, the child's scrawl on the fence, and the crank's message in the marketplace," he told *Playboy* in 1964. "Art is never simple . . . art at its greatest is fantastically deceitful and complex." During his years teaching literature at Wellesley and Cornell, he urged his students to bridge C.P. Snow's

*Two Cultures* dichotomy and equally develop "the passion of the scientist and the precision of the artist."

Nabokov dedicated a great amount of his time to translation and spoke with expertise to journalists about the joys and pitfalls of that unheralded art. In a 1959 interview with the CBC's Kerry Ellard, he asserted a preference in translation for "the specific detail to the generalization, images to ideas; and obscure facts to plain symbols." Having searched in vain for an adequate English language copy of *Eugene Onegin* by Alexander Pushkin which he could use for class lectures, he set himself the task of translating the monumental Russian verse novel. His object was a perfect, literal rendering. "And to the fidelity of transposal," he told Alvin Toffler, "I have sacrificed everything: elegance, euphony, clarity, good taste, modern usage, and even grammar." His definitive four-volume translation, featuring extensive notes and commentary, required ten years of labor.

The most insightful conversations in this book were conducted by Alfred Appel Jr. and Herbert Gold. Appel had attended a literature course at Cornell taught by Nabokov and was one of the earliest academic Nabokovians. He was described by Nabokov as "my pedant. A pedant straight out of *Pale Fire*. Every writer should have such a pedant." Professor Appel produced a stream of scholarly articles, essays, and books, including *The Annotated Lolita*, which provided a line-by-line explication of Nabokov's most famous book. In interviews conducted for *Wisconsin Studies in Contemporary Literature* and *The Atlantic Monthly*, Appel explored the myriad literary, symbolic, and linguistic allusions in his work, with an emphasis on his use of satire and parody. Herbert Gold, the distinguished novelist who replaced Nabokov at Cornell in 1958, interviewed him for *The Saturday Evening Post* and *The Paris Review*. He focused on Nabokov's penchant for elaborate character development, as well as his literary influences and reading preferences.

Nabokov's philosophy on literature and society extend throughout the book and reveal his variegated genius. He opines on a multitude of topics, including censorship, the role of the author, the threat to art posed by authoritarian regimes, and the proper scope of critics and readers. In *The Spectator* profile from 1959, he denominates his audience into groups, stating, "There seem to be three levels of readership: at the bottom, those who go after 'human interest'; in the middle, the people who want ideas, packaged thought about Life and Truth; at the top, the proper readers, who go for *style*." When asked what final emotion the ideal reader should experience on concluding one of his novels, Nabokov answers, "I think that what

I would welcome at the close of a book of mine is a sensation of its world receding in the distance and stopping somewhere there, suspended afar like a picture in a picture."

Time and again, it is that distinctive style which elevates the interviews of Vladimir Nabokov from prose to art.

Many of the interviews in this collection have not appeared since their first publication. Several have been transcribed here for the first time. As is customary with books in the *Literary Conversations* Series, these interviews are published without editorial commentary, allowing readers to appraise Nabokov free from the prism of critical interpretation or conjecture. They are reprinted unaltered from the form of their initial publication. Consequently, the reader will at times encounter repetitious questions and answers, but the evolution of Nabokov's answers, such as his estimation of his best works or *dénouement* preference for writing in English over his native Russian, will hopefully prove of value in their unexpurgated form to scholars and general readers alike.

To comply with Nabokov's preference for writers who end their introductions "with a glowing tribute to Professor Advice, Professor Encouragement, and Professor Every-Assistance," I will conclude by noting that I was greatly aided in assembling the chronology by Professor Brian Boyd's definitive Nabokov biographies, *Vladimir Nabokov: The Russian Years* (Princeton University Press, 1990) and *Vladimir Nabokov: The American Years* (Princeton University Press, 1991). For the bibliography, I utilized the standard reference, Michael Juliar's *Vladimir Nabokov: A Descriptive Bibliography* (Garland, 1986). At the University Press of Mississippi, I relied on Series Editor Monika Gehlawat for her advice and encouragement, and Katie Keene for her editorial assistance. Thanks are also due to the journalists and permission holders who consented to have their interviews included in this book, to Professor Alexandra David for proofreading the manuscript, and to my father for his invaluable contribution.

RG

# Chronology

1899    Vladimir Vladimirovich Nabokov born on April 22, in St. Peters-
        burg, Russia, the eldest child of Vladimir Dmitrievich Nabokov
        and Elena Ivanovna Nabokov. Raised in a cultured, wealthy family.

1900    Birth of brother, Sergey.

1903    Birth of sister, Olga.

1906    Birth of sister, Elena.

1911–17 Attends the Tenishev School in St. Petersburg.

1911    Birth of brother, Kirill.

1916    Death of uncle Vasily Rukavishnikov, who bequeaths his two
        thousand acre estate, "Rozhdestveno," and the equivalent of two
        million dollars to Nabokov. Publication of *Poems*.

1917    Nabokov and brother Sergey flee from St. Petersburg amidst the
        Russian Revolution and settle in Southern Crimea.

1918    Publication of *Almanac: Two Paths*.

1919    The Red Army conquers Crimea as the Nabokov family sails from
        Sebastopol to Athens, and then to London.

1919–22 Studies Modern and Medieval Languages at Trinity College,
        Cambridge.

1922    His father, Vladimir Dmitrievich Nabokov, assassinated in Berlin
        on March 28. Graduates Cambridge with second-class honors
        degree. Became engaged to Svetlana Siewert in Berlin. Publica-
        tion of VN's translation of Romain Rolland's *Colas Breugnon*.
        Publication of *The Cluster*.

1922–37 Lives in Berlin, writes poems and novels in Russian. Supports
        himself by giving Russian, French, tennis and boxing lessons.

1923    Breaks off engagement with Svetlana Siewert. Publication of *The
        Empyrean Path*. Publication of VN's translation of Lewis Carroll's
        *Alice in Wonderland*.

1925    Marries Véra Slonim in Berlin.

1926    Publication of *Mary*.

1928    Publication of *King, Queen, Knave*.

1929    Publication of *The Return of Chorb*.

1930    Publication of *The Defense*.

1932    Publication of *Glory*.

1933    Publication of *Camera Obscura*.

1934    Birth of Nabokov's son, Dmitri Vladimirovich Nabokov.

1936    Publication of *Despair*.

1937–40 Lives in Paris.

1938    Publication of *Laughter in the Dark*. Publication of *The Eye*. Publication of *Invitation to a Beheading*.

1939    Death of mother, Elena, in Prague.

1940    Nabokov emigrates to USA. Lives in New York.

1941–48 Lecturer of Russian and Russian Literature at Wellesley College. Discovers a new species of butterfly at the Grand Canyon, names it *Neonympha dorothea*.

1941    Visiting Lecturer in Slavic Languages at Stanford University. Publication of *The Real Life of Sebastian Knight*.

1942–48 Fellow of the Museum of Comparative Zoology at Harvard University.

1943    Receives Guggenheim Fellowship.

1944    Publication of *Nikolai Gogol*.

1945    Naturalized as a United States citizen. Death of brother, Sergey, in a Nazi concentration camp. Publication of VN's translation, *Three Russian Poets: Selections from Pushkin, Lermontov and Tyutchev*.

1947    Publication of *Bend Sinister*. Publication of *Nine Stories*.

1948–59 Professor of Russian and European Literature at Cornell University.

1950    Discovers rare butterfly species, *Lycaeides samuelis*.

1951    Discovers female butterfly, *Lycaeides sublivens*. Receives Arts and Letters Award from the American Academy of Arts and Letters. Publication of *Conclusive Evidence*.

1952    Visiting Lecturer at Harvard University. Receives Guggenheim Fellowship. Publication of *The Gift*. Publication of *Poems: 1929–1951*.

1955    Publication of *Lolita*.

1956    Publication of *Spring in Fialta*.

1957    Publication of *Pnin*.

1958    Receives National Book Award nomination for *Pnin*. Publication of VN's translation of Mikhail Lermontov's *A Hero of Our Time*. American publication of *Lolita*. Publication of *Nabokov's Dozen*.

1959    Receives National Book Award nomination for *Lolita*. Retires from Cornell University. Travels in Europe. Publication of *Poems*.

1960    Publication of VN's translation of *The Song of Igor's Campaign*. Writes the screenplay for *Lolita* in Los Angeles.

1961–77 Lives in the Palace Hotel, Montreux, Switzerland.

1962    Publication of *Pale Fire*. Release of the film *Lolita*, directed by Stanley Kubrick.

1963    Receives Academy Award nomination for Best Writing, Screenplay Based on Material from Another Medium for *Lolita*. Receives National Book Award nomination for *Pale Fire*. Publication of *Notes on Prosody*. Nominated for the Nobel Prize in Literature.

1964    Death of brother, Kirill. Publication of the four-volume translation of Pushkin's *Eugene Onegin*. Receives Medal for Literature from Brandeis University. American publication of *The Defense*. Nominated for the Nobel Prize in Literature[1].

1965    Receives National Book Award nomination for *The Defense*. Is nominated for the Nobel Prize for Literature.

1966    Publication of *The Waltz Invention*. Publication of *Nabokov's Quartet*.

1967    Publication of *Speak, Memory*.

1968    Publication of *Nabokov's Congeries*. American publication of *King, Queen, Knave*.

1969    Publication of *Ada or Ardor: A Family Chronicle*. Featured on cover of *Time* magazine, May 23. Receives Award of Merit Medal from the American Academy of Arts and Letters. Release of the film *Laughter in the Dark*, directed by Tony Richardson.

1970    American Publication of *Mary*.

1971    Publication of *Poems and Problems*.

1972    Publication of *Transparent Things*. Release of the film *King, Queen, Knave*, directed by Jerzy Skolimowski.

1973    Publication of *A Russian Beauty and Other Stories*. Receives National Book Award nomination for *Transparent Things*. Receives the National Medal for Literature. Publication of *Strong Opinions*.

1974    Publication of *Lolita: A Screenplay*. Publication of *Look at the Harlequins!*

1975    Publication of *Tyrants Destroyed and Other Stories*. Receives National Book Award nomination for *Look at the Harlequins!*

1976    Publication of *Details of a Sunset and Other Stories*. Receives National Book Award nomination for *Tyrants Destroyed and*

*Other Stories.* Receives National Book Critics Circle Award nomination for *Details of a Sunset and Other Stories.*

1977    Vladimir Nabokov dies in Lausanne, Switzerland, July 2.

1978    Release of the film *Despair*, directed by Rainer Werner Fassbinder. Death of sister, Olga.

1979    Publication of *The Nabokov-Wilson Letters: Correspondence Between Vladimir Nabokov and Edmund Wilson 1940–1971.* Publication of *Poems.*

1980    Publication of *Lectures on Literature.* Publication of *Lectures on Ulysses.* National Book Critics Circle Award nomination for *Lectures on Literature.*

1981    Publication of *Lectures on Russian Literature.*

1983    Publication of *Lectures on Don Quixote.*

1984    Publication of *The Man from the USSR and Other Plays.*

1985    Publication of *Letters to His Sister.*

1986    Publication of *The Enchanter.*

1987    Publication of *Carrousel.*

1989    Publication of *Vladimir Nabokov: Selected Letters: 1940–1977.*

1990    Publication of *The Circle.* Publication of *Plays.*

1991    Death of wife, Véra.

1995    Publication of *The Stories of Vladimir Nabokov.*

1997    Release of the film *Lolita*, directed by Adrian Lyne.

2000    Publication of *Nabokov's Butterflies: Unpublished and Uncollected Writings.* Release of the film *The Luzhin Defence*, directed by Marleen Gorris. Death of sister, Elena.

2001    Publication of *Dear Bunny, Dear Volodya: The Nabokov-Wilson Letters, 1940–1971.*

2008    Publication of *Verses and Versions: Three Centuries of Russian Poetry Selected and Translated by Vladimir Nabokov.*

2009    Publication of *The Original of Laura.*

2012    Death of son, Dmitri. Publication of *Selected Poems.* Publication of *The Tragedy of Mister Morn.*

2014    Publication of *Letters to Véra.*

## Notes

1. According to the Statutes of the Nobel Foundation, information about nominations of Nobel Laureates is not to be publicly disclosed for a period of fifty years. Therefore, Nabokov may have been nominated after 1964. In 1965, Nabokov was nominated for the Nobel Prize for Literature.

# Conversations with Vladimir Nabokov

# The Author of *Lolita*—an Unhurried View

## Martha MacGregor / 1958

From the *New York Post Weekend Magazine*, August 17, 1958. © Martha MacGregor.

"*Lolita* is here!" says a triumphant sign taped to the reception desk at G. P. Putnam's Sons. This is the firm whose eager-beaver young head, Walter Minton, also rescued Norman Mailer's controversial *The Deer Park* after its rejection by other publishers in a blaze of sex-sparked publicity.

Banned in Paris, eyed disapprovingly by the British Home Secretary, self-righteously spurned by at least four American publishers, *Lolita* has seduced of all things (or people), the once puritanical U.S. Customs.

Here it is, intact, not a word missing, at three dollars a copy. "I'm very proud that America has not brought charges," says the distinguished Russian-born author, Vladimir Nabokov. "It's wonderful, it's wonderful."

*Lolita* has been dancing in and out of the news for months. An account of a child's affair with a middle-aged man, the novel was received coldly by Virginia Kirkus, whose reviewing service is popular with lending libraries in this country.

### The Hesitant Librarians

"Any librarian will surely question this for anything but the closed shelves," said Miss Kirkus.

Ralph Ginsburg, author of *An Unhurried View of Erotica*, comments: "In certain areas of sex practice this is more forthright than any novel I can recall, but it would be absurd to condemn it as pornographic or obscene."

The author himself says of the charge of pornography: "Foolish." And of conflicting theories on the meaning of *Lolita*: "Just a story, a fairy tale, as all

3

stories are." Nabokov said this with a smile, as if the whole fuss was a great joke.

He is a man of tremendous personal charm and this sense of the comical is perhaps his most attractive characteristic. His conversation is punctuated with smiles, or little quiverings of the lips, as if he were about to explode with laughter at the absurdity of life in general.

Nabokov was born in 1899. His boyhood in Russia has been memorably described in an autobiographical memoir, *Conclusive Evidence*, published in 1951 by Harper.

The whole setting of that boyhood lives again in a few pictures: An uncle's home in the country, a house filled with crucifixes and carnations, his mother in St. Petersburg taking her jewelry from the wall safe—tiaras, chokers, rings—or, fur-coated, riding in a horse-drawn sleigh, a bearskin over her knees.

Or it is a summer afternoon and a French governess reads *Les Misérables* aloud on the veranda, a gardener putters among the peonies and a butterfly shines in the sun. (Nabokov's passion for butterflies dates from his childhood; his parents were also collectors.)

His early education explains to at least some extent his distinguished English prose style. "I had first an English nurse and then a sequence of English governesses," he says. "After that, I had Russian tutors.

"I read English before I read Russian. I spoke English with my mother and my nurse—with my brother, I remember, I always spoke French. That was typical. The children would speak one language together and another language at table and another with their father and mother. Sometimes as many as four languages would be spoken.

"After I started going to school at eleven, my tutor stayed on and would tutor me at night for the next day. You learned a great deal that way.

"And we had wonderful courses in French literature. The French governess would read to us three hours a day—the English governess, too. We had all the English magazines and some of the American ones—*Little Folks* and *St. Nicholas*.

"I started reading Turgenev and Tolstoy when I was very small. My wife read *Anna Karenina* at six. Her nurse said, 'Come, come, I'll tell that to you in my own words.'

"Even then she knew to beware of condensations," Nabokov added, laughing.

"I started writing Russian verse very early—when I was thirteen—and published a little book of verse when I was fifteen."

*Lolita* was written in English, but Nabokov insists that he could have done better in Russian. "It's simply that my knowledge of Russian is infinitely greater than my knowledge of English."

At twenty, Nabokov left Russia with his family. His father, a liberal statesman under the Czar, was killed by Russian monarchists with a bullet intended for another man at a Berlin meeting of Russian exiles in 1922. Nabokov took a B.A. at Cambridge and began writing for *émigré* publications.

"We were desperately poor, you know. I made my living teaching all sorts of things—tennis, boxing, languages. Writing was something that was so natural to me I would sometimes write a poem every day in the week. It was in those Russian newspapers and magazines that came out in Germany, Paris, and later in New York that I published my stories, poems, and then my novels.

"Though they were smuggled into Russia, they were absolutely taboo—banned. Once or twice I was invited to come back to Russia—once was when Prokofiev was asked back. But I knew what to expect, so I just stayed where I was." (Prokofiev returned voluntarily to Russia in 1936.)

Nabokov is volubly anti-Soviet. In his autobiography he says: "My old (since 1917) quarrel with the Soviet dictatorship is wholly unrelated to any questions of property. My contempt for the *émigré* who 'hates the Reds' because they 'stole' his money and land is complete. The most I have been cherishing all these years is a hypertrophied sense of lost childhood, not sorrow for lost banknotes." An uncle left him the equivalent of two million dollars, lost in the revolution.

In 1940, Nabokov was invited to America to teach at Stanford. Of Cornell, where he now teaches, he says: "Oh, I love it. I'm very happy there. I have the most charming colleagues, very nice students, very large classes in European literature—anywhere from 150 to 300.

"Actually, I never understood how I became a professor. But I am a full professor," said Nabokov, looking pleased about it.

A spokesman for Cornell reports that Nabokov is one of the most popular teachers there. "All sorts of students attend his lectures—engineers, pre-meds, not just the arts students. It's partly his knowledge that draws them, partly his humor and, of course, his personality."

His wife, Véra, also an *émigré* of the aristocratic class, whom he met in Berlin and married in 1925, helps with the classroom routine and types his manuscripts. It is obvious that a very tender relationship exists between the two.

They have one son, Dmitri, a Harvard graduate and, his father says, "a wonderful singer." He's now doing leading bass roles with the Broadway Opera Association.

A considerable part of Nabokov's output as a writer remains in the original Russian in which he wrote during the *émigré* years. The press estimate of those novels and stories in English has been kind, even ecstatic. He has been compared with Kafka, Joyce, Proust, Gogol, and Chekhov. *Pnin*, the book before *Lolita*, drew raves and some interesting comment on his work in general.

The *New Statesman and Nation* spoke of his "sweetness" (also, one would guess, a personality trait) and coupled him with a writer little known in this country, William Gerhardi: "Both these young men were young in Russia before the Revolution and it seems as though that experience has endowed them with a sadness at the same time nostalgic and facetious."

### "I Don't Like Groups"

George D. Elliott in *Hudson Review* characterized Nabokov as a "Raconteur with great intelligence" and the Harvard Crimson analyzed his style: "Nabokov's relative detachment from the language permits him to perceive and to exploit means of expression that native English writers often overlook. He gets remarkable mileage out of a part of speech that is more or less neglected nowadays, namely, the adverb."

Two minority reports are worth quoting: Diana Trilling, reviewing *Bend Sinister*, an earlier novel, spoke of Nabokov's "deafness to the music of the English language," and Kingsley Amis, leading Angry Young Man, reviewing *Pnin* in *The Spectator*, found it a mystery that "this limp, tasteless salad of Joyce, Chaplin, and Mary McCarthy had delighted noises made over it by Edmund Wilson, Randall Jarrell, and Graham Greene."

"What do you think of the Angry Young Men?" I asked Nabokov.

"What are they?"

"What do you think of the Beat Generation?"

This drew fire—an outburst in the passionate Russian manner.

"I don't like anything that becomes a movement or a school! I don't like labels, clubs. I don't like groups!

"It just doesn't mean anything to me if you say symbolists or classicists. It doesn't mean anything, and that's what I teach my classes. I teach them books, authors. Not groups or labels.

"Exist—exist—existen—" Nabokov's lips puckered humorously as he made an amusing pretense at being unable to pronounce "existentialism."

"I'm bored by the word itself! I read something Sartre wrote. I didn't know what he was talking about."

How about Freud (of whom Nabokov has in the past been critical)?

"Freudian voodoo!" Nabokov replied vehemently. "That's my *bête noire*. I think he has been one of the most pernicious influences on literature, children, and schools. It's a medieval mind dealing in medieval symbols. The initial witchdoctor and all the little witchdoctors. A rather complicated question on which I will write later. A craze that's passing."

One more hero bit the dust—Albert Schweitzer.

"I would also like to find out who invented Dr. Schweitzer. This is a question I would like to ask at large. I think it's another exaggeration. It's funny how people must have a name to bandy about."

And how does Nabokov feel about politics?

"No interest whatsoever in politics or people with a capital 'P.' I make my own people, my own politics, and my own Gods—if any." His lips puckered in the familiar whimsical way.

Is Nabokov an iconoclast, a rebel, an intellectual anarchist? Says a friend: "I'd say he's a skeptic who calls his own shots. And of course he has a wonderful deadpan humor—it's hard to tell if he's joking or not."

A complicated personality, Nabokov. The same may be said of *Lolita*. To get back to the meaning of the book, here is something that Nabokov himself said in the Cornell Daily Sun when *Pnin* was published: "The book has no message. I'm no messenger boy. A book has to stand on its own two feet or fly on its own two wings, or four."

# Author of *Lolita* Airs Views on Censorship, Role of Artist

## Gladys Kessler / 1958

From *The Cornell Daily Sun*, September 25, 1958. © *The Cornell Daily Sun*. Reprinted by permission.

It isn't often a Cornell professor becomes the center of a literary hurricane—or a tempest in a teapot depending on one's view of *Lolita*, the stylistic masterpiece that has recently caused such a sensation.

Vladimir V. Nabokov is the gentleman in the limelight and his very controversial book *Lolita* is creating the tempest. For those just back from the wilds of Vacationland, *Lolita* is a novel about a European intellectual who has a two-year love affair with a nymphet named Lolita, aged twelve.

Banned in France, the book has turned into a cause célèbre in the United States. But none of this fuss and bother seems to have affected its author at all.

He still lives quietly in a rented home with a seldom-used television set, and plans to continue his teaching and his writing. After all, Professor Nabokov vigorously exclaimed, "I couldn't live without my teaching."

Having had quite a bit of experience with censorship, both Russian and French, Nabokov expressed some very definite ideas on the subject. "Any work of art is above censorship. But censorship, of course, depends on what you call a book. A book, a novel above all, is a work of art and must be above all restrictions."

Professor Nabokov is a man of very firm opinions in regard to the place of the artist in society and his obligations to it and his reader. "The artist has no obligations to the reader," he emphasized. "If no communication exists between writer and reader, then it is either the fault of the reader or it is the work of a poor writer who has no claim to the title of an artist.

"The artist survives and transcends time and place. Above all, I have been trying to root this idea of the artist as a product of his culture out of my classes. I am not influenced by my environment, nor by time nor society. And neither is the true writer."

Discussing his own bestseller (which he claims has no moral whatsoever), the scholarly and very charming gentleman said, "People may take symbolism from *Lolita*, but I put none in. If people take it out, so much the better for them," he concluded.

"But seriously," he continued, "*Lolita* is to be enjoyed as a detached, intellectual exercise. No tears to be shed. You're supposed to enjoy it with your spinal emotions, with a little shiver when you end it."

Mrs. Nabokov is fully as intriguing as her husband. A handsome, white-haired woman, she sits quietly by and listens to every word her husband utters. Previously, she had helped Professor Nabokov by grading some of his students' papers. Now, however, she's kept busy typing her husband's manuscripts.

The Nabokovs have a son, Dmitri, a recent Harvard graduate, who has helped his father in preparing some translations.

An ardent foe of modern, group-oriented, "practical" education, Nabokov pleaded for a return to classical methods with the emphasis on the teaching of Latin and Greek, and a renewed interest in natural history— "not applied natural history for a purpose, but to know the world as it is, to know what makes corn, not cornflakes."

On the university level, he considers the library "the heart and centerpiece of any good institution." To profit from this "our students need more solitude and concentration and, especially, more sleep. There are too many clubs, too many group activities. A university should be quieter; what many students could use is a nice padded cell."

Professor Nabokov loves to write in both Russian and English. Although he prefers Russian because it is his native tongue and he is most at home with it, Nabokov claims that English is "the richest language in the world. The spirit of the language is a harmonious one. It is wonderful for expressing abstractions and for coining the names of things. But, of course, my English is just an echo of my Russian," he quipped.

# Vladimir Nabokov and Lionel Trilling Discuss *Lolita*

## Pierre Berton / 1958

From the Canadian Broadcasting Corporation, November 26, 1958. © CBC Licensing. Reprinted by permission.

**Pierre Berton:** Mr. Trilling, as a critic I think you'd be interested in a remark made about *Lolita*, which I suppose everyone knows by now. It's the so-called "shocking" book about the obsessive love of a middle-aged man for a twelve year old girl, a remark made by a Canadian writer, Nicholas Montserrat, who didn't like the book. He said that he found the subject so debased and horrible that it destroys the book as a work of art. He went on to say that he'd vote to ban it. I'd like to hear what Mr. Nabokov has to say for the defense of this.

**Vladimir Nabokov:** I'm not particularly interested in those foolish attacks. Some of them are very amusing. But I would say that most of the haters of *Lolita* in the US are just common scolds and old philistines.

**PB:** What do you mean by a philistine, Mr. Nabokov?

**VN:** Users of covers and cozies, ready-made souls in plastic bags, negligible generalities.

**PB:** Mr. Trilling, would you identify Mr. Montserrat with that definition of a philistine?

**Lionel Trilling:** In this particular instance, yes, I think I would. I think that the book is shocking. I'm glad that it's shocking. I see a lot of shocking books. I think we need to be shocked. But it's absurd to call it debased; it's anything but that. [The criticism is] ridiculous.

**PB:** The critics, as Mr. Nabokov knows, have said a great many things about this book. I'd like to see if he agrees with them. I'll quote some of them to you. One critic called it "a satire on sex, a mirror of human frailties." Another said it was "a joke on our national cant about youth." A third, that it was "a cutting exposé of chronic American adolescence and shabby materialism." Is this so? Is this what you were intending?

**VN:** I don't think so. First of all, I do not wish to touch hearts and I don't want to affect minds very much. What I want to produce is really that little sob in the spine of the artist-reader. I leave the field of ideas to Dr. Schweitzer and to Dr. Zhivago. And when you say satire you imply a purpose, an object, an awakening, apart from and beyond the dream of the book. I have invented an America, my America, and it's just as fantastic as any inventor's America.

**LT:** Yours is more attractive.

**VN:** I think you have noticed, but some reviewers have not noticed how helpless and how lovely she is. It was fun to breed her in my own laboratory but I am not concerned with holding up public abuses to ridicule or that kind of thing.

**LT:** There is an underlying tone of satire through the book.

**VN:** If you give satire its original sense of *macédoine*, a fruit salad, *satira*, then perhaps my dish is good enough for that purpose.

**PB:** But you say that your book isn't meant to produce emotions in readers. I'd like to ask Mr. Trilling, as we move over here, if it didn't produce some emotion in him? It did in me.

**LT:** Oh, yes, it did indeed. I found it a deeply moving book. Mr. Nabokov may not have meant to move hearts but he moved mine. He may not have meant to affect minds but he did affect my mind.

**PB:** More than just a touch of tingle at the end of your spine, as Mr. Nabokov said?

**LT:** Oh, yes. You can't trust a creative writer to say what he has done. He can say what he meant to do. And even then we don't have to believe him. No, I was deeply moved by the book. I think it was one of the most moving books I've read in a long time.

**PB:** Mr. Nabokov is also saying, as I gather, that he has no message at all in this book.

**VN:** I don't feel I have any special message and if you ask me, for instance, whether my own ideas are those of Humbert Humbert, I would say no. Of course, he's a European and a man of letters as I am, but I've taken great care to separate myself from him. For instance, the good reader notices that Humbert Humbert confuses, just to take an instance, hummingbirds with hawk moths. Now, I would never do that, being an entomologist.

**PB:** You're an expert in butterflies.

**VN:** I am to a certain extent. And I would never do that. Well, there are many other things, many other matters, which I leave to him.

**LT:** I think nobody would suppose that the author and the hero were to be in any way identified.

**VN:** Well, it has been supposed.

**PB:** Humbert Humbert, besides several odd tastes, also hates American motels. He despises them. Have you this feeling?

**VN:** No. I must say there are some absolutely delightful motels where I've been very happy; very happy with Humbert Humbert writing the book but which I could not use because the book is slanted in a different way.

**PB:** He would see a motel as something rather grotesque.

**VN:** Not necessarily. A motel can be anything.

**PB:** Let's get down to the really intriguing point, Mr. Nabokov. What gave you the idea for *Lolita*, the story of a middle-aged man and a twelve year old girl and their love affair? How did you start it?

**VN:** In a little afterpiece which I have to my book, I talk about a certain ape who was taught to use charcoal, and the first thing the poor little animal did was to sketch the bars of its own cage.

**PB:** Is this an analogy?

**VN:** Yes. I read that story in a newspaper and if I try to rationalize the impact of that image I would say that my baboon, Humbert Humbert—and after all, Humbert Humbert is a baboon, a baboon of genius, perhaps, but a baboon—is doing exactly that. He is drawing and shading and erasing and redrawing the bars of his cage. The bars between him and what he terms "the human herd."

**PB:** And this cage, I take it, is this obsessive and rather frightening love for this girl?

**VN:** It is, yes. It is his passion—the pattern of his passion.

**PB:** But let's get down to the more specific point. Why did you choose this rather odd, and something that's never been done before, this curious and debased love?

**VN:** I think because on the whole it afforded me all kinds of interesting possibilities. I'm not so much interested in the philosophy of the book as I am in weaving the thing in a certain way. In those intergradations and inter-weavings of certain themes and subthemes, for instance the semantic line of Mr. Quilty, whom Humbert will kill, and does kill, and whom Humbert mentions as early as page thirty-three. And he appears several times throughout the book.

**PB:** But you must have read a newspaper, been aware of this strange sexual symbolism or this oddity in a minority of humans which has shocked so many people about *Lolita*?

**VN:** I have read a considerable number of case histories. I would say I became quite an expert in those matters. I have not combined them for the purpose of writing the book, but they have influenced me in one way or another, just giving me certain information.

**PB:** Mr. Trilling has a very intriguing theory about *Lolita*. He thinks it's a return to the old kind of romantic shocking love, but I'll let him explain it. I'd like to hear what you have to say about it.

**LT:** Well, Mr. Burton, it isn't quite to be dignified by calling it a theory. But my reading of the book led me to feel that, in spite of the judgments that a good many people have made on it as a book about sex and sexual obsession—although it is indeed a very erotic book, a very sexual book, if you wish—it is not a book so much about an aberration as about an actual love. And a love that makes all the terrible demands that almost any love makes, certainly that any sexual love makes, but that is very full of tenderness and very full of compassion, as well as passion. It occurred to me to say that this particular love that Mr. Nabokov had chosen as the love object of his hero, a young girl—someone who is usually preserved from the sexual attentions of men—a very young girl of twelve because he wanted to reconstitute the scandalous nature that once used to characterize the famous love affairs, the love affairs of great stars.

**PB:** Do you think love should be scandalous and is no longer scandalous? Is that what you're trying to say?

**LT:** I don't think love should be scandalous. I'm a very respectable man. I think that all the great love stories have been scandalous. They, for example, have been adulterous. They have been stories not of love between married people but between people who ought not be in love.

**PB:** Let me interrupt you here and let Mr. Nabokov have his say here.

**VN:** It seems to me that all worthwhile novels, after all, are concerned with passioned love. Apart from Humbert's and a nymphet's, [passioned love] has always existed in novels as well as in life. If you take a novel, take Tolstoy's *Anna Karenina* with Kitty and Levin, [who] have a relationship which in ordinary life in Europe and America may be termed passionate love, co-amorous love, within the terms of normal marriage; so we have that, too.

**LT:** Yes, we do, but it's not called "Kitty" and it's not called "Levin," it's called *Anna Karenina*.

**VN:** I'm not sure of that. I think Kitty and Levin are just as alive as Anna is and the rather dummy-like Vronsky.

**LT:** Yes, but it seems to me that all great love affairs are tragic. They all end in death, as yours does.

**VN:** I would put it this way, that if sex is the sermon made of art, love is the lady of that tower.

**PB:** What Mr. Trilling is saying, I think, is your book is about love and not about sex.

**VN:** I agree with him perfectly in that.

**PB:** But a great many people who are shocked by this book think it is a book about sex, right?

**LT:** Oh, yes. And because it is destructive and because the love is destructive or cruel or many other things, it is no less love. In fact, that is why it is love. Love is these things very often.

**VN:** That is because they think in clichés. For them, sex is something so well-defined, there's a kind of gap between it and love. They don't know what love is, perhaps. And perhaps they don't know what sex is either.

**PB:** Has sex become a literary cliché so that people can't recognize anything else?

**LT:** I'll say yes.

**VN:** I have to agree with you.

**PB:** Let me ask you one fast question before we close, Mr. Nabokov: You've put a word in the language, "nymphet." Is this going to be your monument? Do you feel you've accomplished something?

**VN:** It is a very small monument, it is a delicate monument, and it is pleasant to have it somewhere in the garden, in the shade.

**PB:** It is a word that is cropping up. You must see this word staring out at you.

**VN:** I see it constantly. It is a pleasant feeling.

**LT:** There'll be nymphet clothes very soon.

**PB:** Thank you very much Mr. Trilling, Mr. Nabokov. Talking about *Lolita*.

# What Hath *Lolita* Wrought?

## Edward E. Van Dyne / 1958

From *The Elmira Telegram*, December 14, 1958. Courtesy of Star-Gazette, Elmira, N.Y.

Since his controversial novel *Lolita* flashed to the top of the bestseller lists, Vladimir Nabokov, Russian-born professor of literature at Cornell University, has been one of America's most discussed writers.

But long before *Lolita*, he had a small, devoted following. His memoirs, first published in magazines, later in a slim volume called *Conclusive Evidence*, contain some of the most beautiful prose in the language.

The chance to meet him recently in his home in Cayuga Heights was—for this country correspondent and long-time fan—a small triumph.
Emitting a series of sonorous chuckles, Nabokov opened the door of a large, red brick house.

The scantly furnished interior had a transitory air which Nabokov quickly explained: "We are birds of passage. When someone goes on leave, we take over. We've never owned a home."

This statement had unintended pathos. Nabokov and his Russian-born wife, a trim, gray haired woman with intense dark eyes, are permanent exiles from their native land. Like many exiles, they've never really taken root in their adopted country.

Nabokov was born to an old and aristocratic family in 1899. His grandfather was Minister of Justice under two czars. His father was a liberal statesman whose democratic views put him at odds equally with the opposing cancers of czarism and communism.

Nabokov escaped the Soviet regime to lead the drifting, insecure life of the Russian *émigré*. He attended Cambridge University, then eked out an existence in various European countries. In 1940, he sailed with his wife and small son for America. He has taught eleven years at Cornell.

In the drab living room in Ithaca, little bespoke this colorful past save a stiffly posed photograph of Nabokov Sr., who died at the hands of czarist assassins in 1922.

The interview was to be mostly about butterflies. Entomology is more than a hobby with Nabokov: he's a recognized authority in the field. As it turned out, butterflies were scarcely mentioned. *Lolita* was too much with us.

The Nabokovs are genuinely distressed by some reactions to the book. It has often been dismissed with shrill indignation, smirks, elevated eyebrows and the pursed lips of maiden ladies in libraries and bookstores.

"Some simply haven't read the book or don't understand it," he said. "It is not obscene; it has none of the dirt of many so-called realistic modern novels."

"Most critics have failed to stress the pathetic side," said Mrs. Nabokov. "It's really a tragic story. Here, in the hands of this maniac is this poor girl . . ."

"And a very ordinary girl . . ." Nabokov put in.

At first, many critics either confessed to bafflement or else roundly damned the book. Then, presumably after soul-searching and reading other reviews, some came forth with second thoughts. *The New Yorker* finally placed it in "a special class of satire." Three words used by a *Time* critic— "Brilliant, hilarious, horrifying"—form a neat capsule comment.

"Recently, we've received some wonderful reviews from smaller newspapers in Texas and places like that," the author said. "We didn't expect them and it's gratifying. America has lived up to her liberal heritage in this."

What adverse effect has the controversy had on a quiet Ivy League professor living in a respectable, upper middle class neighborhood?

"Absolutely none. Both faculty and students have been extremely serious and intelligent in their approach. It has made me feel very warm inside."

And what of that other Russian's controversial work, *Doctor Zhivago*, bestseller of Nobel Prize fame?

"The political aspect does not interest me. Of course, I'm sure the Soviets are really pleased with the whole thing. They've attracted a lot of attention and they get the royalties.

"However, my concern is with the artistic character of a novel. From this point of view, *Doctor Zhivago* is a sorry thing, full of clichés, clumsy, trivial and melodramatic."

What of the immediate Nabokov future?

"Just now there is a great deal to be done. I'm controlling a French translation of *Lolita*. Some of my early novels, originally written in Russian, will be coming out. I'm applying for a sabbatical leave. We'll probably go to California next summer, then to Europe."

# My Child *Lolita*

## Alan Nordstrom / 1959

From *Ivy Magazine*, February, 1959. © Alan Nordstrom, Professor of English, Rollins College. Reprinted by permission.

A few months back the long-buried phenomenon of the *bête noire* reared its head and caused the biggest storm of the literary season. Unjust as it was to compare the delicately textured *Lolita* of Vladimir Nabokov to the licentious doodlings of Grace Metalious, the same indignant eyebrows arched and the same righteous epithets flew around the sewing circles. Mention of the ban in France fed the flames of a substantial controversy. Champions arose on either side to praise the book's "artistry" or condemn its "filth." But while the literary winds blow outside, the man in the quiet eye of the storm remains relatively unperturbed and inaccessible at his Cornell "retreat."

Slouching comfortably in his armchair, walled from the world and notoriety by dusty stacks of Pushkin, Mr. Nabokov could not have contrasted more to the image that some of his stronger critics have of the creator of the mad Humbert. He seems the professorial prototype, as his tortoiseshell glasses move from his nose bridge, leap forth to emphasize a point and return again to their perch. More noticeable than this is his acute linguistic sensitivity, suggesting the literary craftsman. He looks more British than Russian. Yet his speech rolls gently in Slavic fashion, though considerably mellowed in years spent abroad. His conversations range from butterflies (he and his wife chase them each summer) to his special interest, Russian literature. They fairly glitter with lively anecdotes and pungent observations on the American academic scene.

Born in Russia, Nabokov departed for England and Cambridge when the impending threat of revolution swelled in his homeland. The years between the wars were spent in Germany and France, where he concentrated on developing his immaculate literary style. In 1940, his "Columbian urge" to see America was realized when Stanford University offered him a position teaching "The Art of Writing." ("Solely," injected Mrs. Nabokov, "on his literary reputation.") Appointed to a professorship by Cornell, for the past ten years he has been occupied with teaching Russian and European novels and with continuous literary research and writing.

The idea of *Lolita* had occupied Mr. Nabokov's mind for many years, finding vague and partial expression in some of his early Russian stories. From a filed mass of indexed ideas and information, the characters of the perverted Humbert and "nymphet" Lolita gradually took recognizable shape. (Campus scuttlebutt recounts the hours he spent on school buses observing young girls, nine to fourteen). When he canvassed the country for details (studying American motels), he did most of his writing in his car, "the only place in America with no noise and no draft."

Nabokov's dignified independence makes him a stimulating lecturer. In training his students to scrutinize the complete assemblage of a novel, he urges: "You do not read, you reread. The first time through read to learn and understand; the second reading is for enjoyment." The professor's lectures stress style and structure as the basis of literary study rather than generalized speculation about "father images or personal philosophies." "You only know the author through his book," he declares. "An artist is original. He first assimilates his experience and then recreates and invents a world in his book." In answer to those who would like to see Mr. Nabokov in terms of the perverted Humbert, the professor's lectures are marked with a perfervid repetition of his thesis that an artist *invents* his characters, rather than projecting his own personality into them.

"The ideal method of teaching," avowed the perspicacious professor, "is to pass out recorded lectures which have been carefully and concisely prepared in the quiet of the teacher's study. With the present system the lecturer undermines his effect with hems and haws, while the student, perhaps, transcribes a name, a dash, and a date."

"The highest virtue of a writer, of any artist, is to stimulate in others an inward *thrill.*" Claiming not to belong to any school himself, Mr. Nabokov objects to the generality of such an appellative as vehemently as he does to the works of many members of certain schools. Sartre and Faulkner ("They are not artists.") bore the brunt of his criticism. J. D. Salinger, on the other hand, is "a great, wonderful writer—the best American novelist." Mention of Mr. Nabokov's highly controversial Russian contemporary, Boris Pasternak, drew a series of interesting comments. "Pasternak is a poet, not a prose writer. *Doctor Zhivago*, as a novel, is nowhere—though quite in line with the Soviet conservative literary style. It wanders like *Gone with the Wind* and is filled with all kinds of blunders and melodramatic situations. Compared to Pasternak, Mr. Steinbeck is a genius."

"Literary expression," the professor maintains, "must first of all be clear, even when treating obscurities; it must be a unique approach to what the artist feels. This must be the constant quest of the writer." Through his writings Nabokov has realized this ultimate goal. The lucidity of his style and the freshness of his phrasing best illustrate the natural artistic sensitivity of the man whose child is *Lolita*.

# An Absence of Wood Nymphs

## Robert H. Boyle / 1959

From *Sports Illustrated*, September 14, 1959. © Robert H. Boyle. Reprinted by permission.

To an army of admirers, Vladimir Nabokov, a balding Russian *émigré* of sixty, is known as the author of that spectacular bestseller, *Lolita*. To a comparative handful, however, he is revered as V. Nabokov, lepidopterist. Respectful colleagues have named four species after him. He is the discoverer of at least two subspecies of butterflies, one of which, it should be noted, is called (accidentally, but prophetically) Nabokov's wood nymph.

Nabokov has described his findings in a number of scientific periodicals ranging from *Psyche*—"A Third Species of *Echinargus* Nabokov (*Lycaenidae, Lepidoptera)*"—to the *Bulletin of the Museum of Comparative Zoology at Harvard College*—"The Nearctic Members of the Genus *Lycaeides Hubner* (*Lycaenidae, Lepidoptera*)." Rarely can the reader deduce that V. Nabokov, the naturalist, is Vladimir Nabokov, the novelist. Only when writing for the *Lepidopterists' News*, a rather chatty journal, is V. likely to peep through as Vladimir: "Every morning the sky would be an impeccable blue at six A.M. when I set out. The first innocent cloudlet would scud across at seven thirty A.M. Bigger fellows with darker bellies would start tampering with the sun around nine A.M., just as I emerged from the shadow of the cliffs and onto good hunting grounds." (Conversely, Vladimir sometimes artfully assumes V.'s vocabulary, as in describing Humbert Humbert's first wife in *Lolita*: "The bleached curl revealed its melanic root." Melanic is a butterfly word meaning dark.)

Nabokov has had a passionate interest in butterflies since he was a boy of six in Russia. By the time he was ten, he had made such a nuisance of himself with the net that solemn Muromtsev, the president of the first Russian Duma, intoned, "Come with us by all means, but do not chase butterflies, child. It mars the rhythm of the promenade." In 1919 in the Crimea, a bowlegged Bolshevik sentry, patrolling "among shrubs in waxy bloom," attempted to arrest him for allegedly signaling with the net to a British warship in the Black Sea. Later, in France, a fat policeman wriggled on his belly through parting grass, suspicious that Nabokov was netting birds. Shortly after Nabokov arrived in the United States in 1940, he became a Research Fellow in the Museum of Comparative Zoology at Harvard, one place, presumably, where his passion was better appreciated. Since 1948 he has been a member of the Department of Literature at Cornell, but he has kept his summers free for his beloved butterflies. Net in hand, he roams the West, unmindful of hooting motorists, chiding cowpokes or snarling dogs.

"This, to me," Nabokov explains, "is most pleasurable—to collect on mountain tops or bogs. It is nostalgic perhaps, but there is also the pleasant feeling of being familiar with a place and surprised when you get more than you expect. You can get as close as possible to these living creatures and see reflected in them a higher law. Mimicry and evolution are for me more and more fascinating . . . I cannot separate the aesthetic pleasure of seeing a butterfly and the scientific pleasure of knowing what it is."

Last month Nabokov and his charming snow-haired wife, Véra, were staying in a cabin at Forest Houses in Oak Creek Canyon, a sort of watchpocket Grand Canyon, eighteen serpentine miles south of Flagstaff, Arizona. There, tucked away in the woods, Nabokov devoted himself to literature (working over translations of the *Song of Igor's Campaign*, a twelfth century Russian epic, and *Invitation to a Beheading*, a novel he wrote in Paris during the thirties) and Lepidoptera. Lepidoptera, for several days at least, won out.

On a Monday morning, for instance, Nabokov, bundled up in dungarees, sport shirt and sweater, emerged from his pine cabin to sniff the air and see the morning sun. "It is now nine o'clock," he said, lying. It was really only 8:30 or thereabouts, but Nabokov keeps moving all clocks and watches within his reach ahead to make Mrs. Nabokov move faster so he can get to his butterflies all the sooner. "The butterflies won't be up for another hour," he admitted however. "This is a deep canyon, and the sun has to go some way up the rim of the mountain to cast its light. The grass is damp, and the butterflies generally come out when it's dry. They are late risers."

He moved inside, sat down on a sofa and picked up a thick brown volume entitled *Colorado Butterflies*. He opened to Nabokov's wood nymph on page 11. "This butterfly which I discovered has nothing to do with nymphets," he said, smiling. "I discovered it in the Grand Canyon in 1941. I know it occurs here, but it is difficult to find. I hope to find it today. I'll be looking for it.

It flies in the speckled shade early in June, though there's another brood at the end of the summer, so you came at the right time." He picked up another book, Alexander Klots' *A Field Guide to the Butterflies*, and opened to the page on the orange-margined blues. Proudly, he pointed to a sentence which read, "The recent work of Nabokov has entirely rearranged the classification of this genus." A look of bliss spread across his face. "The thrill of gaining information about certain structural mysteries in these butterflies is perhaps more pleasurable than any literary achievement."

Mrs. Nabokov called him to breakfast. "The Southwest is a wonderful place to collect," he said over soft-boiled eggs. "There's a mixture of arctic and subtropical fauna. A wonderful place to collect."

At 9:35, Nabokov standard time, he got up to get his net and a blue cloth cap. The thrill of the chase was upon him as he left the cabin and headed south down a foot trail paralleling Oak Creek. "This Nabokov's wood nymph is represented by several subspecies, and there's one here," he said, his eyes sweeping the brush on either side. "It is in this kind of country that my nymph occurs."

He stopped and pointed with the handle of his net to a butterfly clinging to the underside of a leaf. "Disruptive coloration," he said, noting white spots on the wings. "A bird comes and wonders for a second. Is it two bugs? Where is the head? Which side is which? In that split second the butterfly is gone. That second saves that individual and that species. You may call it a large skipper."

Nabokov walked on. At 9:45, he gave a quick flick with the net. "This is a checkered butterfly," he said, looking at his catch. "There are countless subspecies. The way I kill is the European, or Continental, way. I press the thorax at a certain point. If you press the abdomen, it just oozes out." He took the butterfly from the net and held it in the palm of his hand. "This," he exclaimed, "is a beauty! Such a beautiful fresh specimen. *Melitaea anicia.*" He took a Band-Aid box from his pocket, shook loose a glassine envelope and slid *Melitaea anicia* home to rest. "It's safe in the envelope until I can get to a laboratory and spread it."

In good spirits, he pushed on. Something fluttered across the trail. "A common species," he said, walking on, maneuvering the net before him. "The thing is," he said, "when you hit the butterfly, turn the net at the same time to form a bag in which the butterfly is imprisoned."

Nearby, another butterfly was feeding on a flower, but Nabokov ignored it. "A dusky-wing skipper. Common." At 10:03, he passed a clarus sitting on a bare twig. "I've seen that same individual on that same twig since I've been here," he said. "There are lots of butterflies around, but this individual will chase away the others from its perch."

At 10:45, Nabokov lunged wildly off the trail and raced up a rocky incline. Whatever it was escaped in the underbrush. At eleven o'clock, he stopped short. "Ah," he said, a tremor of delight rocking him ever so lightly. "Ah. Oh, that's an interesting thing! Oh, gosh, there it goes. A white skipper mimicking a cabbage butterfly belonging to a different family. Things are picking up. Still, they're not quite right. Where is my wood nymph? It is heartbreaking work," he complained. "Wretched work."

Back at the cabin, Mrs. Nabokov, fresh from writing letters, greeted her husband in Russian. "Let us hurry, darling," he said. Mrs. Nabokov smiled indulgently and followed him down the porch steps to their car, a black 1957 Buick, where she got behind the wheel.

**Journey in a Nervous Car**

The car wouldn't start. "The car is nervous," Nabokov said. At last it started. Mrs. Nabokov drove onto Highway Alt. 89 and headed to a butterfly camping ground several miles north. At 11:26 (Nabokov standard time), Mrs. Nabokov swung over to the left side of the road and parked by Oak Creek. Nabokov leaped out. "Now we'll see something spectacular, I hope!" He waved farewell to Mrs. Nabokov with his net and jogged down a rough trail. He stopped. A butterfly was sipping nectar from yellow asters. "Here's a butterfly that's quite rare. You find it here and there in Arizona. *Lemonias zela*. I've collected quite a few. It will sit there all day. We could come back at four and it would still be here. The form of its wings and its general manner are very mothlike. Quite interesting. But it is a real butterfly. It belongs to a tremendous family of South American butterflies."

The morning turned up a few more interesting specimens, but still no wood nymph, Nabokov noted sadly. Once he swished the net triumphantly and trapped two butterflies. He grinned savagely. "Lygdamus Blue—female," he said. "This other, by freakish chance, is a male blue of another species that was flying with it. That's adultery. Or a step toward adultery." He let the offending male fly free, unpunished.

Another time, Nabokov swung and netted three butterflies, one an angle wing. "It has a curiously formed letter C. It mimics a chink of light through a dead leaf. Isn't that wonderful? Isn't that humorous?"

Still shy of a bona fide wood nymph, the Nabokovs headed south to Sedona for lunch. "I lost two butterfly collections," Nabokov recalled, as the car sped along. "One to the Bolsheviks, one to the Germans. I have another I gave to Cornell. I dream of stealing it back."

Lunch over, the Nabokovs drove farther south. Nabokov's eyes wallowed in the gorgeous windswept buttes. "It looks like a giant chess game is being played around us." At 2:20, Mrs. Nabokov parked the car by the side of the road. Nabokov, net at the ready, was off like an eager boy. Mrs. Nabokov, retrieving another net from the rear seat, joined him. "You should see my wife catch butterflies," he said. "One little movement and they're in the net."

The grove was disappointing. "Rien," he muttered. He probed some bushes. "There is nothing," he said. "A hopeless place." They gave up the hunt and drove back to Sedona to shop. Vladimir followed Mrs. Nabokov into the supermarket. "When I was younger I ate some butterflies in Vermont to see if they were poisonous," he said, as his wife hovered over the cold cuts counter. "I didn't see any difference between a monarch butterfly and a Viceroy. The taste of both was vile, but I had no ill effects. They tasted like almonds and perhaps a green cheese combination. I ate them raw. I held one in one hot little hand and one in the other. Will you eat some with me tomorrow for breakfast?" His visitor declined.

That night, still not surfeited with the day's steady diet of butterflies, Nabokov burrowed into a pile of scientific papers and pulled out the thickest one, his article on the Nearctic members of the genus *Lycaeides Hubner.* "This work took me several years and undermined my health for quite a while. Before, I never wore glasses. This is my favorite work. I think I really did well there." Yes, the Soviets were aware of his work on butterflies. As recently as last November, one Lubimov had attacked him in the *Literary Gazette.* "He said that I was starving in America, 'compelled to earn a precarious existence selling butterflies.'" Nabokov laughed merrily.

The next morning, Nabokov was as chipper and as restless as ever. "Come on, darling," he called to Mrs. Nabokov during breakfast. "The sun is wasting away! It's a quarter to ten." Mrs. Nabokov took her time. "He doesn't know that everyone is wise to him," she said. At 10:10, Nabokov at last succeeded in luring her behind the wheel. "We are going to Jerome," he said happily. "The wood nymph should be out, I hope, on Mingus Mountain." While the car sped swiftly through a veritable Lolitaland, Nabokov said, "Butterflies help me in my writing. Very often when I go and there are no butterflies, I am thinking. I wrote most of *Lolita* this way. I wrote it in motels or parked cars."

The Nabokovs reached Jerome ("Welcome to Ghost City. Three places to eat") at 11:10. "Shall we catch my butterfly today?" Nabokov asked.

At a marker announcing the elevation to be 7,023 feet, Mrs. Nabokov parked. Both took nets from the back seat and walked up a dirt road bordered by pines. A yellow butterfly danced crazily by. Nabokov swung and missed. "Common," he said. "I'm just getting warmed up." Unfortunately, a fifteen minute search of the terrain revealed nothing. Nabokov turned toward an iris-covered meadow. "I can't believe there won't be butterflies here," he said. He was mistaken. "I'm very much disappointed," Nabokov said after searching the meadow. "Rien. Rien."

Nabokov returned to the car. "It was very sad. 'And then I saw that strong man put his head on his forearms and sob like a woman.'" At 12:40, Mrs. Nabokov stopped again. "This will be our last stop today," Nabokov said. "It is this kind of place that my wood nymph should be flying, but with the exception of three cows and a calf, there is nothing." "Do we have to mix with cows?" asked Mrs. Nabokov.

They got back in the car and drove toward Jerome. "Sad," said Nabokov. "'His face was now a tear-stained mask.'" Five minutes later, he had Mrs. Nabokov stop at Mescal Canyon. "We may be in for a surprise here," he said. Alas, there was none. He walked up a dirt road alone. Mrs. Nabokov lent her net to their visitor. With a whoop of joy, the visitor snared a white-winged beauty. Cupping it in his hands, he showed it to Nabokov who dismissed it airily. "A winged cliché." It had been a poor day for hunting. There would be other days to come, but the visitor wouldn't be there. As the car swung out for the journey home, Nabokov spread his arms and said sadly, "What can I say? What is there to say? I am ashamed for the butterflies. I apologize for the butterflies."

The apology was, of course, gracefully rejected.

# The Author of *Lolita*

## Neil Hickey / 1959

From *American Weekly*, October 4, 1959. © Neil Hickey, Adjunct Professor, Columbia University Graduate School of Journalism. Reprinted by permission.

There's a new word in the English language, one that inspires a welter of reaction from uncontrolled indignation to sly, surreptitious laughter. The word is "Lolita" and it's the title of the most wildly controversial bestseller since James Joyce's *Ulysses*.

So far-reaching has been its influence that Paris high-fashion designers are now displaying dresses for the fall of 1959 with the titles "Lolita" and "Nymphet."

The man who started it all is a bit surprised by the fuss it has stirred up. Russian-born, balding, good-humored, professor of European literature at a staid Ivy League university: this is Vladimir Nabokov (pronounced Na-*bow*-kov), whose vivid tale of a gum-chewing, comic-book-reading American schoolgirl and her unsavory adventures with a middle-aged *émigré* writer has earned for him descriptions ranging all the way from: "an artist of rare comic genius" to "a doddering and willful pornographer."

Whatever the truth, readers, critics, educators and parents have stormed the author ever since the novel's appearance early last year and, with a collective, open-armed gesture, inquired, "Why have you done this thing?" To which Nabokov replies, with a shake of the head, "What did I do? I'm no messenger boy. If the novel conveys some kind of moral, then God bless those who find it."

But more important than messages or Paris fashions for the fall is the matter of pornography and whether *Lolita* qualifies as such. Many critics insist that the tale of Humbert Humbert's passion for a twelve-year-old schoolgirl is a tale of pure satiric genius, written in a new, marvelously inventive kind of language; that the unwholesome situation it describes detracts not at all from its importance as a work of art. (It was still lodged firmly on the bestseller lists a year after publication.)

Vladimir Nabokov took time out recently to discuss *Lolita* with *The American Weekly*. He reviewed the details of his celebrated novel, which appeared first, illegally, in France in [1955]. Humbert Humbert (a nonsense name that sets the tone of the book) contrives to become the guardian of one Dolores (Lolita) Haze, a pre-teener for whom he has developed an uncommon yen. He embarks with her on a cross-country debauch unprecedented in American literature.

Lolita is no innocent, however. In her own precocious way she knows more about the game of love and how to win it than does the cloying Humbert, who appears to her little more than a comic, pathetic figure. "Modern coeducation, juvenile mores, the campfire racket and so forth had utterly and hopelessly depraved her," says the author.

She deserts Humbert, finally, for a goon-like husband and manages to attain something like conventional respectability. In a terrifying, farcical finale, Humbert collars a wealthy writer with whom Lolita had an earlier affair and shoots him. Lolita dies in childbirth. Humbert succumbs to a heart attack while awaiting trial.

Does all this add up to pornography? A majority of the reviewers say no, but the untidy spectacle of love between a fifty-year-old neurotic and a gum-chewing sub-teen has thrust the book into international fame—even among the habitués of Paris dress salons.

Says Nabokov, "My definition of pornography is 'a copulation of clichés' in which an author puts the reader on familiar ground and then makes a direct attempt at provoking the most basic response. This is not the case with *Lolita*."

How did he go about gathering such detailed information on nymphets (Nabokov's own word for young love sprites)? Is there anything personal in his interest in them? He laughs at this.

"My knowledge of nymphets is purely scholarly, I assure you," he says. "In fact, I don't much care for little girls. I have a twenty-five-year-old son, so I'm probably better qualified to write about little boys."

Sometime around the fall of 1960, a motion picture on the adventures of Lolita will go into production (Harris and Kubrick, who made *Paths of Glory* and *The Killing*, will produce) and Nabokov is not at all concerned with the obvious difficulties of translating his rather explicit tale into manageable fare for the "family" moviegoer. "A motion picture has a life of its own," he says. "As to who should play the main roles, I'm not movie fan enough to say."

At sixty, Nabokov lives the quiet life of a university professor at Cornell, in Ithaca, New York. His chief interest, outside of writing and teaching, is chasing butterflies, a passion he indulges with enormous energy to the far reaches of the American continent. It's a pastime that dates from his child-hood in Russia, where his father (later assassinated by Russian monarchists) was the founder and leader of the Constitutional Democratic Party, the lib-eral party of Russia.

Despite censorship problems, particularly in Great Britain, where *L'affaire Lolita* has become a political football involving a seat in Parliament, the British obscenity laws and heated words between major literary figures, Nabokov is firmly in favor of censorship to protect the public from pornog-raphy, an unusual attitude for a man whose career has been bedeviled by censors.

What about the American sex symbols—Marilyn Monroe and Jayne Mansfield? Do they represent sex for the author of *Lolita*?

Says Nabokov: "Well, first of all, Miss Marilyn Monroe is one of the greatest comedy actresses of our time. She is simply superb. Miss Mansfield I've never seen. But the usual concept of the bosomy female does not repre-sent sex from my point of view. Sexual appeal seems, to me, something far more subtle than that."

As an educator, Nabokov is firmly against coeducation on any but the grade-school level. "Young girls," he says, "mature so much faster than boys. They become voluptuous and get into the habit of wearing tight woolen sweaters that make for enormous distraction. That just defeats the whole process of education."

Beginning a year's leave of absence from his post at Cornell to hunt but-terflies in Arizona, Nabokov insisted he plans no *Son of Lolita* to capitalize on the earlier novel's notoriety. (Grace Metalious, author of *Peyton Place*, will soon publish *Return to Peyton Place*.) "Lolita is dead," he says. "I have no plans to resurrect her."

# Nabokov

## John Coleman / 1959

From *The Spectator*, November 6, 1959. © *The Spectator*. Reprinted by permission.

*Lolita* rolls slowly down its London slipway this week and the author and his wife are here with us to preside over what practically everyone except John Gordon hopes will be a serene launching. I talked to Mr. Nabokov at his hotel a few days ago, a Mr. Nabokov disappointingly free of the "five body-guards" accredited to him by one of our more inflamed dailies. Mrs. Nabokov, a charming, elegant woman with a fine profile and white hair, assisted at the interview but showed no signs of carrying a gun. It was an occasion without formality, rather like a supervision with the unusually sympathetic don that Mr. Nabokov not surprisingly resembles: after all, no one really expected Humbert Humbert. The twenty-year-old Vladimir left Russia with his family in 1919 and has never been back. In his autobiographical volume *Speak, Memory*, he writes of his beloved St. Petersburg and the surrounding countryside with longing (it is typical of their absolute rejection of "that trite *deus ex machina* the Russian Revolution" that Leningrad exists for neither Mr. Nabokov nor his wife). "Sometimes I fancy myself revisiting them with a false passport, under an assumed name. It could be done." But it never will be now. That Russia has gone: all he needs of it he has preserved in the lavishly furnished nostalgia of *Speak, Memory*, that magnificent succession of Proustian *madeleines*, and his eight Russian novels and many stories; "my artificial but beautifully exact Russian world." He was at Cambridge till 1922, reading Modern Languages; then in Berlin, where he taught English and tennis, translated *Alice in Wonderland* into Russian, helped to compile a Russian grammar for foreigners ("Madam, I am a doctor, here is a banana"), and produced a daily crossword puzzle for an *émigré* paper. He left Paris for America in 1940.

Why did he choose America? It seems America chose him. "I came to Cambridge again in 1938 to give some lectures and readings, a disappointing visit in bad weather. I went to see my old tutor"—the story is in his memoirs—"whose tea things I had crushed underfoot at our first meeting sixteen years before, and, walking into a dark room, stepped on them again." Recognition was, apparently, immediate. There was unfulfilled talk of a post at Leeds and nothing doing at Oxford or Cambridge. "Then I had the offer of some lecturing in America. In fact, I went in place of a friend of mine, and in 1942 was taken on at Wellesley College. It's funny how that happened. I'm certain it was because of that *Alice* translation, not the first in Russian, but the best." You believe Mr. Nabokov. There is nothing immodest about the delight he shows in some of his achievements. "They have a unique collection of Aliceana of which they're very proud. So they wanted me in it, I suppose. I was very happy there, but it was an exhausting time. I was also curator of Lepidoptera at Harvard!" From Wellesley he went to Cornell as Professor of Russian and European Literature. They have a champion soccer team and he relived his goalkeeping days ("I had the Mediterranean, *prima-donna* style, out of place in England") on the touchline. Mr. Nabokov as Mr. Nabokov obviously feels warmly towards America: the slanting gibes of H. H. and Pnin are not to be taken out of context. "It's such a *receptive* country. *Lolita* went to four publishers who turned it down in horror—there had been all that fuss over Edmund Wilson's *Hecate County*—then, of course, it came out in Paris in the Olympia Press edition. But it was able to be published in America, finally, because critics of Trilling's calibre have helped to create the climate of opinion over there. You feel they really have some influence." Mr. Nabokov politely refused to be drawn when I invited his opinion of our greater squeamishness. "Perhaps because you're so close to France." The dubious reputation of Olympia Press hadn't helped. Yes, there should certainly be some forms of censorship against commercial pornography.

We turned to language. "My English is getting better." Mr. Nabokov's English is impeccable, spoken with a gentle accent. "I have no ear for dialogue, you know. Yes, I managed the American rhythms in the end in *Lolita*, but it was exacting work. I'd be at sea if I had to do, oh, Dorsetshire farmers, or Londoners even . . . even harder—London is very difficult. He turned to his wife and chuckled. "The hardest of all for me now, of course, would be two *Soviet* farmers. Yes, the language has changed a great deal. It is Basic Russian now; provincial." I asked him which of his three languages (French is the other) he commonly thought and spoke in these days; all of them, he decided. And, after all, a lot of thinking was done in images, not words. But he always spoke Russian when he was at home and, when he hurt himself, swore in Russian anywhere. Talk of debased speech currency led us to the

Russian literary language today. Could *Zhivago* conceivably be called "provincial?" Had he liked the book—and its translation? "The English was better." It was a poor book. Mr. Nabokov invoked the word "bourgeois," lending it a solid Flaubertian emphasis while I caught my breath. "All that about the Bolsheviks—so confused. And the symbolism—what is it supposed to be doing?" (Mr. Nabokov, as I already knew, is a stout foe of symbols and allegory, "partly due to my old feud with Freudian voodooism and partly to my loathing of generalizations devised by literary mythists and sociologists." In the margin, I might add that, when I taxed him later with his confessed admiration for Kafka, he refused to accept him as a wielder of symbols, darkly hinting it had been a put-up job by an early aficionado, after which the world had followed suit.) No, *Zhivago*'s reputation astonished him. He sighed. "All those artificial snow storms!" We agreed there was certainly a lot of weather in Pasternak and passed on.

We may expect to read at least one of Mr. Nabokov's Russian novels soon. His son Dmitri—"he speaks beautiful English"—has just completed a translation. "It has really come out wonderfully. And *my* translation into English of *Eugene Onegin* is finished at last—in five volumes. One of poem, four of annotations!" Mr. Nabokov has erratic writing habits. "Sometimes I'll do nothing for days or weeks, then, suddenly, all through the night. And always in longhand. I use these file cards." He pulled some out of an inside pocket and began reading one. "Yes, here's a note about the etiquette in giving your name or someone else's to a new subspecies of butterfly. A delicate business." He cheerfully acknowledged that there was more certainty of posterity for Nabokov's Wood Nymph, netted twenty years ago, than for Nabokov's nymphet, and read some wittily appropriate stanzas from a very slim volume of verse ("my fourteen collected English poems").

The conversation grew increasingly discursive. "When I lecture my students, I make them examine even Madame Bovary's hairstyle—details are *important* . . . I don't believe at all in didactic art. There seem to be three levels of readership: at the bottom, those who go after 'human interest'; in the middle, the people who want ideas, packaged thought about Life and Truth; at the top, the proper readers, who go for *style*. Tolstoy's books suffer from injections of *ideas* . . . English writers who have moved my pen to the right or left? No one, really. I don't believe in movements. But, of course, I enormously admire Shakespeare, Keats—not Shelley, not Swinburne." Little was said about contemporary English letters, but the feeling communicated itself somehow that our new comic novelists are not exactly Mr. Nabokov's idea of fun. "The literary achievements that most satisfy me now are a paper

I wrote on South American Blue Butterflies—and *Lolita*." Inevitably, the "event" of *Lolita* rounded off the questioning. "It hasn't really changed our lives much. I was going to retire from Cornell, in any case. You can say, oh, two shirts instead of one—and lots of trouble with the taxmen."

# Vladimir Nabokov Discusses *Lolita*

## Kerry Ellard / 1959

From the Canadian Broadcasting Corporation, November 30, 1959. © CBC Licensing. Reprinted by permission.

**Narrator:** Probably the most talked-of book in the past decade has been *Lolita* by Vladimir Nabokov. The most recent development of this book was its publication in England earlier this month. Tonight, "Assignment" begins a three-part profile of Mr. Nabokov. Kerry Ellard talks to this novelist, who has also been Professor of Russian and European Literature at Cornell University and curator of butterflies at Harvard. At one time, Mr. Nabokov believed that his claim to immortality would stem from the fact that he has a butterfly named after him. It's the Nabokov Wood Nymph, discovered twenty years ago and bearing a name strangely similar to his nymphet of *Lolita*. The question of his book is the first interest of nearly everyone.

**Vladimir Nabokov:** I wrote this book because I had to write it. I thought it was an interesting problem to solve in artistic terms, but I never thought of its being controversial or not. As a matter of fact, I never bothered about what would happen to it after I had written it.
**Kerry Ellard:** When did you write it?
**VN:** I started writing it as early as '48 and I went on [writing it] in my spare time well into '54. As soon as it was finished I sent a copy to my agent in Paris, who arranged for its publication in English. The book was published in '55 and was published in New York three years later in the American edition.

**KE:** One of the big discussion points of *Lolita* to most people is: Is it pornography or is it not?
**VN:** This is a question which is very easily answered. I gave a complete, detailed answer to that question, if that question be raised at all, in a kind

of afterpiece appended to the American edition of *Lolita*, where I explained that pornography was, first of all, I used the term "copulation of clichés"; something which is fundamentally banal, something which is for a very primitive type of reader. That type of reader, if he acquires *Lolita* for that special purpose, will not get anywhere because he'll get bored after the first page. He'll get more and more bored and will never read the book to the end. So this is not what I would call pornography. This is what I would call a very, very simple term: Art.

KE: Mr. Nabokov, you were originally Russian, weren't you?
VN: I was born in Russia in 1899 and I had been writing in Russian since 1925. I am a "White Russian." That is the technical term for a Russian *émigré*. I left Russia in 1919, and since 1925 I've been writing novels and short stories and poems in Russian. These were published by *émigré* firms in Berlin and Paris and New York. Eight in all. Banned in Soviet Russia, I'm sure they are somewhere there in libraries or smuggled in by my fellow writers. The books which I and other writers, such as Bunin or Aldonov, brought out had a comparatively wide circulation.

KE: In which language do you prefer to write then, English or Russian?
VN: Now I think I would prefer English because I gave up my extremely rich and comfortable Russian language for another tongue in which I am more or less at home because I always knew English. When I was a little boy I had an English nurse and then a whole series of English governesses. I knew French, too. I've always had three languages. And, unlike Joseph Conrad, I had written in my mother tongue before, and indeed was an established author in emigration when I switched to English. This was difficult because it was a kind of diminishment from what I would term my palatial Russian to the narrow quarters of my English. It was like moving from a darkened house to another on a starless night during a strike of candle makers and torchbearers. After a period of panic and groping, I managed to settle down rather comfortably. Now I know what a caterpillar must feel on the rack of metamorphosis in the straightjacket of the chrysalis. Now I'm in the last stage, what in science we call the "imago" stage, and I hope to stay in that stage as long as I write because I could not repeat that performance again.

KE: Mr. Nabokov, what are you doing at the moment?
VN: I have just completed a huge work on my favorite Russian writer, the

romantic poet, the classical Russian writer Pushkin, of the early nineteenth century. And it is a translation of Pushkin's *Eugene Onegin*, which will have a huge commentary. It will be brought out by the Bollingen Press in New York in five handsome volumes of about five hundred pages each. During my years of teaching literature, I demanded of my students the passion of science and the patience of poetry. As an artist and a scholar I always prefer the specific detail to the generalization, images to ideas; and obscure facts to plain symbols are always more interesting. So this was my treatment of the Pushkin theme. I had worked for ten years, on and off, on this translation and on those notes. It is an absolutely literal translation of the thing. I do not believe in paraphrases, that would be too easy. It has no rhymes. It is honest and clumsy and ponderous and miraculously faithful. It is what an English schoolboy would call a "crib," and it is meant to be a crib. I have notes to every stanza and to the commentary I really gave a discussion of such things as irrational associations and a complete *Explication de Texte*, as the French say.

**Narrator:** Now we're continuing Kerry Ellard's talk with Vladimir Nabokov. Mr. Nabokov, himself a controversial author, has very definite views on other writers. He discounts almost entirely the other recent Russian novel *Doctor Zhivago* by Boris Pasternak. He doesn't like the English poets Shelley or Swinburne, but he does admire Shakespeare and Keats. Referring to his own work, Mr. Nabokov feels that his two best works are *Lolita* and a paper he wrote dealing with South American blue butterflies. Kerry Ellard has now some more questions for Mr. Nabokov.

**KE:** What about *Pnin*? *Pnin* is a book of yours which was written quite a while ago, I believe, and has suddenly become popular through the fame which came to you from *Lolita*. Is it doing very well right now?

**VN:** This is not quite exact because *Pnin* was published serially. It came out in chapters in *The New Yorker*. At the time it enjoyed a certain success among people who like literature as much as I do. But finally it came out as a book. It came out, as a matter of fact, after *Lolita* had been published by Olympia in Paris. Its success was a gradual development of the general success attending my other works because it is not true that I was a completely obscure, unknown writer before *Lolita* came out. I was very well known in those circles who were interested in literature. It is only what the French call *le gros public* that discovered my work [later on]. Others knew it before.

**KE:** Mr. Nabokov, I've read *Lolita* and enjoyed it immensely. You seem to write with a gusto. An awful lot of fun seems to have been had by somebody in writing this book. At least in *Lolita* I had the feeling you got a real boot out of writing this thing.

**VN:** Yes, "a real boot" is good. I did. I got a kick out of it as we say in New York State and I thought it was fun. It was also very difficult. It was a very arduous task and there were many times when I told myself, "Well, perhaps I'd better stop and do something else easier than that." But for me, art is difficult. Art is never easy. A good book is never a simple book. Good litera-ture is always elaborate, always complex; and this idea, this feeling, led me on and helped me to stick to the task I had set to myself. I was having fun, but it was the kind of fun that one has in paddling down one of those rapids that you have in Canada and elsewhere in the Rockies, where everything is very difficult and very dangerous and you are very cold and wet, but still it is fun.

**KE:** Yesterday I was riding on the Metro with a friend and we were talking about *Lolita*, and we were thoroughly astonished. Someone turned around as they were getting off the Metro train and said, "Tell Mr. Nabokov for me, I think his book is lousy." Do you get this kind of reaction from people because *Lolita* is such a controversial novel?

**VN:** That's a rather rare reaction. Perhaps it does occur more usually than I know. But it is also true that among the thousands of letters that my wife and I got in reference to *Lolita*, there were only three or four that were criti-cal of the book and that were downright insulting; so that when my wife told a journalist in America that there had been only two insulting letters, [the] next week we got one which said: "This is the third. I have not read *Lolita* but it is a wicked book and it should be banned."

**KE:** What do you think about book banning?

**VN:** Generally speaking, the banning of books is a medieval custom, a medieval tradition. I'm not speaking of censorship. I think there should be some kind of censorship against downright pornography and that kind of thing, there's no doubt about that. But the banning of books just because they displease some cranky old party, some philistine, some postmaster, or some head librarian—I think that's silly.

**KE:** Mr. Nabokov, you have coined a word in English now. "Lolita" has come to apply to a nymphet, as you call her in your book, and this was a classification which hitherto had never existed. You invented the classification of a nymphet.

**VN:** That's right, I invented the classification. I invented the appliance of that term but I did not invent the word. The word is a diminutive of "nymph," which had been used before by early French poets, by Ronsard for instance, and by English writers of the time, of Shakespeare's time as a matter of fact, who have used the word nymphet before in poems. But in those days it just meant a small, a nice, a gentle, a charming nymph. It had not that special tang that I gave it. And it is not I who gave it. It is my hero, Mr. Humbert Humbert, who concocted the term in order to apply it to very young girls.

**KE:** Do nymphets exist? Was this a figment of your imagination or has it got some basis in fact?

**VN:** It was a figment of my imagination but I suppose they will exist now, as often happens. Say a painter draws a fog on a river. Then the next man who sees a fog on the river says, "Oh, that's just like Turner's. That's his kind of fog." And so everybody starts to see that fog in terms of the picture which first expressed it. I suppose that's the same thing with those graceful girls, of which that particular nymphet is a representative.

**KE:** You have immortalized yourself by putting a name to something which hitherto did not have a name.

**VN:** Immortalize is, of course, a ponderous word. I hope I will continue to be happier than my poor little girl is.

**Narrator:** Tonight, we're completing the story of Vladimir Nabokov, author of the bestseller *Lolita*. Many of Mr. Nabokov's earlier works are written in Russian and, as yet, unavailable in North America. However, this situation may be changed shortly, as the author's son, Dmitri, is currently translating one of his father's Russian novels. Tonight, Kerry Ellard talks with Mr. Nabokov about his views concerning *Lolita* and nymphets in general.

**KE:** Mr. Nabokov, how did you pick America as a set for this particular book? Some people I think would—certainly myself, living in France –find that this would apply even more so to Paris.

**VN:** Curiously enough, when I first started to toy with this theme I thought of staging the whole thing in France and I even wrote a first draft of *Lolita*, a kind of sketch or short story of some thirty pages or so. Then I realized that I didn't know France well enough. Though I don't know any American little girl, I can imagine an American little girl . . . but I just could not imagine a French little girl clearly enough, lucidly enough and poetically, artistically enough to use that as a term of reference. In America I found, to my intense relief and gratitude, a country that I could use and an America that I could reimagine. The America in *Lolita* is my own America. It's a Nabokovian America, a kind of world that I have recreated. I've been very happy there, very content, and I've found it the place for writing books.

**KE:** Are you going now to write another book?

**VN:** I'm planning another novel, which will not be a continuation of *Lolita* as one newspaper in London had me say. This book will probably be set in America as [was] *Lolita*. I'm going back to America in a few months and I'll put myself into the task of writing it.

**KE:** When people interview you, and I'm sure you've been interviewed thousands of times now, what do they usually ask you?

**VN:** They generally ask me about my book; why I wrote it. This is one of those questions I find unanswerable. Any kind of theme which I would choose would also require the same answer.

**KE:** Mr. Nabokov, I know quite a few Russians in Paris and I've met them before in other places. The Slavic temperament has got something that [makes] people always want to go back to Russia. I know Americans who live out of America and Canadians who live out of Canada and they don't particularly harp on going home again. But Russians—maybe it's because some of them had to get out—have a certain love of Russia that nobody else has. Every time they have three or four vodkas they stand around together and say "Those were the days on the Volga."

**VN:** I think you are right in half-suggesting that the reason for that passion to go back is the sudden cutting away of a country. Otherwise, if you know that you can go back, and if the parting has been more or less gradual and you have some contact with the old country, that's another kind of thing. I know many Irishmen who would like to go back to Ireland. They have their friends and their old aunts there, and sometimes their father and their mother and so on, and they go back with pleasure. But it is not this kind of keen spiritual pang which an *émigré* feels. If I went back to Russia I would look up the places of my childhood, the landscape of my youth. It would be a very small country that I would be going back to because it would come to me, not in terms of a huge national, geographic and political kind of country, but in terms of the garden, of the park, of the grove, where I played as a child.

**KE:** Thank you very much, Mr. Nabokov, for talking to us this afternoon. I hope that a lot of us will be looking forward to your next book and I think a lot of people will get hold of *Pnin* and take a look at Nabokov in a broader view.

**VN:** And remember that there is nothing between the 'P' and the 'N.' It is *Pnin* and not "Penin," which is, of course, difficult for the Anglo-Saxon tongue to achieve.

**KE:** Thank you very much, Mr. Nabokov. This is Kerry Ellard reporting to "Assignment" from Paris.

# After *Lolita*: A Conversation with Vladimir Nabokov—with Digressions

## John G. Hayman / 1959

From *The Twentieth Century*, December, 1959. © John G. Hayman. Reprinted by permission.

The series of events leading to the American publication of Vladimir Nabo-kov's *Lolita* read like a highly contrived fantasy. Rejected by four American publishers on the grounds that parts of it were pornographic, the novel was finally published by the Olympia Press in Paris. According to one account, however, so many copies of this edition found their way into England that the English Home Office called for its suppression. The truth of this account, however, has been denied. The subject matter, which was at first found objectionable, is, as most people now know, the love of a mature man, Humbert, for a girl of twelve—a "nymphet" in Humbert's terminology. One of the American publishers felt that he might be able to print the work if a boy of the same age were substituted for the girl.

All this is somewhat unfortunate since the significance of the work as literature tends to be overlooked in the side issues. In America, for example, the fantasy continues. The film rights have been sold for $150,000 (plus fif-teen percent of the film's revenue) and it is *Time*'s guess that the chief roles will go to Maurice Chevalier and Brigitte Bardot. The work is also being translated into various languages, and Mr. Nabokov recently discovered a Swedish version that was about to be published, the slightness of which sug-gested to him that certain portions had been deleted. On scrutiny he found that only the "purple patches" had been selected. Naturally, Mr. Nabokov suppressed the edition.

When I suggested to Nabokov that he might reasonably feel outraged at the charges of pornography, he replied that he thought they were "just plain silly." Talking with Nabokov in his office at Cornell University, I frequently met this mildness. He was unwilling, for example, either to speak harshly of any living writer or to select any for particular praise. Those earlier writers he criticized, too, were nearly always commended on some personal grounds. ("Galsworthy was a good *man*, I believe . . . Gorky was a great *character*.") And yet his mildness is mingled with excitement—an excitement which will often reveal itself in a sudden aside and which makes conversation with Nabokov a little like riding on a switchback.

Nabokov's casual attitude towards the publication of *Lolita* is connected, it seems to me, with his general unconcern with his audience. I recalled that a number of English critics and writers have suggested that the writer in America is "isolated," that he is never quite sure who, if anyone, is going to read his work. Nabokov said that he had never been troubled by this: "I write for myself," he said, "and hope for hundreds of little Nabokovs." So far there have been over one hundred thousand little Nabokovs who have read *Lolita*, so perhaps such a rejoinder was to be expected. And yet the question of the writer's public in America (which remains for me, at least, an interesting one) was posed recently concerning *Lolita* in a cartoon in *The New York Times Book Review*. A carefully dressed office worker was reading a copy of *Lolita* over the shoulder of a man partially engaged in working down a manhole. The caption was an order from the workman: "Go and buy your own copy." Possibly the little Nabokovs are thus diversified—and possibly the trouble with much American writing is that it is aimed too calculatedly at certain small and different sections of the public. Nabokov, however, is not particularly interested in any of this.

That many of the problems normally experienced by writers emigrating to America seem irrelevant to Nabokov is partly to be explained by his special background. Prior to the Revolution, his family were members of the Russian nobility, and there is a fascinating account of his early life in a series of autobiographical sketches published under the title *Conclusive Evidence*. There was extensive travel at an early age (Paris, Biarritz, Berlin, Abbazia), and this gave Nabokov an early familiarity with a number of foreign languages and a certain cosmopolitanism. There was also an Englishness surrounding his early existence (Pears Soap, imported Golden Syrup and English governesses). It would be wrong, however, to feel that this led to a "rootless" existence. There was Russia, always Russia. Nabokov says, however, that "the fertile emotion of nostalgia" for his country was liberated long ago in the writing of a novel. He now feels nostalgic only when confronted with a region of America strikingly reminiscent of Russia.

The "American Scene"—something most emigrant writers have attempted to analyze at some time—does not as an entity interest Nabokov.

He has, he says, no idea even what the term means. I quoted as a guide an extract of W.H. Auden. In a preface to some essays of Henry James, Auden once listed such phenomena of American life as "the unspeakable jukeboxes, the horrible Rockettes, the insane salads, etc." and added that without these things "the analyst and the emigrant alike would never understand by contrast the nature of the Good Place nor desire it with sufficient desperation to stand a chance of arriving." The quotation, however, didn't seem of very much use; Nabokov seemed more interested in the idea of insane salads than in any other part of the remark. Finally, he said that it was the generality of the statement that made him suspicious: "A little town in New England is so entirely different from a little town in Oregon. And a little town in one part of Oregon is so entirely different from a little town in another part." The standardized and frequently ugly features connected with the mechanics of living simply do not trouble him. Quite the opposite, in fact; he has suggested in writing that "there is nothing more exhilarating than philistine vulgarity."

The reason for Nabokov's fresh approach to such things as soda fountains and motels is, however, probably less the result of a certain temperament and more a matter of language. Even today, after eighteen years in America, he will experience difficulty with the inflection of an idiom and repeat it several times, varying the position of the emphasis (sometimes sadly abandoning the phrase altogether). He had, he recalled in conversation, not only to create his imaginative world out of America on arriving there; he had to form a new language. I asked him how he went about this: "I read *Webster's Dictionary* for one thing," he replied. And it is perhaps as a result of this that one occasionally meets such words as 'alembic,' 'achromatic,' 'aquarelle' and 'ikontinct' in the space of a couple of pages of his writing. The process of building a vocabulary was obviously a laborious one, but in his writing one often feels that Nabokov is actually building a language as he writes. There is a sense in which this is true of any major writer, but it is more obvious in one who is using a language which is not his native one. One of the ways in which this peculiar effect shows itself is in the slight distance existing between Nabokov's personal use of words and the more conventional. He will criticize the word "skyscraper," for example, and move into a beautiful description of the buildings, "remote and lilac colored, and strangely aquatic, mingling their first cautious lights with the colors of the sunset and revealing, with a kind of dreamy candor, the pulsating inside of their semi-transparent structure." He makes Humbert, in *Lolita*, turn a neon sign advertising Gulfex Lubrication into one declaring Genuflexion

Lubricity. To the English or American reader this verbal awareness and wit seems a full recompense for the loss Nabokov laments—the loss of his "untrammelled, rich, and infinitely docile Russian tongue . . . the baffling mirror, the black-velvet backdrop, the implied associations and traditions." Nabokov himself, however, is unwilling to acknowledge that the freshness of viewpoint and language that we notice results in any major way from his using a language other than his native one. "My Russian novels," he said, "were just as far from the cliché."

Nabokov's position as a specifically American writer has a curious ambivalence about it. One critic, for example, has said of *Lolita* that it has "a style, an individuality, a brilliance which may yet create a tradition in American letters"—a strange notion by any standards and significant only in its expression of the need felt in America for a "tradition." Nevertheless, Nabokov's treatment of a concern which seems to preoccupy many American novelists at the moment is an interesting one. This concern has been defined by at least one English critic as an unfortunate obsession with the nervous system. "It becomes," one critic has written, "a matter of nerves rather than of a finer and more rigorous perception." This might conceivably make sense when applied to, let us say, a novel of Jack Kerouac. *The Subterraneans*, for example, begins with the statement: "Once I was young and had so much more orientation and could talk with nervous intelligence about everything and with clarity and without so much literary preambling as this . . ." And the irony which may be evident here disappears as the novel advances; the interest is centered firmly in the protagonist's nervous system. Nabokov's own creation, Humbert, is certainly, by most people's definition, neurotic. He twists, he turns, he shouts, he cries, he addresses his remarks in the course of the novel at a jury, at a doctor, at the reader, at "folks" in general. But the interest in *Lolita* is not restricted to Humbert's nervous twitches. One often feels the pressure of his neuroticism, but there are also sections of the book where one is kept at an intentional distance from Humbert. One views his obsession in all its grotesqueness. It is in insuring this that Nabokov seems to me to differ from most American writers at the moment. In most novels we are invited to suffer and sympathize with the protagonist—perhaps because the novelist is afraid to relax his grasp even for a moment on the reader.

This liberation from Humbert's neurotic viewpoint (which is paradoxically achieved by giving him *many* viewpoints) evokes in the reader the final emotion Nabokov says he *should* experience.

"For me a work of fiction exists only in so far as it affords me what I shall bluntly call aesthetic bliss; that is, a sense of being somehow, somewhere, connected with other states of being where art (curiosity, tenderness, kindness, ecstasy) is the norm. There are not many such books. All the rest is either topical trash or what some call the Literature of Ideas, which very often is topical trash coming in huge blocks of plaster that are carefully transmitted from age to age until somebody comes along with a hammer and takes a good crack at Balzac, at Gorky, at Mann."

In our conversation Nabokov took a crack at a few more writers. I suggested that different periods seemed to me to call for different interests on the part of the writer and that there might be a period in which moral problems were especially relevant. Rashly, I hazarded the eighteenth century and mentioned Richardson. "A third-rate writer," Nabokov retorted. "Such frigidity." Pleased with the word, he repeated it several times, making it sound very chilling. "But there was Sterne," he added. "Sterne was a first-rate writer."

The instantaneous vision, the immediate which is also timeless—this is what interests Nabokov and makes him contemptuous of the social and didactic writer. The problem is, how to express the instantaneous vision in a sequence of words. I asked if he had tried to do this in *Lolita* by breaking down the language and by the frequent use of phrases instead of sentences. Nabokov was skeptical. "I sometimes think one could best describe lightning in a long, elaborately built sentence," he said, simulating the quality of lightning by gestures. "But one could also do it by using two words. Truth is what matters, isn't it?" There was a pause; and then, as often after a pause, Nabokov began talking about Russian writers. "Gorky," he said, "once wrote: 'The sea is laughing.' But then Gorky was a bad writer. As Chekhov commented, the only thing you can say about the sea is: 'The sea is *big*.'"

However achieved, this attempt to communicate a sense of the instantaneous vision and to leave the reader with a single impression is something which, Nabokov feels, calls for peculiarly sensitive reading, as well as writing. "You see," he said, "you cannot read a novel (there is all the physical effort of moving the eye from left to right—of turning over all the pages). No, you can only reread a novel. Or re-reread a novel." We arrive at a single impression, it seems, by increasingly refining our separate impressions. Such an approach to reading a novel is obviously open to attack, but it is closely connected with Nabokov's own achievement as a novelist. One isn't asked to identify oneself with any of the characters in a novel; this, Nabokov says, is "a low pleasure—one for minor readers (you see, there must be minor readers because there are minor writers)." No, the good reader maintains a delicately suspended attitude: "He takes pleasure in his aloofness and yet enjoys the shivers along the spine and the tears . . ." With most novels, this can be achieved by rereading. But it seems to me that with Nabokov's own work the changing focus ensures that a first reading is of this nature.

Nabokov enjoys talking about literature and he communicates this enjoyment in his university lectures on selected European novels as well as in his conversation. There are periods in a lecture when it is fortunately quite impossible for anyone to take notes. It is enough simply to sit back and follow the flow of imagery, the sudden changes in direction; to listen to controlled talk of shivers, enchantment, semicolons, passion and patience, patience and passion . . . and to stories of the birth of literature: "It was not," Nabokov says, "when a boy saw an animal in a clearing and said: 'That is a wolf.' That was not the birth of literature. It was when a boy cried: 'Wolf . . . wolf . . . wolf.' And there was no wolf. That was the Birth of Literature." In the early stages of the term his pupils may be a little uncertain about the tone of a remark. When he says: "Consider these eight sorts of readers"; the heads bow to their notebooks and an expectant list of figures is outlined in the margin. But soon the heads are raised and the faces have mystified expressions. For Nabokov has continued:"There is the reader who belongs to a book club. The reader who has seen the movie of the book he is reading. The budding-author-reader. The reader who approaches everything from the social and economic angle. The reader who has a dictionary. The reader with artistic sense. The reader with imagination. The reader with memory."

Which are the good readers, he will ask. Why, the last four, of course. (A good dictionary is very important; "buy a dictionary the size of an elephant," he urges his class.) Once again, one is made aware of Nabokov's attitude to the reader and, with his university audience as with his reader, he creates the mood and attitude by which he can be understood and enjoyed. "The jaws stop chewing gum and the spine starts to shiver," as one coed put it. "You stop taking notes and actually listen." Nabokov, at any rate, is stimulating and original in everything he does. His occupation as a professional lepidopterist has even led to his discovering several previously unknown species of butterflies.

# The Man Who Scandalized the World

## Helen Lawrenson / 1960

From *Esquire*, August, 1960. © Johanna Lawrenson, Estate of Helen Lawrenson.
Reprinted by permission.

One of the more diverting aspects of *Lolita*, the most controversial best-seller of the century, has been the considerable speculative curiosity about the private life and personality of Vladimir Nabokov, the virtually unknown university professor who now, at the age of sixty-one, finds himself world famous as the author of this nettlesome novel. The book, denounced in the British Parliament and formerly banned in France, has sold, midst a cacophonic medley of rapturous encomium and emetic distaste, an estimated three million copies in the United States, has been translated into fifteen foreign languages, including the Japanese, and is now, incredibly enough, being made into a Hollywood movie.

What manner of man is it whose mind could conceive a book like this? Among the wildly disparate views of the critics ("a great book," "a distinguished book," "the filthiest book I have ever read," "exquisitely distilled sewage," "the funniest book I have ever read," "a sad book," "undoubtedly one of the great comic novels of all time," "dull, dull, dull") there has been one point of unanimity: the subject matter is abnormal and decadent. J. Donald Adams, contributing editor of *The New York Times* Sunday book review section, who found the novel revolting but not pornographic, wrote that he was reminded of John Randolph's excoriation of Edward Livingston: "He is a man of splendid abilities, but utterly corrupt. He shines and stinks like rotten mackerel by moonlight."

By all rights, Nabokov could turn out to be in real life either a sort of priapic pundit with a frosty contempt for the homely virtues or a demoniac neurotic whose past history reveals a flair for the cruel and the shocking. He seems to be neither. Nor is he merely a merry grig with a peculiarly audacious imagination. Instead, he appears as a disarmingly pleasant and serene man whose personal life has been untouched by even a wisp of scandal. He is a loving and proud father, a faithful husband who leads a snugly domestic Darby-and-Joan existence with his wife—to whom he has been married for thirty-five years—and a gentleman scholar of simple, quiet tastes, whose wildest pleasure is chasing butterflies.

When I met him, he was staying with Mrs. Nabokov in a small residence hotel on the upper west side of Manhattan, comfortable but far from chic. More good-looking than his photographs indicate, he is a tall, well-built man with a strong nose, quizzical eyes, a dimple in his chin, and quite a resemblance to George Sanders, the movie star. One of his professorial colleagues has told me that when Nabokov first joined the Cornell University faculty in 1948, he was "an incredibly handsome man." He must have been very attractive to women all his life, and still is, I imagine. There is no evidence, however, that he has availed himself of this attribute. His devotion to his wife, Véra, is something of a legend among their friends and is apparent even to the casual interviewer. Mrs. Nabokov is a slender woman with delicate wrists and ankles, snow-white hair worn unwaved in a cropped bob, an aquiline nose, and the *bluest* blue eyes I have ever seen. Her manner toward her husband is at once protective and admiring, tender and respectful—but no more so than is his toward her. One gets the feeling, almost immediately, of an unusual relationship.

During the interview, I found the Nabokovs friendly, charming and courteous. There was a cheerful unpretentiousness about them. They called each other "darling," and seemed delighted to talk about their son, Dmitri, an only child, now a tall, handsome young man of twenty-five, who graduated from Harvard with honors. His ambition is to be an opera singer—he is a *basso profundo*—and his parents were planning to send him to study in Italy, going along themselves in order to be near him. With obvious parental pride, they told me about his proficiency in sports-car racing, tennis, waterskiing, mountain climbing—"He has led several climbing expeditions. We would encourage him, but then we would sit home and worry and wait and wait and wait!"—and the time when, on a youthful spree, he drove a pink hearse from Cambridge to Mexico in two days. ("You should have seen Nabokov when his boy was a child," says a friend. "He was the most doting father in the world and bored everyone to death.")

Our whole conversation was of such an innocent, sunshiny, wholesome nature that I hesitated even to bring up a subject like *Lolita*. I needn't have. Both Nabokov and his wife reject with well-bred amusement any hint that they or their son or their professorial friends could regard the book with anything but proud delight and fond admiration. Between them, they manage to give the impression that anyone who would be so uncouth as to question *Lolita*'s value is indeed a yahoo and beneath civilized notice. In fact, said Nabokov, after the novel's publication and the ensuing hullabaloo, he was even invited to address the woman's auxiliary of the local Presbyterian Church in Ithaca, and he has received a whole slew of offers to lecture and teach, including one to give a course at the University of California in Berkeley. As to the situation at Cornell, he commented that not only the faculty but also the trustees and the students "were all quite interested in the book and its success," which seems to me to have the earmarks of an understatement.

Mrs. Nabokov serves as her husband's secretary and business manager. She writes his letters, makes his telephone calls for him, cuts out clippings about him and pastes them in scrapbooks, drives his car for him, keeps house and cooks for him, and even cuts his hair. During his tenure at Cornell, she went to class with him every day, sat on the platform while he lectured, cleaned the blackboard, collected the test papers, and, on occasion, gave his lectures for him when he was sick. After school, from three-thirty to five, they would go for a walk together, side by side, rain or shine. During summer vacations, for ten years, she chauffeured him around the western United States to pursue his scientific passion for butterfly chasing.

This idyllic domestic picture, with its almost folksy touches, is verified by their friends. No one, apparently, has ever seen them quarrel. The wife of one professor told me of an evening spent with the Nabokovs at the home of a third professor. During the evening, the host professor got in a snit at his wife and bawled her out in front of the guests. To assuage her embarrassment, the other wife said tactfully that her own husband often flew off the handle like that and she guessed all husbands were alike. "No," said Mrs. Nabokov calmly, "Vladimir isn't. Perhaps it is because when we were very poor in Paris I supported him by working as a milliner, and he has always been so grateful that he never gets angry at me."

In all this amiable and homey setting, as cozy as a teakettle and a purring cat on the hearth, there is little to suggest the emotional origins of *Lolita*. Why did he write it?

He certainly didn't do so, as some other authors might have, because he was trying to write a sensational bestseller which would make a lot of money. He believed that it could probably never be published. Nor did he do it as a diabolic joke. He is a seriously creative writer who would hardly expend such a tremendous amount of time, energy, thought and caressing attention to detail just for a lark. It was in Paris in 1939 that he wrote the first version in Russian as a short story. He read it to some friends, who were horrified and advised him to tear it up. Instead, he put the manuscript in a trunk, but carried the story around in his mind and began to work on it again at Cornell ten years later, this time in English. Much of it was written on summer cross-country butterfly hunts in 1951 and 1952. He wrote the whole book in longhand on six-by-four-inch filing cards, often working in motels or parked in his car, and finally finished it in the summer of 1953 in a rented house in Oregon.

To one interviewer, he has explained that he *had* to write it as a satisfaction of his need for self-expression. But again, why? Why did he *have* to write it? He, himself, has written, and he told me again that the original inspiration was an item in the French newspaper *Paris-Soir*, describing a scientist's attempts to persuade an ape in the zoo to draw with charcoal. After months of coaxing, the animal produced a sketch which showed the bars of its cage. Nabokov told me that there was no rational connection between the item and *Lolita*. "My point," he said, "is that in a sense the book, which is kind of a memoir, represents the grating of Humbert's personality, which he tries to break through."

It has been suggested by his admirers that the book is pure satire, representing variously "old Europe debauching young America," "young America debauching old Europe," and "Nabokov's love affair with the romantic novel." This, I think, is piffle. It is interesting, if not significant, that *Lolita* is not his first literary effort dealing with a sexual relationship between a grown man and a child. Twenty-five years ago, the original Russian version of *Invitation to a Beheading* was published in Paris. In this novel, twelve-year-old Emmie keeps darting into the hero's cell to snuggle with him. Evidently aware that some might regard this as more than coincidence, Nabokov has added to the recently published English version one of his arrogantly caustic caveats to the reader, in which he attempts to head off any odious comparisons by flatly stating that it is "the evil-minded who will perceive in little Emmie a sister of little Lolita."

This is all very well, but there was also another novel, *Laughter in the Dark*, published here in 1938, in which a married man deserts his wife and daughter to live—"in a thin, slimy layer of turpitude"—with greedy, scheming, immoral little Margot, aged sixteen. This novel was described by critic Clifton Fadiman as "combining Chekhovian lassitude with surrealist degeneracy."

Delving further into Nabokov's writings, we find another provocative similarity, this time between *Lolita* and an admittedly autobiographical short story. In *Lolita*, Humbert traces his perverse lust for nymphets back to his childhood when, at thirteen, he fell passionately in love on a Riviera beach with a child whom he calls Annabel Leigh: "We loved each other with a premature love, marked by a fierceness that so often destroys adult lives." She was, he said, "the initial fateful elf" in his life, and ever afterward he was to be haunted by her memory.

In the collection of short stories, *Nabokov's Dozen*, there is one called *First Love*, written in Boston in 1948. Of this story, Nabokov says that, except for a change of names, "it is true in every detail to the author's remembered life." It deals with a summer spent at Biarritz when Nabokov was ten, and tells of a nine-year-old French girl, with green eyes and "delicate, downy forearms," whom he met on the beach and with whom he fell in love.

Would it not seem possible that the tender memory of her, and not that artistic ape in Paris, was the true emotional impetus for *Lolita*? Just as it is impossible to shrug off a weird nightmare by saying, "After all, it wasn't me; it was only a dream"—because *you* were the one who dreamed it! So is it true that everyone who writes a book reveals a great deal of himself in it (no matter how fanciful a product of the conscious imagination he may claim it) if only because he chose to write *that* particular book. It is interesting to toy with the notion that perhaps for all these years Vladimir Nabokov may have been faithful, in his fashion, to a little girl on the beach at Biarritz.

In attempting to unravel the riddle of Nabokov by interviewing his professorial colleagues—brilliant, perceptive men like Arthur Mizener of Cornell and Harry Levin of Harvard—one finds that these men who have known him at close range agree that none of them *really* knows him. "He is an incorrigible mystificator, a leg-puller," said Levin, while Mizener described him as "wheels within wheels, whose writing is a joke within a joke within a joke, an enormously complicated and subtle joke which is deadly serious."

Whether dazzling listeners with the eximious quality of his sophistication, or cultivating an attitude of excessively inefficient unworldliness, Nabokov manages to charm his associates into a mood of puzzled admiration. When it amuses him, he has a tendency to overplay the middle-age professor, walking with an exaggerated stoop and acting benign and innocent. One of his girl students once sought to curry favor with him by making conversation after class. "Isn't it a *beautiful* day, professor?" she cooed. Nabokov assumed a beatific expression and intoned solemnly, "The little trees will love it."

In a 1947 essay, Jean-Paul Sartre speaks of Nabokov's writing as belonging to the "curious literature of the Russian *émigrés* or *déracinés*. They do not care for any society, not even to revolt against it, because they do not belong to any society." He adds that Nabokov "never writes without *seeing himself* write, as others listen to themselves talk, and what interests him almost uniquely are the subtle deceptions of his own conscience . . . One would swear that he writes for masochism."

To try to understand Nabokov, one must first try to understand his background, a difficult trick for any native American. He belonged to the aristocracy of Czarist Russia and until he was twenty he inhabited a fabulous world glimpsed by us only through the novels of Tolstoy or an occasional Hollywood super-spectacle. It was a world of enormous wealth, pomp, and luxury. His family had been for generations people of high position and influence: generals, diplomats, members of the nobility, privileged participants in the most glittering court life of the Western world. His grandmother was a baroness and his aunt a princess. It is not unusual for scions of the aristocracy to be cultural cretins, but Nabokov was fortunate in that his family were not only patrician but rich, not only but rich but cultured, scholarly and—for their era and social status—rather liberal. His father was one of the founders of the Constitutional Democratic Party in 1905 and later forfeited his court title, refused to drink the Czar's health at a banquet, and advertised for sale his gorgeous court uniform.

Vladimir Nabokov (pronounced with the accent on the second syllable in both names) was born in 1899 in St. Petersburg and spent his childhood in his families palatial pink-granite townhouse or on their huge country estate, to which he now refers as "our pleasant house," which is a little as if England's Prince Charles should in future years look back on Buckingham Palace as "a nice place." A permanent staff of fifty servants was kept at the country place alone, and Nabokov grew up surrounded by butlers, maids, footmen, coachmen, chauffeurs, valets, cooks, gardeners, and other lackeys. He had four or five female English governesses in turn, all of whom lived with the Nabokovs and, later on, two male English tutors who lived out. He also had a French mademoiselle, a Swiss tutor, a French boxing and fencing instructor, and a drawing master. When the Nabokovs traveled to Biarritz or the Riviera, an entourage of maids, valets, and tutors accompanied them. One of Vladimir's early memories is of walking with his mother and an English governess in Nice when he was four and being stopped by the Queen of Belgium, who inquired about his grandfather's health.

A great to-do has been made over how astonishing it is that Nabokov can write so well in English, but the fact is that he learned it before he learned

Russian. By the time he was six, he could read and write in English, but not in Russian, so a schoolmaster was hired to come every afternoon and give him lessons in his native tongue. His father and mother, like many of the Russian aristocracy, spoke French to each other much of the time. They also liked to talk to the children in English, and his mother used to read to Vladimir in that language every night, after which he would be turned over to an English governess to be undressed and put to bed.

Nabokov's favorite relative was his Uncle Vasili, a dashing diplomat who spent a lot of time riding to hounds in England and adorning society gatherings in New York and Paris. He owned a chateau near Paris, a villa near Rome and another in Egypt, and a country estate which had once been the home of Peter the Great's son, the Czarevitch Alexei. Uncle Vasili died when Vladimir was seventeen, leaving him two million dollars and the country estate. It might have seemed as if Vladimir was well-fixed for life. But the year was 1916, and in Russia the vast political and social changes which were to alter the history of the world were already underway. The Nabokovs fled to the Crimea, taking with them jewels hidden in a can of talcum powder, and spent sixteen months there, living with a Countess. Other friends sent them money, and the time passed not too unpleasantly.

For a brief period Vladimir's father served as Minister of Justice in Kerensky's provisional government (Vladimir is still on close terms with Kerensky who now lives in California), but he resigned in 1917. When the Bolsheviks took the Crimea in 1919, Vladimir and his family left Russia forever on a small Greek cargo ship bound for Constantinople and Piraeus. Using the Nansen passports provided for stateless Russian, Armenian and Greek refugees, they arrived ultimately in London. Vladimir and his brother went to Cambridge on scholarships awarded, according to the former, "for political tribulation." His brother went to Christ College, Vladimir to Trinity. After his graduation in 1922, he joined his father in Berlin, were the latter was editing a newspaper for Russian refugees. It was in that same year that the elder Nabokov, attending a political lecture, attempted to shield the lecturer from the bullets of two assassins and was himself killed. (Vladimir's widowed mother died in 1930 in a suburb of Prague, where she lived for several years on a pension granted her by the Czech government.)

Vladimir stayed on in Berlin, eking out a living by giving lessons in boxing, tennis, English and French, writing poetry and fiction for Russian *émigré* publications, and performing various odd-job intellectual chores. He did a Russian translation of *Alice in Wonderland*, for which he was paid five dollars; he originated Russian crossword puzzles; he wrote a Russian grammar for foreigners, with exercise sentences like, "Madam, I am the doctor. Here is a banana."

In Berlin, in 1923, he met his wife, also a refugee, the daughter of the former owner of the largest and most important publishing house in Russia. They were married in April, 1925. Mrs. Nabokov is Jewish, and they left Germany for France before Hitler came to power. Again, with the advent of World War II, they were forced to move on. Eventually, they escaped through Lisbon and arrived in New York in May, 1940. Shortly afterward, Nabokov became a Research Fellow in the Museum of Comparative Zoology at Harvard, where he reclassified the butterfly collection and wrote technical papers on the subject. He gave lectures on Russian literature at Wellesley and continued to write poetry and fiction for the Russian-language Chekhov Press, which was sponsored by the Ford Foundation. In 1948 he got a job as European Professor of Russian Literature at Cornell.

Looking back, he seems rather proud of the fact that in his ten years there he never attended a single faculty meeting or official social gathering, never joined the faculty club or any other club, and lived only in furnished houses rented from other professors who were on leave, a temporary living arrangement resulting in the Nabokovs having to move sometimes twice a year. He has never had a house of his own since he left Russia over forty years ago.

Nabokov's lecture courses were popular with the undergraduates, not only because he was known as one of the softest markers ever in Cornell, but also because the students were fascinated by him and generally fond of him in sort of a "My God, what next?" way. The publication of *Lolita* understandably increased this feeling. In the opinion of some of his colleagues, if the book had not been such a success he would probably have been fired. As it was, the university trustees were inclined to view it as something of a publicity windfall. "If the most expensive public relations firm in New York had been retained to handle the university, they couldn't have done as spectacular a job," commented one of the professors.

As almost everyone must know by now, *Lolita* was turned down by all the American publishers to whom Nabokov, mostly for the hell of it, sent the manuscript. One of them wrote the author a letter urging him to burn all copies, while another suggested that it might be more acceptable if Lolita were changed into a small boy. The book was first published in Paris by Olympia Press, a firm which had made a living mostly by publishing pornography. Tourists began bringing home copies, and eventually book-sellers in England and America were importing copies and selling them for twelve dollars and fifteen dollars each. The United States Customs permitted importation of the novel, but the British government, viewing with alarm the number of copies brought home, sent a letter to the French Ministry of the Interior calling attention to the International Convention for the Suppression of Obscene Publications. Subsequently, Paris gendarmes swooped down on the Olympia offices, confiscated all copies and forbade further sales. Olympia promptly issued a pamphlet, *L'Affaire Lolita*, reproducing the letter from the British Home Office in Whitehall and appealing to all loyal Frenchmen to rally round the cause of national sovereignty and liberty.

As a result of all the publicity, *Lolita* became more widely known in America and editor Jason Epstein published excerpts from it in the *Anchor Review*, with an enthusiastic introduction by F.W. Dupee, Professor of English at Columbia University. The magazine caught the eye of a tall, pretty, ex-Latin Quarter showgirl named Rosemary Ridgewell, who brought it to the attention of Walter Minton, President of Putnam's, whom she knew. Although Olympia owned all the English rights and insisted on fifty percent of the basic royalties and thirty-three and a third percent of publishers' profits on paperbacks, Minton took a gambler's chance and brought the book out here in August, 1958. After that, the deluge.

Within five weeks after publication, *Lolita* had become the No. 1 best-seller in the country. It remained on the bestseller list for fifty-six weeks. Last December, Fawcett published the paperback edition with a prepublication printing of two million copies. For her historic part in the whole publishing saga, the statuesque Miss Ridgewell received a tidy nest egg: a sizeable equivalent of some of the author's royalties for the first year, plus an equally sizeable share of the publisher's subsidiary rights for the next two years. She has been quoted as saying, "I thought Nabokov had a very interesting way of writing, very, you know—crystalline?"

In general, the intellectual and emotional repercussions varied in vehemence. A state senator in Massachusetts tried unsuccessfully to prohibit the sale of "this vile book." A staff member resigned in protest when the Cincinnati public library banned it from the shelves. In Lolita, Texas, a deacon of the First Baptist Church circulated a petition to change the name of the town to Jackson. A vice president of a major oil company announced that he had thrown his new copy into the wastebasket without reading it because

"I didn't want to carry it around with me." On the other hand, Jack Kerouac called it "a classic old love story."

In the torrent of critical appraisal which has appeared in print, Nabokov has been compared as a writer to Balzac, F. Scott Fitzgerald, Aristophanes, James Thurber, Freud, Krafft-Ebing, Lewis Carroll, Dickens, Joyce, Proust, Kafka, Oscar Wilde, Gogol, Conrad, Laurence Sterne, Henry Fielding, and Dostoyevsky crossed with Voltaire. Perhaps the most piquant suggestion of all was that of *The New York Times'* Gilbert Millstein, who asked: "Who else is Humbert Humbert but Daddy Long Legs?"

(Incidentally, everything written about *Lolita* refers to a "middle-aged man and a twelve-year-old girl," but the chronology in the book, itself, would make Humbert either thirty-five or thirty-seven, which is not exactly "middle-aged"—at least not from where I sit.)

Although now translated into Greek, Serbian, Hebrew, Dutch, Polish—to name only a few—*Lolita* had tough sledding for a while in France, where a French version was prohibited until last winter; in Argentina, which banned it last summer; and in England, where one publisher destroyed the copy sent him (he was reported to have torn it up, page by page) and another threatened to resign if his firm took it. In December, 1958, it was the subject of a two hour Parliament debate, in the course of which Mr. Nigel Nicolson, a Conservative from Bournemouth and also a partner in the firm which finally accepted the book, defended it by stating that, despite its theme, it carries a built-in condemnation since "it leads to utter misery, suicide, prison, murder and great unhappiness." Mr. Nicolson, previously in hot water for opposing government policy on Suez, ran into a sticky wicket when he sought reelection to the House of Commons. "A director of a firm intending to publish this vulgar novel is no fitting representative for good Bournemouth citizens," declared a member of his local political group, and a Conservative M.P. remarked, "*Lolita* is the main issue. Suez has been replaced."

Nevertheless, the book was published in England last November by Weidenfeld & Nicolson and the whole edition sold out on the first day, despite the antipathy of the critics, who failed to duplicate the American relish for Nabokov's elegantly randy wit. Typical of the reviews was that of the *Daily Telegraph & Morning Post*, which said: "Let us hear no more high-flown stuff about Mr. Nabokov having written a great work of art. His theme is unlikely to corrupt; his manner almost certain to anesthetize." *The Spectator*'s acrid Kingsley Amis gave the book the old heave-ho by remarking that while "Few books published in this country since the King James Bible can have set up more eager expectation . . . it is thoroughly bad in both senses: bad as a work of art, that is, and morally bad."

Although probably disappointed by the English reviews, Nabokov has remained imperturbably confident of his own talent, while anything but reticent about what he considers the lack of it in others. He has referred to both Conrad and Hemingway as "writers for little boys," called Dostoyevsky "a cheap sensationalist, clumsy and vulgar," attacked Balzac, Dreiser and Thomas Mann, and, at the mention of Thomas Wolfe, snorted, "Mediocrity!"

His opinions on other subjects are equally outspoken. Music bores him, and he has commented that it affects him "merely as an arbitrary succession of more or less irritating sounds." Of psychiatry he has said, "I reject completely the vulgar, shabby, fundamentally medieval world of Freud . . . what matters is *what* people think, not *why*." He dismisses all politics as bad and, of course, feels that in the good old days of the Czar, "a freedom-loving Russian had more freedom than under Lenin," without, however, specifying whether he meant freedom-loving aristocrats or freedom-loving serfs.

While publishers were cagily rushing into print translations of his earlier works—he wrote eight novels in Russian before switching to English—and reissuing books like *The Real Life of Sebastian Knight*, Nabokov, himself, put the final polish on a labor of scholarly love, his translation of Pushkin's *Eugene Onegin*, on which he worked off and on for nine years. The Bollingen Foundation is publishing it in five volumes, of which one is the translation and the other four contain Nabokov's commentaries. And Random House will publish *The Song of Igor's Campaign*, one of the greatest epics of medieval Europe, which Nabokov has translated and annotated. The work of an anonymous Russian poet in 1187, it is, according to Nabokov, "a colorful, resounding poem, much more gusty than the *Chanson de Roland*."

Last spring Nabokov interrupted his European holiday to return to America at the request of James Harris and Stanley Kubrick, who bought the film rights to *Lolita* for $150,000, plus fifteen percent of the producers' net profits. They persuaded Nabokov to go to Hollywood to write the script.

As far as the film version of *Lolita* is concerned, the burning question in everyone's mind is: How in God's name can they do it? However, Harris and Kubrick, both in their early thirties, are two of the brightest and most unorthodox of the new type of filmmakers and, if anyone can pull off the feat of successfully translating the book to the screen, they are about the likeliest candidates. They would prefer Sir Laurence Olivier or David Niven as Humbert, but justifiably feel that the casting of the title role presents a problem. All this year their offices have been besieged by ambitious mothers who want to see their small daughters play Lolita, while hundreds of others, unable to make the trek to Hollywood, mail in photos of their subteen female progeny, accompanied by enthusiastic sales pitch letters, a chilling commentary on American mother love.

Since Nabokov is a complex and protean man, he can probably latch onto the intricacies of Hollywood with more adaptability than would other men of his background. Indeed, one of the surprises of *Lolita* was that this foreign-born, aristocratic, elderly university professor should reveal such an astounding knowledge of our more coarsely demotic American slang. Coupled with his often irritating tendency to strew his text with unnecessary French phrases—as when he describes a trip south by saying, "we dipped deep into *ce qu'on appelle* Dixieland"—this produces an effect of which one might well say that *vraiment*, it is, *comme on dit*, a gasser.

Aware of these qualities, it was with a combination of confidence, hope and trepidation that Harris and Kubrick hired him to do the cinema version. They know that whatever else he may be, he is unpredictable—and a persistent intellectual prankster. At this writing, no one knows the eventual fate of the script. Producer Harris feels that Nabokov's exposure to the film colony may open up an entirely new career for him and that he could develop into one of the titans of the movie world. On the other hand, it seems just as likely that his experiences there could imaginably result in an abrupt departure and, subsequently, the book on Hollywood to end Hollywood.

# V. Nabokov Unresting

## Phyllis Meras / 1962

From *The Providence Sunday Journal*, May 13, 1962. © 2011 *The Providence Journal*. Reprinted by permission.

"All writers that are worth anything are humorists," Vladimir Nabokov said. "I'm not P.G. Wodehouse. I'm not a funny man, but give me an example of a great writer who is not a humorist. The best tragedian is O'Neill. He is probably the worst writer. Dostoyevsky's slapstick is wonderful, but in his tragedy he is a journalist."

But didn't he consider the satirical *Lolita* a humorous book?

"It's not humor," he replied. "It's not a story. It's a poem."

Although reluctant to talk about *Pale Fire* before publication, the author did say that it was not at all like *Lolita*, except for "a kind of bizarre streak running through it."

To illustrate his point about humor, he explained that in *The Gift*, another novel due next year, there is a scene where a number of people are sitting in a small room and generally falling over each other. "A very serious and important thought is revealed in this scene," he said, "but there still is humor."

The Nabokovs are temporarily residing in Montreux, principally to be near their son, who is living in Milan.

"You really can't define humor, though," the author continued. "In Russian and in French there is no word for humor. In English, it has a kind of cozy sound, but there is a savage humor, too. Perhaps humor is simply seeing things in a singular, unique, extraordinary way. This almost always sounds funny to the average person."

"When our son was very small," Mrs. Nabokov interjected, "they asked him in school, 'What does rain remind you of,' and he said 'It gives goose skin to the puddles.' 'This is too unusual,' the teacher said."

"Yes, the unusual is funny in itself," Nabokov agreed. "A man slips and falls down. It is the contrary of gravity in both senses—that's a great pun, by the way."

Remarking that the writer, in brief, must see both the comic and the cosmic in life, he said that he generally writes more than one book at a time.

"Plots have a way of breeding—of living in sneaky little labs. Then they break out of their cocoons and I have to mop up the mess.

"When I was writing *Lolita*, I was doing *Pnin* for *The New Yorker* at the same time. And then I was translating Pushkin's *Eugene Onegin* as well. It's Russia's most famous novel and it has never been adequately translated. It will come out in four volumes with a special commentary, and be printed by the Bollingen Foundation. Would you like to see it?"

He rose and disappeared from the room briefly to return with a mound of galley proofs.

"It's taken me ten years to do this," he said with a contented sigh. "Of course, it all started when my wife said, 'Why don't you translate it?' The Guggenheim people gave me a grant for the work."

One spur for the work was his desire to have a good translation for his students. He has taught both at Cornell and Wellesley.

The translation, he said, kept him busy between novels, and when not writing he keeps occupied with research, chess problems, and his great passion, the study of butterflies.

"For seven years, you see, I was responsible for the butterflies at Harvard. I was practically curator there. There's a butterfly in every one of my novels. One of the first things I ever wrote in English was a paper on Lepidoptera I prepared at the age of twelve. It wasn't published because a butterfly I described had been described by somebody else. But the paper itself was written in beautiful, precise English."

He was born in Russia in 1899, and he described his parents as belonging to "the heights of intellectual Russia." He himself has "always" known French and English as well as Russian. He writes for the most part in English now. Of his seventeen books, ten were in Russian and the rest in English. One book, *Invitation to a Beheading* was translated by the son in Milan.

"It doesn't matter to me in what language I write," he said. "Language is just another instrument. Except that, of course, English is the language with the richest literature. It breaks my heart to say it, but after English there comes a little gap. Then I would say Russian and French were on a par as far as literature is concerned. But English literature is huge—especially in its poets. English poetry is supreme.

"Russian literature only got started in the eighteenth century, and then it had only a century and a half in which it could go before the Revolution occurred. Of course, during that period it had such prose writers as Tolstoy—and, well—I don't think he has any peer in any other country. I think he's much greater than Proust or James Joyce, to take two other greats. But then in the twentieth century in Russia, it all stopped.

"I suppose there is still some goodish writing in Russia—Mandelstam, who died in a concentration camp, was a wonderful poet, for example, but literature can't thrive where limits are set to human fantasy.

"My books? They are absolutely banned in Russia. Every word of mine, after all, is filled with contempt for the police state.

"When do I write? Whenever I feel like it. I write in shorthand—sometimes on a bench in the garden, or in the park, or in the car, or in bed. I always write in pencil on index cards. When the whole thing is one grey smudge of writing and erasing, I tear the whole thing up and make a fair copy. Then all the cards go to the Library of Congress, and they cannot be consulted for fifty years."

Nabokov said he hadn't expected *Lolita* to become a bestseller. "And I didn't know that the first company that agreed to print it—that was the Olympia Press in Paris—printed mostly pornography. I was a little taken aback. But it happened that way because after I could not find a publisher in America, my agent said perhaps we could find an English language publisher in Paris to do it."

He put down his wine glass and looked out the window toward the Jura Mountains and the Lake of Geneva. The Chateau de Chillon made famous by Lord Byron is not far from Montreux on the lake shore.

"Besides all these books, lectures, short stories, essays, and poems," he suggested, "you might want to note that I have also written four books on butterflies."

# Vladimir Nabokov on his Life and Work

## Peter Duval Smith / 1962

From *The Listener*, November 22, 1962. © The Estate of Peter Duval Smith. Reprinted by permission.

**Peter Duval Smith:** Would you ever go back to Russia?

**Vladimir Nabokov:** I will never go back for the simple reason that all the Russia I need, after all, is always with me: literature, language, and my own Russian childhood. I will never return. I will never surrender. And anyway, the grotesque shadow of a police state will not be dispelled in my lifetime. I don't think they know my works there—oh, perhaps a number of readers exist there in my special secret service, but let us not forget that Russia has grown tremendously provincial during these forty years, apart from the fact that people there are told what to read, what to think. In America I'm happier than in any other country. It is in America that I found my best readers, minds that are closest to mine. I feel intellectually at home in America. It is a second home in the true sense of the word.

**PDS:** You're a professional lepidopterist?

**VN:** Yes, I'm interested in the classification, variation, evolution, structure, distribution, habits, of Lepidoptera: this sounds very grand, but actually I'm an expert in only a very small group of butterflies. I have contributed several works on butterflies to the various scientific journals—but I want to repeat that my interest in butterflies is exclusively scientific.

**PDS:** Is there any connection with your writing?

**VN:** There is, in a general way, because I think that in a work of art there is a kind of merging between the two things, between the precision of poetry and the excitement of pure science.

**PDS:** In your new novel *Pale Fire*, one of the characters says that reality is neither the subject nor the object of real art, which creates its own reality. What is that reality?

**VN:** Reality is a very subjective affair. I can only define it as a kind of gradual accumulation of information; and as specialization. If we take a lily, for instance, or any other kind of natural object—a lily is more real to a naturalist than it is to an ordinary person. But it is still more real to a botanist. And any further stage of reality is reached with that botanist who is a specialist in lilies. You can get nearer and nearer, so to speak, to reality; but you never get near enough because reality is an infinite succession of levels, levels of perception, of false bottoms, and hence unquenchable, unattainable. You can know more and more about one thing but you can never know everything about one thing: it's hopeless. So, we live surrounded by more or less ghostly objects—that machine there, for instance. It's a complete ghost to me—I don't understand a thing about it and, well, it's a mystery to me, as much of a mystery as it would be to Lord Byron.

**PDS:** You say that reality is an intensely subjective matter, but in your books it seems to me that you seem to take an almost perverse delight in literary deception.

**VN:** The fake move in a chess problem, the illusion of a solution or the conjurer's magic: I used to be a little conjurer when I was a boy. I loved doing simple tricks—turning water into wine, that kind of thing; but I think I'm in good company because all art is really deception and so is nature; all is deception in that good cheat, from the insect that mimics a leaf to the popular enticements of procreation. Do you know how poetry started? I always think that it started when a cave boy came running back to the cave through the tall grass, shouting as he ran, "Wolf, wolf," and there was no wolf. His baboon-like parents, great sticklers for the truth, gave him a hiding, no doubt, but poetry had been born—the tall story had been born in the tall grass.

**PDS:** You talk about games of deception, like chess and conjuring. Are you, in fact, fond of them yourself?

**VN:** I am fond of chess but deception in chess, as in art, is only part of the game; it's part of the combination, part of the delightful possibilities, illusions, vistas of thought, which can be false vistas, perhaps, but I think a good combination should always contain a certain element of deception.

**PDS:** You spoke about conjuring in Russia as a child, and one remembers that some of the most intense passages in a number of your books are concerned with the memories of your lost childhood. What is the importance of memory to you?

**VN:** Memory is, really, in itself a tool, one of the many tools that an artist uses; and some recollections, perhaps intellectual rather than emotional, are very brittle and sometimes apt to lose the flavor of reality when they are immersed by the novelist in his book, when they are given away to characters.

**PDS:** Do you mean that you lose the sense of a memory once you have written it down?

**VN:** Sometimes, but that only refers to a certain type of intellectual memory. But, for instance—oh, I don't know, the freshness of the flowers being arranged by the under-gardener in the cool drawing-room of our country house as I was running downstairs with my butterfly net on a summer day half a century ago: that kind of thing is absolutely permanent, immortal, it can never change, no matter how many times I farm it out to my characters it is always there with me. There's the red sand, the white garden bench, the black fir trees, everything, a permanent possession. I think it is really all a matter of love: the more you love a memory, the stronger and stranger it is. I think it's natural that I have a more passionate affection for my old memories, the memories of my childhood, than I have for later ones, so that Cambridge in England or Cambridge in New England are less vivid in my mind and in myself than some kind of nook in the park on our country estate in Russia.

**PDS:** Do you think that such an intense power of memory as yours has inhibited your desire to invent in your books?

**VN:** No, I don't think so.

**PDS:** The same sort of incident turns up again and again, sometimes in slightly different forms.

**VN:** That depends on my characters.

**Tribute to Russia**

**PDS:** Do you still feel Russian, in spite of so many years in America?

**VN:** I do feel Russian and I think that my Russian works, the various novels and poems and short stories that I have written during these years are a kind of tribute to Russia. And I might define them as the waves and ripples of the shock caused by the disappearance of the Russia of my childhood, and recently I have paid tribute to her in an English work on Pushkin.

**PDS:** Why are you so passionately concerned with Pushkin?

**VN:** It started with a translation, a literal translation. I thought it was very difficult and the more difficult it was, the more exciting it seemed. So it's not so much caring about Pushkin—I love him dearly, of course, he is the greatest Russian poet, there is no doubt about that—but it was again the combination of the excitement of finding the right way of doing things and a certain approach to reality, to the reality of Pushkin through my own translations. As a matter of fact, I am very concerned with things Russian and I have just finished revising a good translation of my novel, *The Gift*, which I wrote about thirty years ago. It is the longest, I think the best, and the most nostalgic of my Russian novels. It portrays the adventures, literary and romantic, of a young Russian expatriate in Berlin in the twenties; but he's not myself. I am very careful to keep my characters beyond the limits of my own identity. Only the background of the novel can be said to contain some biographical touches. And there is another thing about it that pleases me: probably my favorite Russian poem is the one that I happened to give to my main character in that novel.

**PDS:** Written by yourself?

**VN:** Which I wrote myself, of course; and now I'm wondering whether I would be able to recite it in Russian. Let me explain it: There are two persons involved, a boy and a girl, standing on a bridge above the reflected sunset and there are swallows skimming by. The boy turns to the girl and says to her "Tell me, will you always remember *that* swallow?—not any kind of swallow, not those swallows there, but that particular swallow that skimmed by?" And she says "Of course I will," and they both burst into tears.

**PDS:** What language do you think in?

**VN:** I don't think I think in any language. I think in images. I don't believe that people think in languages. They don't move their lips when they think. It is only a certain type of illiterate person who reads a newspaper in a tram who moves his lips as he reads or as he thinks. No, I think in images, and now and then a Russian phrase or an English phrase will crop up with the foam of the brainwave, but that's about all.

### Success of *Lolita*

**PDS:** You started writing in Russian and then you switched to English, didn't you?

**VN:** Yes, that was a very difficult kind of switch. My private tragedy, which cannot, indeed should not, be anybody's concern, is that I had to abandon my natural language, my natural idiom, my rich, infinitely rich and docile Russian tongue, for a second-rate brand of English.

**PDS:** You have written a shelf of books in English as well as your books in Russian. And of them only *Lolita* is well known. Does it annoy you to be the *Lolita* man?

**VN:** No, I wouldn't say that, because *Lolita* is a special favorite of mine. It was my most difficult book—the book that treated of the theme which was so distant, so remote, from my own emotional life that it gave me a special pleasure to use my combinational talent to make it real.

**PDS:** Were you surprised at the wild success when it came?

**VN:** I was surprised that the book was published at all.

**PDS:** Did you, in fact, have any doubts about whether *Lolita* ought to be printed, considering its subject matter?

**VN:** No; after all, when you write a book you generally envisage its publication in some far future. But I was pleased that the book was published.

**PDS:** What was the genesis of *Lolita*?

**VN:** She was born a long time ago, it must have been in 1939, in Paris; the first little throb of *Lolita* went through me in Paris in thirty-nine, or perhaps early in forty, at a time when I was laid up with a first attack of intercostal neuralgia, which is a very painful complaint. As far as I can recall, the first shiver of inspiration was somehow prompted in a rather mysterious way by a newspaper story, I think it was in the *Paris Soir*, about an ape in the Paris Zoo, who after months of coaxing by scientists produced finally the first drawing ever charcoaled by an animal, and this sketch, reproduced in the paper, showed the bars of the poor creature's cage.

**PDS:** Did Humbert Humbert, the middle-aged seducer, have any original?

**VN:** No. He's a man with a mind and a man with an obsession, and I think many of my characters have sudden obsessions, different kinds of obsessions; but he never existed. He did exist after I had written the book. While I was writing the book, here and there in a newspaper I would read all sorts of accounts about elderly gentlemen who seduced little girls: a kind of interesting coincidence but that's about all.

**PDS:** Did Lolita herself have an original?
**VN:** No, Lolita didn't have any original. She is perhaps a great-grand-niece, born in my own mind. She never existed. As a matter of fact, I don't know little girls very well. When I think about the subject, I don't think I know a single little girl. I've met them socially now and then, but Lolita is a figment of my imagination.

**PDS:** Why did you write *Lolita*?
**VN:** It was an interesting thing to do. Why did I write any of my books, after all? For the sake of the pleasure, for the sake of the difficulty. I have no social purpose, no moral message; I've no general ideas to exploit but I like composing riddles and I like finding elegant solutions to those riddles that I have composed myself.

**Seeing Letters in Color**

**PDS:** How do you write? What are your methods?
**VN:** I find now that index cards are really the best kind of paper that I can use for the purpose. I don't write consecutively from the beginning to the next chapter and so on to the end. I just fill in the gaps of the picture, of this jigsaw puzzle which is quite clear in my mind, picking out a piece here and a piece there and filling out part of the sky and part of the landscape and part of the—I don't know, the carousing hunters.

**PDS:** Another aspect of your not entirely usual consciousness is the extraordinary importance you attach to color.
**VN:** Color. I think I was born a painter, really! And up to my fourteenth year, perhaps, I used to spend most of my time drawing and painting and I was supposed to become a painter in due time. But I don't think I had any real talent there. However, the sense of color, the love of color, I've had all my life: and also I have this rather strange and freakish gift of seeing letters in color. Yes, yes: that's called color hearing. Perhaps one in a thousand has that. But I'm told by psychologists that most children have it, that later they

lose that aptitude when they are told by their parents that it's all nonsense, that an 'A' isn't black, and a 'B' isn't brown—that you should not say that. It's stupid, you know, that kind of thing.

**PDS:** What colors are your own initials, "V. N."?

**VN:** "V" is a kind of pale, transparent pink: I think it's called, technically, quartz pink: this is one of the closest colors that I can connect with the "V." And the "N," on the other hand, is a greyish-yellowish oatmeal color. But a funny thing happens: my wife has this gift of seeing letters in color, too, but her colors are completely different. There are, perhaps, two or three letters where we coincide, but otherwise the colors are quite different. It turned out, we discovered one day, that my son, who was a little boy at the time—I think he was ten or eleven—sees letters in colors, too. Quite naturally he said, "Oh, this isn't that color, this is this color," and so on. Then we asked him to list his colors and we discovered that in one case, one letter which he sees as purple, or perhaps mauve, is pink to me and blue to my wife. This is the letter "M." So the combination of pink and blue makes lilac in his case. Which is as if his genes were painting in aquarelle.

**PDS:** Whom do you write for? What audience?

**VN:** I don't think that an artist should bother about his audience. His best audience is the person he sees in his shaving mirror every morning. I think that the audience that an artist imagines, when he imagines that kind of a thing, is a room filled with people wearing his own mask.

**PDS:** In your books there is an almost extravagant concern with masks and disguises: almost as if you were trying to hide yourself behind something, as if you'd lost yourself.

**VN:** Oh, no. I think I'm always there; there's no difficulty about that. Of course, there is this certain type of critic who, when reviewing a work of fiction, keeps dotting all the "i's" with the author's head. Recently one anonymous clown, writing on *Pale Fire* in a New York book review, mistook all the declarations of my invented commentator in the book for my own. It is also true that some of my more responsible characters are given some of my own ideas. There is John Shade in *Pale Fire*, the poet. He does borrow some of my own opinions. There is one passage in his poem, which is part of the book, where he says something I think I can endorse. He says— let me quote it, if I can remember; yes, I think I can do it: "I loathe such things as jazz, the white-hosed moron torturing a black bull, rayed with red, abstractist bric-a-brac, primitivist folk masks, progressive schools, music in supermarkets, swimming pools, brutes, bores, class-conscious philistines, Freud, Marx, fake-thinkers, puffed-up poets, frauds, and sharks." That's how it goes.

**PDS:** It is obvious that neither John Shade nor his creator are very clubbable men.

**VN:** I don't belong to any club or group. I don't fish, cook, dance, endorse books, sign books, co-sign declarations, eat oysters, get drunk, go to church, go to analysts, or take part in demonstrations.

**PDS:** It sometimes seems to me that in your novels there is a strain of perversity amounting to cruelty. In *Laughter in the Dark*, for instance, the tribulations of the hero, Albinus, are really dreadful after he has gone blind, and his mistress and her lover tease him.

**VN:** Well, what difference do you see between perversity and cruelty? I mean, could you define perversity, perhaps?

**PDS:** Cruelty is perverse.

**VN:** Oh, cruelty *is* perverse. Always perverse. Is a butcher always perverse? A butcher is cruel by definition. I don't know. But I think that in that novel to which you refer, a novel that I wrote when I was a boy of twenty-six, say, I tried to express a world in terms as candid, as near to my vision of the world as I could. If I was cruel, I suppose it was because I saw the world as cruel in those days. I don't think that there is a specially perverse or cruel streak in my writing. In life I'm a mild old gentleman. I'm very kind. There's nothing cruel or brutal in me whatsoever.

# Playboy Interview: Vladimir Nabokov

## Alvin Toffler / 1964

From *Playboy Magazine*, January, 1964. © Playboy Enterprises International, Inc. and Alvin Toffler. All Rights Reserved. Reprinted by permission.

Few authors of this generation have sparked more controversy with a single book than a former Cornell University professor with the resoundingly Russian name of Vladimir Vladimirovich Nabokov. *Lolita*, his brilliant tragicomic novel about the nonplatonic love of a middle-aged man for a twelve-year-old nymphet, has sold 2,500,000 copies in the United States alone.

It has also been made into a top-grossing movie, denounced in the House of Commons, and banned in Austria, England, Burma, Belgium, Australia, and even France. Fulminating critics have found it to be "the filthiest book I've ever read," "exquisitely distilled sewage," "corrupt," "repulsive," "dirty," "decadent" and "disgusting." Champions of the book, in turn, have proclaimed it "brilliantly written" and "one of the great comic novels of all time"; while Nabokov himself has been compared favorably with every writer from Dostoyevsky to Krafft-Ebing, and hailed by some as the supreme stylist in the English language today. Pedants have theorized that the book is actually an allegory about the seduction of the Old World by the New—or perhaps the New World by the Old. And Jack Kerouac, brushing aside such lascivious symbolism, has announced that it is nothing more than a "classic old love story."

Whatever it is, Nabokov would seem to be incongruously miscast as its author. A reticent Russian-born scholar whose most violent passion is an avid interest in butterfly collecting, he was born in 1899 to the family of a wealthy statesman in St. Petersburg. Fleeing the country when the Bolsheviks seized power, he made his way to England, where he enrolled as an undergraduate at Trinity College in Cambridge. In the twenties and thirties he drifted between Paris and Berlin earning a spotty living as a tennis instructor and tutor in English and French; achieving a modest degree of fame as an author of provocative and luminously original short stories, plays, poems, and book reviews for the *émigré* press; and stirring praise and puzzlement with a trio of masterful novels in Russian—*Invitation to a Beheading, The Gift*, and *Laughter in the Dark*. Finding himself again a refugee when France fell to the Nazis in 1940, Nabokov emigrated with his wife to the United States, where he began his academic career as a research fellow at Harvard's Museum of Comparative Zoology. Now writing in English—in a style rich with inventive metaphors and teeming with the philosophical paradoxes, abstruse ironies, sly *non sequiturs*, multilingual puns, anagrams, rhymes, and riddles which both illuminate and obscure his work—he produced three more novels during his subsequent years as a professor in Russian and English literature at Wellesley, and then at Cornell. First came *Bend Sinister*, an unsettling evocation of life under a dictatorship; then *Pnin*, the poignant, haunting portrait of an aging *émigré* college instructor; and finally the erotic tour de force which was to catapult him almost overnight to worldwide eminence—*Lolita*.

This brief recital of biographical facts, however, outlines only the visible Nabokov, revealing nothing of the little-known interior man; for the labyrinth of his creative intellect has remained a hall of mirrors to all who have attempted to explore it. And his amused indifference to the most erudite appraisal of his work and worth has served merely to enhance the legend of his inscrutability. Shunning personal publicity, he grants interviews only rarely—having consented to see *Playboy* only after satisfying himself that the subjects we proposed to discuss were worthy of his attention.

Tweedy, bespectacled, absentmindedly professorial in mien, the sixty-four-year-old author greeted our interviewer, freelance writer Alvin Toffler, at the door of Nabokov's quiet apartment on the sixth floor of an elegant old hotel on the banks of Switzerland's Lake Geneva[1], where he has lived and worked for the past four years—most recently producing *Pale Fire*, the extraordinary story of a gifted poet as seen darkly through the eyes of his demented editor, and a belated English translation of *The Gift*. In a week-long series of conversations which took place in his study, Nabokov parried our questions with a characteristic mixture of guile, candor, irony, astringent wit, and eloquent evasiveness. Speaking in a curiously ornate and literary English lightly tinctured with a Russian accent, choosing his words with self-conscious deliberation, he seemed somewhat dubious of his ability to make himself understood—or perhaps skeptical about the advisability of doing so. Despite the good humor and well-bred cordiality which marked our meetings, it was as though the shadowed universe within his skull was forever beckoning him away from a potentially hostile world outside. Thus his conversation, like his fiction—in which so many critics have sought vainly to unearth autobiography—veils rather than reveals the man; and he seems to prefer it that way. But we believe our interview offers a fascinating glimpse of this multileveled genius.

**Playboy:** With the American publication of *Lolita* in 1958, your fame and fortune mushroomed almost overnight from high repute among the literary *cognoscenti*—which you had enjoyed for more than thirty years—to both acclaim and abuse as the world-renowned author of a sensational bestseller. In the aftermath of this *cause célèbre*, do you ever regret having written *Lolita*?

**Vladimir Nabokov:** On the contrary, I shudder retrospectively when I recall that there was a moment, in 1950 and again in 1951, when I was on the point of burning Humbert Humbert's little black diary. No, I shall never regret *Lolita*. She was like the composition of a beautiful puzzle—its composition and its solution at the same time, since one is a mirror view of the other, depending on the way you look. Of course, she completely eclipsed my other works—at least those I wrote in English: *The Real Life of Sebastian Knight*, *Bend Sinister*, my short stories, my book of recollections; but I cannot grudge her this. There is a queer, tender charm about that mythical nymphet.

**Playboy:** Though many readers and reviewers would disagree that her charm is tender, few would deny that it is queer—so much so that when director Stanley Kubrick proposed his plan to make a movie of *Lolita*, you were quoted as saying, "Of course, they'll have to change the plot. Perhaps they will make Lolita a dwarfess. Or they will make her sixteen and Humbert twenty-six." Though you finally wrote the screenplay yourself, several reviewers took the film to task for watering down the central relationship. Were you satisfied with the final product?

**VN:** I thought the movie was absolutely first-rate. The four main actors deserve the very highest praise. Sue Lyon bringing that breakfast tray or childishly pulling on her sweater in the car—these are moments of unforgettable acting and directing. The killing of Quilty is a masterpiece, and so is the death of Mrs. Haze. I must point out, though, that I had nothing to do with the actual production. If I had, I might have insisted on stressing certain things that were not stressed—for example, the different motels at which they stayed. All I did was write the screenplay, a preponderating portion of which was used by Kubrick.

**Playboy:** Do you feel that *Lolita*'s twofold success has affected your life for the better or for the worse?
**VN:** I gave up teaching—that's about all in the way of change. Mind you, I loved teaching, I loved Cornell, I loved composing and delivering my lectures on Russian writers and European great books. But around sixty, and especially in winter, one begins to find hard the physical process of teaching, the getting up at a fixed hour every other morning, the struggle with the snow in the driveway, the march through long corridors to the classroom, the effort of drawing on the blackboard a map of James Joyce's Dublin or the arrangement of the semi-sleeping car of the St. Petersburg-Moscow express in the early 1870's—without an understanding of which neither *Ulysses* nor *Anna Karenina*, respectively, makes sense. For some reason my most vivid memories concern examinations. Big amphitheater in Goldwin Smith. Exam from eight A.M. to ten thirty A.M. About one hundred and fifty students—unwashed, unshaven young males and reasonably well-groomed young females. A general sense of tedium and disaster. Half-past eight. Little coughs, the clearing of nervous throats, coming in clusters of sound, rustling of pages. Some of the martyrs plunged in meditation, their arms locked behind their heads. I meet a dull gaze directed at me, seeing in me with hope and hate the source of forbidden knowledge. Girl in glasses comes up to my desk to ask: "Professor Kafka, do you want us to say that . . . ? Or do you want us to answer only the first part of the question?" The great fraternity of C-minus, backbone of the nation, steadily scribbling on. A rustle arising simultaneously, the majority turning a page in their bluebooks, good teamwork. The shaking of a cramped wrist, the failing ink, the deodorant that breaks down. When I catch eyes directed at me, they are forthwith raised to the ceiling in pious meditation. Windowpanes getting misty. Boys peeling off sweaters. Girls chewing gum in rapid cadence. Ten minutes, five, three, time's up.

**Playboy:** Citing in *Lolita* the same kind of acid-etched scene you've just described, many critics have called the book a masterful satiric social commentary on America. Are they right?
**VN:** Well, I can only repeat that I have neither the intent nor the temperament of a moral or social satirist. Whether or not critics think that in

*Lolita* I am ridiculing human folly leaves me supremely indifferent. But I am annoyed when the glad news is spread that I am ridiculing America.

**Playboy:** But haven't you written yourself that there is "nothing more exhilarating than American philistine vulgarity?"

**VN:** No, I did not say that. That phrase has been lifted out of context, and like a round, deep-sea fish, has burst in the process. If you look up my little afterpiece, "On a Book Entitled Lolita," which I appended to the novel, you will see that what I really said was that in regard to philistine vulgarity—which I do feel is most exhilarating—no difference exists between American and European manners. I go on to say that a proletarian from Chicago can be just as philistine as an English duke.

**Playboy:** Many readers have concluded that the philistinism you seem to find the most exhilarating is that of America's sexual mores.

**VN:** Sex as an institution, sex as a general notion, sex as a problem, sex as a platitude—all this is something I find too tedious for words. Let us skip sex.

**Playboy:** Not to belabor the subject, some critics have felt that your barbed comments about the fashionability of Freudianism, as practiced by American analysts, suggest a contempt based upon familiarity.

**VN:** Bookish familiarity only. The ordeal itself is much too silly and disgusting to be contemplated even as a joke. Freudism and all it has tainted with its grotesque implications and methods, appear to me to be one of the vilest deceits practiced by people on themselves and on others. I reject it utterly, along with a few other medieval items still adored by the ignorant, the conventional, or the very sick.

**Playboy:** Speaking of the very sick, you suggested in *Lolita* that Humbert Humbert's appetite for nymphets is the result of an unrequited childhood love affair; in *Invitation to a Beheading* you wrote about a twelve-year-old girl, Emmie, who is erotically interested in a man twice her age; and in *Bend Sinister*, your protagonist dreams that he is "surreptitiously enjoying Mariette [his maid] while she sat, wincing a little, in his lap during the rehearsal of a play in which she was supposed to be his daughter." Some critics, in poring over your works for clues to your personality, have pointed to this recurrent theme as evidence of an unwholesome preoccupation on your part with the subject of sexual attraction between pubescent girls and middle-aged men. Do you feel that there may be some truth in this charge?

**VN:** I think it would be more correct to say that had I not written *Lolita*, readers would not have started finding nymphets in my other works and in their own households. I find it very amusing when a friendly, polite person says to me—probably just in order to be friendly and polite—"Mr. Naborkov," or "Mr. Nabahkov," or "Mr. Nabkov" or "Mr. Nabohkov," depending on his linguistic abilities, "I have a little daughter who is a regular Lolita." People tend to underestimate the power of my imagination and my capacity of evolving serial selves in my writings. And then, of course, there is that special type of critic, the ferrety, human-interest fiend, the jolly vulgarian. Someone, for instance, discovered telltale affinities between Humbert's boyhood romance on the Riviera and my own recollections about little Colette, with whom I built sand castles in Biarritz when I was ten. Somber Humbert was, of course, thirteen and in the throes of a pretty extravagant sexual excitement, whereas my own romance with Colette had no trace of erotic desire and indeed was perfectly commonplace and normal. And, of course, at nine and ten years of age, in that set, in those times, we knew nothing whatsoever about the false facts of life that are imparted nowadays to infants by progressive parents.

**Playboy:** Why false?
**VN:** Because the imagination of a small child—especially a town child—at once distorts, stylizes or otherwise alters the bizarre things he is told about the busy bee, which neither he nor his parents can distinguish from a bumblebee, anyway.

**Playboy:** What one critic has termed your "almost obsessive attention to the phrasing, rhythm, cadence and connotation of words" is evident even in the selection of names for your own celebrated bee and bumblebee—Lolita and Humbert Humbert. How did they occur to you?
**VN:** For my nymphet I needed a diminutive with a lyrical lilt to it. One of the most limpid and luminous letters is "L." The suffix "-ita" has a lot of Latin tenderness, and this I required too. Hence: Lolita. However, it should not be pronounced as you and most Americans pronounce it: Low-lee-ta, with a heavy, clammy "L" and a long "o." No, the first syllable should be as in "lollipop," the "L" liquid and delicate, the "lee" not too sharp. Spaniards and Italians pronounce it, of course, with exactly the necessary note of archness and caress. Another consideration was the welcome murmur of its source name, the fountain name: those roses and tears in "Dolores." My little girl's heart-rending fate had to be taken into account together with the cuteness

and limpidity. Dolores also provided her with another, plainer, more familiar and infantile diminutive: Dolly, which went nicely with the surname
"Haze," where Irish mists blend with a German bunny—I mean a small German hare.

**Playboy:** You're making a word-playful reference, of course, to the German
term for rabbit—*Hase*. But what inspired you to dub Lolita's aging inam-
orato with such engaging redundancy?
**VN:** That, too, was easy. The double rumble is, I think, very nasty, very sug-
gestive. It is a hateful name for a hateful person. It is also a kingly name, and I
did need a royal vibration for Humbert the Fierce and Humbert the Humble.
Lends itself also to a number of puns. And the execrable diminutive "Hum" is
on a par, socially and emotionally, with "Lo," as her mother calls her.

**Playboy:** Another critic has written of you that "the task of sifting and
selecting just the right succession of words from that multilingual memory,
and of arranging their many-mirrored nuances into the proper juxtapositions, must be psychically exhausting work." Which of all your books, in this
sense, would you say was the most difficult to write?
**VN:** Oh, *Lolita*, naturally. I lacked the necessary information—that was the
initial difficulty. I did not know any American twelve-year-old girls, and I
did not know America; I had to invent America and Lolita. It had taken me
some forty years to invent Russia and Western Europe, and now I was faced
by a similar task, with a lesser amount of time at my disposal. The obtaining
of such local ingredients as would allow me to inject average "reality" into
the brew of individual fancy proved, at fifty, a much more difficult process
than it had been in the Europe of my youth.

**Playboy:** Though born in Russia, you have lived and worked for many years
in America as well as in Europe. Do you feel any strong sense of national
identity?
**VN:** I am an American writer, born in Russia and educated in England
where I studied French literature, before spending fifteen years in Germany.
I came to America in 1940 and decided to become an American citizen and
make America my home. It so happened that I was immediately exposed
to the very best in America, to its rich intellectual life and to its easygo-
ing, good-natured atmosphere. I immersed myself in its great libraries and
its Grand Canyon. I worked in the laboratories of its zoological museums.

I acquired more friends than I ever had in Europe. My books—old books and new ones—found some admirable readers. I became as stout as Cortez—mainly because I quit smoking and started to munch molasses candy instead, with the result that my weight went up from my usual 140 to a monumental and cheerful 200. In consequence, I am one-third American—good American flesh keeping me warm and safe.

**Playboy:** You spent twenty years in America, and yet you never owned a home or had a really settled establishment there. Your friends report that you camped impermanently in motels, cabins, furnished apartments and the rented homes of professors away on leave. Did you feel so restless or so alien that the idea of settling down anywhere disturbed you?

**VN:** The main reason, the background reason, is, I suppose, that nothing short of a replica of my childhood surroundings would have satisfied me. I would never manage to match my memories correctly—so why trouble with hopeless approximations? Then there are some special considerations: for instance, the question of impetus, the habit of impetus. I propelled myself out of Russia so vigorously, with such indignant force, that I have been rolling on and on ever since. True, I have lived to become that appetizing thing, a "full professor," but at heart I have always remained a lean "visiting lecturer." The few times I said to myself anywhere: "Now, that's a nice spot for a permanent home," I would immediately hear in my mind the thunder of an avalanche carrying away the hundreds of far places which I would destroy by the very act of settling in one particular nook of the earth. And finally, I don't much care for furniture, for tables and chairs and lamps and rugs and things—perhaps because in my opulent childhood I was taught to regard with amused contempt any too-earnest attachment to material wealth, which is why I felt no regret and no bitterness when the Revolution abolished that wealth.

**Playboy:** You lived in Russia for twenty years, in West Europe for twenty years, and in America for twenty years. But in 1960, after the success of *Lolita*, you moved to France and Switzerland and have not returned to the U.S. since. Does this mean, despite your self-identification as an American writer, that you consider your American period over?

**VN:** I am living in Switzerland for purely private reasons—family reasons and certain professional ones too, such as some special research for a special book. I hope to return very soon to America—back to its library stacks and mountain passes. An ideal arrangement would be an absolutely sound-proofed flat in New York, on a top floor—no feet walking above, no soft music anywhere—and a bungalow in the Southwest. Sometimes I think it might be fun to adorn a university again, residing and writing there, not teaching, or at least not teaching regularly.

**Playboy:** Meanwhile, you remain secluded—and somewhat sedentary, from all reports—in your hotel suite. How do you spend your time?

**VN:** I awake around seven in winter: my alarm clock is an Alpine chough—big, glossy, black thing with a big yellow beak—which visits the balcony and emits a most melodious chuckle. For a while I lie in bed mentally revising and planning things. Around eight: shave, breakfast, meditation, and bath—in that order. Then I work till lunch in my study, taking time out for a short stroll with my wife along the lake. Practically all the famous Russian writers of the nineteenth century have rambled here at one time or another: Zhukovsky, Gogol, Dostoyevsky, Tolstoy—who courted the hotel chambermaids to the detriment of his health—and many Russian poets. But then, as much could be said of Nice or Rome. We lunch around one P.M., and I am back at my desk by half-past one and work steadily till half-past six. Then a stroll to a newsstand for the English papers, and dinner at seven. No work after dinner. And bed around nine. I read till half-past eleven, and tussle with insomnia from that time till one A.M. About twice a week I have a good, long nightmare with unpleasant characters imported from earlier dreams, appearing in more or less iterative surroundings—kaleidoscopic arrangements of broken impressions, fragments of day thoughts, and irresponsible mechanical images,

**Playboy:** Is it true that you write standing up, and that you write in longhand rather than on a typewriter?

**VN:** Yes. I never learned to type. I generally start the day at a lovely old-fashioned lectern I have in my study. Later on, when I feel gravity nibbling at my calves, I settle down in a comfortable armchair at an ordinary writing desk; and finally, when gravity begins climbing up my spine, I lie down on a couch in a corner of my small study. It is a pleasant solar routine. But when I was young, in my twenties and early thirties, I would often stay all day in bed, smoking and writing. Now things have changed. Horizontal prose, vertical prose, and sedent scholia keep swapping qualifiers and spoiling the alliteration.

**Playboy:** Can you tell us something more about the actual creative process involved in the germination of a book—perhaps by reading a few random notes for or excerpts from a work in progress?

**VN:** Certainly not. No fetus should undergo an exploratory operation. But I can do something else. This box contains index cards with some notes I made at various times more or less recently and discarded when writing *Pale Fire.* It's a little batch of rejects. I'll read a few [Reading from cards]:

"Selene, the moon. Selenginsk, an old town in Siberia: moon-rocket town" . . . "Berry: the black knob on the bill of the mute swan" . . . "Dropworm: a small caterpillar hanging on a thread" . . . "In *The New Bon Ton Magazine,* volume five, 1820, page 312, prostitutes are termed 'girls of the town'" . . . "Youth dreams: forgot pants; old man dreams: forgot dentures" . . . "Student explains that when reading a novel he likes to skip passages 'so as to get his own idea about the book and not be influenced by the author'" . . . "Naprapathy: the ugliest word in the language."

"And after rain, on beaded wires, one bird, two birds, three birds, and none. Muddy tires, sun" . . . "Time without consciousness — lower animal world: time with consciousness — man; consciousness without time — some still higher state" . . . "We think not in words but in shadows of words. James Joyce's mistake in those otherwise marvelous mental soliloquies of his consists in that he gives too much verbal body to words" . . . "Parody of politeness: That inimitable 'Please' — 'Please send me your beautiful –' which firms idiotically address to themselves in printed forms meant for people ordering their product."

"Naive, nonstop, peep-peep twitter in dismal crates late, late at night, on a desolate frost-bedimmed station platform" . . . "The tabloid headline 'TORSO KILLER MAY BEAT CHAIR' might be translated: '*Celui qui tue un buste peut bien battre une chaise*'" . . . "Newspaper vendor, handing me a magazine with my story: 'I see you made the slicks.'"

"Snow falling, young father out with tiny child, nose like a pink cherry. Why does a parent immediately say something to his or her child if a stranger smiles at the latter? 'Sure,' said the father to the infant's interrogatory gurgle, which had been going on for some time, and would have been left to go on in the quiet falling snow, had I not smiled in passing" . . . "Intercolumniation: dark-blue sky between two white columns."

"'I,' says Death, 'am even in Arcadia' — legend on a shepherd's tomb". . . "Marat collected butterflies". . . "From the aesthetic point of view, the tapeworm is certainly an undesirable border. The gravid segments frequently crawl out of a person's anal canal, sometimes in chains, and have been reported a source of social embarrassment."

**Playboy:** What inspires you to record and collect such disconnected impressions and quotations?

**VN:** All I know is that at a very early stage of the novel's development I get this urge to collect bits of straw and fluff, and to eat pebbles. Nobody will ever discover how clearly a bird visualizes, or if it visualizes at all, the future nest and the eggs in it. When I remember afterwards the force that made me jot down the correct names of things, or the inches and tints of things, even before I actually needed the information, I am inclined to assume that what I call, for want of a better term, inspiration, had been already at work, mutely pointing at this or that, having me accumulate the known materials for an unknown structure. After the first shock of recognition—a sudden sense of "*this* is what I'm going to write"—the novel starts to breed by itself; the process goes on solely in the mind, not on paper; and to be aware of the stage it has reached at any given moment, I do not have to be conscious of every exact phrase. I feel a kind of gentle development, an uncurling inside, and I know that the details are there already, that in fact I would see them plainly if I looked closer, if I stopped the machine and opened its inner compartments; but I prefer to wait until what is loosely called inspiration has completed the task for me. There comes a moment when I am informed from within that the entire structure is finished. All I have to do now is take it down in pencil or pen. Since this entire structure, dimly illumed in one's mind, can be compared to a painting, and since you do not have to work gradually from left to right for its proper perception, I may direct my flashlight at any part or particle of the picture when setting it down in writing. I do not begin my novel at the beginning, I do not reach chapter three before I reach chapter four, I do not go dutifully from one page to the next, in consecutive order; no, I pick out a bit here and a bit there, till I have filled all the gaps on paper. This is why I like writing my stories and novels on index cards, numbering them later when the whole set is complete. Every card is rewritten many times. About three cards make one typewritten page, and when finally I feel that the conceived picture has been copied by me as faithfully as physically possible—a few vacant lots always remain, alas—then I dictate the novel to my wife who types it out in triplicate.

**Playboy:** In what sense do you *copy* "the conceived picture" of a novel?

**VN:** A creative writer must study carefully the works of his rivals, including the Almighty. He must possess the inborn capacity not only of recombining but of recreating the given world. In order to do this adequately, avoiding duplication of labor, the artist should *know* the given world. Imagination without knowledge leads no farther than the backyard of primitive art, the child's scrawl on the fence, and the crank's message in the marketplace. Art is never simple. To return to my lecturing days: I automatically gave low marks when a student used the dreadful phrase "sincere and simple"— "Flaubert writes with a style which is always simple and sincere"—under the impression that this was the greatest compliment payable to prose or poetry. When I struck the phrase out, which I did with such rage in my pencil that it ripped the paper, the student complained that this was what teachers had always taught him: "Art is simple, art is sincere." Someday I must trace this vulgar absurdity to its source. A schoolmarm in Ohio? A progressive ass in New York? Because, of course, art at its greatest is fantastically deceitful and complex.

**Playboy:** In terms of modern art, critical opinion is divided about the sincerity or deceitfulness, simplicity or complexity of contemporary abstract painting. What is your own opinion?

**VN:** I do not see any essential difference between abstract and primitive art. Both are simple and sincere. Naturally, we should not generalize in these matters: it is the individual artist that counts. But if we accept for a moment the general notion of "modern art," then we must admit that the trouble with it is that it is so commonplace, imitative, and academic. Blurs and blotches have merely replaced the mass prettiness of a hundred years ago, pictures of Italian girls, handsome beggars, romantic ruins, and so forth. But just as among those corny oils there might occur the work of a true artist with a richer play of light and shade, with some original streak of violence or tenderness, so among the corn of primitive and abstract art one may come across a flash of great talent. Only talent interests me in paintings and books. Not general ideas, but the individual contribution.

**Playboy:** A contribution to society?

**VN:** A work of art has no importance whatever to society. It is only important to the individual, and only the individual reader is important to me. I don't give a damn for the group, the community, the masses, and so forth. Although I do not care for the slogan "art for art's sake"—because unfortunately such promoters of it as, for instance, Oscar Wilde and various dainty poets, were in reality rank moralists and didacticists—there can be no question that what makes a work of fiction safe from larvae and rust is not its social importance but its art, only its art.

**Playboy:** Do you expect your own work to remain "safe from larvae and rust?"

**VN:** Well, in this matter of accomplishment, of course, I don't have a thirty-five-year plan or program, but I have a fair inkling of my literary afterlife. I have felt the breeze of certain promises. No doubt there will be ups and downs, long periods of slump. With the Devil's connivance, I open a newspaper of 2063 and in some article on the books page I find: "Nobody reads Nabokov or Fulmerford today." Awful question: Who is this unfortunate Fulmerford?

**Playboy:** While we're on the subject of self-appraisal, what do you regard as your principal failing as a writer—apart from forgettability?

**VN:** Lack of spontaneity; the nuisance of parallel thoughts, second thoughts, third thoughts; inability to express myself properly in any language unless I compose every damned sentence in my bath, in my mind, at my desk.

**Playboy:** You're doing rather well at the moment, if we may say so.

**VN:** It's an illusion.

**Playboy:** Your reply might be taken as confirmation of critical comments that you are "an incorrigible leg puller," "a mystificator" and "a literary *agent provocateur.*" How do *you* view yourself?

**Nabokov:** I think my favorite fact about myself is that I have never been dismayed by a critic's bilge or bile, and have never once in my life asked or thanked a reviewer for a review. My second favorite fact—or shall I stop at one?

**Playboy:** No, please go on.

**VN:** The fact that since my youth—I was nineteen when I left Russia—my political outlook has remained as bleak and changeless as an old gray rock. It is classical to the point of triteness. Freedom of speech, freedom of thought, freedom of art. The social or economic structure of the ideal state is of little concern to me. My desires are modest. Portraits of the head of the government should not exceed a postage stamp in size. No torture and no executions. No music, except coming through earphones, or played in theaters.

**Playboy:** Why no music?

**VN:** I have no ear for music, a shortcoming I deplore bitterly. When I attend a concert—which happens about once in five years—I endeavor gamely to follow the sequence and relationship of sounds but cannot keep it up for more than a few minutes. Visual impressions, reflections of hands in lacquered wood, a diligent bald spot over a fiddle, take over, and soon I am bored beyond measure by the motions of the musicians. My knowledge of music is very slight; and I have a special reason for finding my ignorance and inability so sad, so unjust: There is a wonderful singer in my family—my own son. His great gifts, the rare beauty of his bass, and the promise of a splendid career—all this affects me deeply, and I feel a fool during a technical conversation among musicians. I am perfectly aware of the many parallels between the art forms of music and those of literature, especially in matters of structure, but what can I do if ear and brain refuse to cooperate? But I have found a queer substitute for music in chess—more exactly, in the composing of chess problems.

**Playboy:** Another substitute, surely, has been your own euphonious prose and poetry. As one of few authors who have written with eloquence in more than one language, how would you characterize the textural differences between Russian and English, in which you are regarded as equally facile?

**VN:** In sheer number of words, English is far richer than Russian. This is especially noticeable in nouns and adjectives. A very bothersome feature that Russian presents is the dearth, vagueness, and clumsiness of technical terms. For example, the simple phrase "to park a car" comes out—if translated back from the Russian—as "to leave an automobile standing for a long time." Russian, at least polite Russian, is more formal than polite English. Thus, the Russian word for "sexual"—*polovoy*—is slightly indecent and not to be bandied around. The same applies to Russian terms rendering various anatomical and biological notions that are frequently and familiarly expressed in English conversation. On the other hand, there are words rendering certain nuances of motion and gesture and emotion in which Russian excels. Thus by changing the head of a verb, for which one may have a dozen different prefixes to choose from, one is able to make Russian express extremely fine shades of duration and intensity. English is, syntactically, an extremely flexible medium, but Russian can be given even more subtle twists and turns. Translating Russian into English is a little easier than translating English into Russian, and ten times easier than translating English into French.

**Playboy:** You have said you will never write another novel in Russian. Why?
**VN:** During the great, and still unsung, era of Russian intellectual expatriation—roughly between 1920 and 1940—books written in Russian by *émigré* Russians and published by *émigré* firms abroad were eagerly bought or borrowed by *émigré* readers but were absolutely banned in Soviet Russia—as they still are, except in the case of a few dead authors such as Kuprin and Bunin, whose heavily censored works have been recently reprinted there—no matter the theme of the story or poem. An *émigré* novel, published, say, in Paris and sold over all free Europe, might have, in those years, a total sale of one thousand or two thousand copies—that would be a bestseller—but every copy would also pass from hand to hand and be read by at least twenty persons, and at least fifty annually if stocked by Russian lending libraries, of which there were hundreds in West Europe alone. The era of expatriation can be said to have ended during World War II. Old writers died, Russian publishers also vanished, and worst of all, the general atmosphere of exile culture, with its splendor, and vigor, and purity, and reverberative force, dwindled to a sprinkle of Russian-language periodicals, anemic in talent and provincial in tone. Now to take my own case: It was not the financial side that really mattered; I don't think my Russian writings ever brought me more than a few hundred dollars per year, and I am all for the ivory tower, and for writing to please one reader alone—one's own self. But one also needs some reverberation, if not response, and a moderate multiplication of one's self throughout a country or countries; and if there be nothing but a void around one's desk, one would expect it to be at least a sonorous void, and not circumscribed by the walls of a padded cell. With the passing of years I grew less and less interested in Russia and more and more indifferent to the once-harrowing thought that my books would remain banned there as long as my contempt for the police state and political oppression prevented me from entertaining the vaguest thought of return. No, I will not write another novel in Russian, though I do allow myself a very few short poems now and then. I wrote my last Russian novel a quarter of a century ago. But today, in compensation, in a spirit of justice to my little American muse, I am doing something else. But perhaps I should not talk about it at this early stage.

**Playboy:** Please do.

**VN:** Well, it occurred to me one day—while I was glancing at the vari-colored spines of *Lolita* translations into languages I do not read, such as Japanese, Finnish or Arabic—that the list of unavoidable blunders in these fifteen or twenty versions would probably make, if collected, a fatter volume than any of them. I had checked the French translation, which was basically very good but would have bristled with unavoidable errors had I not corrected them. But what could I do with Portuguese or Hebrew or Danish? Then I imagined something else. I imagined that in some distant future somebody might produce a Russian version of *Lolita*. I trained my inner telescope upon that particular point in the distant future and I saw that every paragraph could lend itself to a hideous mistranslation, being pock-marked with pitfalls. In the hands of a harmful drudge, the Russian version of *Lolita* would be entirely degraded and botched by vulgar paraphrases or blunders. So I decided to translate it myself. Up to now I have about sixty pages ready.

**Playboy:** Are you presently at work on any new *writing* project?

**VN:** Good question, as they say on the lesser screen. I have just finished correcting the last proofs of my work on Pushkin's *Eugene Onegin*—four fat little volumes which are to appear this year in the Bollingen Series; the actual translation of the poem occupies a small section of volume one. The rest of the volume and volumes two, three and four contain copious notes on the subject. This opus owes its birth to a casual remark my wife made in 1950—in response to my disgust with rhymed paraphrases of *Eugene Onegin*, every line of which I had to revise for my students—"Why don't you translate it yourself?" This is the result. It has taken me some ten years of labor. The index alone runs five thousand cards in three long shoe boxes; you see them over there on that shelf. My translation is, of course, a literal one, a crib, a pony. And to the fidelity of transposal I have sacrificed everything: elegance, euphony, clarity, good taste, modern usage, and even grammar.

**Playboy:** In view of these admitted flaws, are you looking forward to reading the reviews of the book?

**VN:** I really don't read reviews about myself with any special eagerness or attention unless they are masterpieces of wit and acumen—which does happen now and then. And I never reread them, though my wife collects the stuff, and though maybe I shall use a spatter of the more hilarious

*Lolita* items to write someday a brief history of the nymphet's tribulations. I remember, however, quite vividly, certain attacks by Russian *émigré* critics who wrote about my first novels thirty years ago; not that I was more vulnerable then, but my memory was certainly more retentive and enterprising, and I was a reviewer myself. In the 1920s I was clawed at by a certain Mochulski who could never stomach my utter indifference to organized mysticism, to religion, to the church—any church. There were other critics who could not forgive me for keeping aloof from literary "movements," for not airing the "*angoisse*" that they wanted poets to feel, and for not belonging to any of those groups of poets that held sessions of common inspiration in the back rooms of Parisian cafes. There was also the amusing case of Georgy Ivanov, a good poet but a scurrilous critic. I never met him or his literary wife Irina Odoevtsev; but one day in the late 1920s or early 1930s, at a time when I regularly reviewed books for an *émigré* newspaper in Berlin, she sent me from Paris a copy of a novel of hers with the wily inscription "*Thanks for King, Queen, Jack*"—which I was free to understand as "thanks for writing that book," but which might also provide her with the alibi: "Thanks for sending me your book," though I never sent her anything. *Her* book proved to be pitifully trivial, and I said so in a brief and nasty review. Ivanov retaliated with a grossly personal article about me and my stuff. The possibility of venting or distilling friendly or unfriendly feelings through the medium of literary criticism is what makes that art such a skewy one.

**Playboy:** What is your reaction to the mixed feelings vented by one critic in a review which characterized you as having a fine and original mind, but "not much trace of a generalizing intellect," and as "the typical artist who distrusts ideas?"
**VN:** In much the same solemn spirit, certain crusty lepidopterists have criticized my works on the classification of butterflies, accusing me of being more interested in the subspecies and the subgenus than in the genus and the family. This kind of attitude is a matter of mental temperament, I suppose. The middlebrow or the upper philistine cannot get rid of the furtive feeling that a book, to be great, must deal in great ideas. Oh, I know the type, the dreary type! He likes a good yarn spiced with social comment; he likes to recognize his own thoughts and throes in those of the author; he wants at least one of the characters to be the author's stooge. If American, he has a dash of Marxist blood, and if British, he is acutely and ridiculously class-conscious; he finds it so much easier to write about ideas than about words; he does not realize that perhaps the reason he does not find general

ideas in a particular writer is that the particular ideas of that writer have not yet become general.

**Playboy:** Dostoyevsky, who dealt with themes accepted by most readers as universal in both scope and significance, is considered one of the world's great authors. Yet you have described him as "a cheap sensationalist, clumsy and vulgar." Why?

**VN:** Non-Russian readers do not realize two things: that not all Russians love Dostoyevsky as much as Americans do, and that most of those Russians who do, venerate him as a mystic and not as an artist. He was a prophet, a claptrap journalist, and a slapdash comedian. I admit that some of his scenes, some of his tremendous, farcical rows are extraordinarily amusing. But his sensitive murderers and soulful prostitutes are not to be endured for one moment—by this reader anyway.

**Playboy:** Is it true that you have called Hemingway and Conrad "writers of books for boys?"

**VN:** That's exactly what they are. Hemingway is certainly the better of the two; he has at least a voice of his own and is responsible for that delightful, highly artistic short story, *The Killers*. And the description of the fish in his famous fish story is superb. But I cannot abide Conrad's souvenir-shop style, and bottled ships, and shell necklaces of romanticist clichés. In neither of these two writers can I find anything that I would care to have written myself. In mentality and emotion, they are hopelessly juvenile, and the same can be said of some other beloved writers, the pets of the common room, the consolation and support of graduate students, such as—but some are still alive, and I hate to hurt living old boys while the dead ones are not yet buried.

**Playboy:** What did you read when *you* were a boy?

**VN:** Between the ages of ten and fifteen in St. Petersburg, I must have read more fiction and poetry—English, Russian and French—than in any other five-year period of my life. I relished especially the works of Wells, Poe, Browning, Keats, Flaubert, Verlaine, Rimbaud, Chekhov, Tolstoy, and Alexander Blok. On another level, my heroes were the Scarlet Pimpernel, Phileas Fogg, and Sherlock Holmes. In other words, I was a perfectly normal trilingual child in a family with a large library. At a later period, in Cambridge, England, between the ages of twenty and twenty-three, my favorites were Housman, Rupert Brooke, Joyce, Proust and Pushkin. Of these top favorites, several—Poe, Verlaine, Jules Verne, Emmuska Orczy, Conan Doyle, and Rupert Brooke—have faded away, have lost the glamour and thrill they held for me. The others remain intact and by now are probably beyond change as far as I am concerned. I was never exposed in the twenties and thirties, as so many of my coevals have been, to the poetry of Eliot and Pound. I read them late in the season, around 1945, in the guest room of an American friend's house, and not only remained completely indifferent to them, but could not understand why anybody should bother about them. But I suppose that they preserve some sentimental value for such readers as discovered them at an earlier age than I did.

**Playboy:** What are your reading habits today?
**VN:** Usually I read several books at a time—old books, new books, fiction, nonfiction, verse, anything—and when the bedside heap of a dozen volumes or so has dwindled to two or three, which generally happens by the end of one week, I accumulate another pile. There are some varieties of fiction that I never touch—mystery stories, for instance, which I abhor, and historical novels. I also detest the so-called "powerful" novel—full of commonplace obscenities and torrents of dialog—in fact, when I receive a new novel from a hopeful publisher—"hoping that I like the book as much as he does"—I check first of all how much dialog there is, and if it looks too abundant or too sustained, I shut the book with a bang and ban it from my bed.

**Playboy:** Are there any contemporary authors you *do* enjoy reading?
**VN:** I do have a few favorites—for example, Robbe-Grillet and Borges. How freely and gratefully one breathes in their marvelous labyrinths! I love their lucidity of thought, the purity and poetry, the mirage in the mirror.

**Playboy:** Many critics feel that this description applies no less aptly to your own prose. To what extent do you feel that prose and poetry intermingle as art forms?
**VN:** Poetry, of course, includes all creative writing; I have never been able to see any generic difference between poetry and artistic prose. As a matter of fact, I would be inclined to define a good poem of any length as a concentrate of good prose, with or without the addition of recurrent rhythm and rhyme. The magic of prosody may improve upon what we call prose by bringing out the full flavor of meaning, but in plain prose there are also certain rhythmic patterns, the music of precise phrasing, the beat of thought rendered by recurrent peculiarities of idiom and intonation. As in today's

scientific classifications, there is a lot of overlapping in our concept of poetry and prose today. The bamboo bridge between them is the metaphor.

**Playboy:** You have also written that poetry represents "the mysteries of the irrational perceived through rational words." But many feel that the "irrational" has little place in an age when the exact knowledge of science has begun to plumb the most profound mysteries of existence. Do you agree?

**VN:** This appearance is very deceptive. It is a journalistic illusion. In point of fact, the greater one's science, the deeper the sense of mystery. Moreover, I don't believe that any science today has pierced any mystery. We, as newspaper readers, are inclined to call "science" the cleverness of an electrician or a psychiatrist's mumbo jumbo. This, at best, is applied science, and one of the characteristics of applied science is that yesterday's neutron or today's truth dies tomorrow. But even in a better sense of "science"—as the study of visible and palpable nature, or the poetry of pure mathematics and pure philosophy—the situation remains as hopeless as ever. We shall never know the origin of life, or the meaning of life, or the nature of space and time, or the nature of nature, or the nature of thought.

**Playboy:** Man's understanding of these mysteries is embodied in his concept of a Divine Being. As a final question, do you believe in God?

**VN:** To be quite candid—and what I am going to say now is something I never said before, and I hope it provokes a salutary little chill: I know more than I can express in words, and the little I can express would not have been expressed, had I not known more.

## Notes

1. Lake Geneva is Lake Léman.

# On the Banks of Lake Léman: Mr. Nabokov Reflects on *Lolita* and *Onegin*

## Douglas M. Davis / 1964

From *The National Observer*, June 29, 1964. Copyright © 1964 Dow Jones and Company, Inc. All Rights Reserved Worldwide. Reprinted with permission of *The National Observer*.

For lovers of Russian literature—and lovers of Vladimir Nabokov—last week was a milestone. It was the week Pantheon Press published Mr. Nabokov's four-volume translation of Alexander Pushkin's great narrative poem, *Eugene Onegin*, complete with footnotes and commentary.

To people who think of Mr. Nabokov as the gay, mad author of novels like *Lolita* and *Pale Fire*, this latest work may seem incongruous. No doubt it will leave them wondering what kind of man this Nabokov is.

I wondered the same thing as I traveled by train from Geneva to Montreux, a small resort town on the far side of Lake Léman, where Mr. Nabokov now lives with his wife and son. I wanted to know, too, why Mr. Nabokov had apparently deserted his "new home," the United States, as soon as *Lolita* began to bring him long-denied financial rewards in 1959 and 1960.

Before I had gone very far, though, I began to think that the countryside alone was reason enough for Mr. Nabokov's move to Switzerland. No lake in the world can rival the beauty of Léman. No town owns a better view of Léman than Montreux, perched on the edge of a steep hill towering above the lake. And in Montreux no hotel suite fronts the lake more directly than Mr. Nabokov's.

### Why He's at Lake Léman

Shortly after my arrival at this suite, as if reading my mind, Mr. Nabokov threw open the French doors and gestured at the lake. Then he explained why he was there. "I am working on a novel which 'happens' on Lake Léman," he said, adding that he planned to return to the United States as soon as it was finished.

Which came first—the novel or the move to Montreux? He wouldn't say. He uncorked a bottle of red wine instead, and talked of Switzerland. "It is the most pleasant and poetical country in Europe. Gogol, Tolstoy, Byron, Dostoyevsky walked here. Gogol wrote *Dead Souls* here. Dostoyevsky found himself penniless here. Tolstoy caught a good case of venereal disease here. As I say, it is a poetical country."

Mr. Nabokov—in his sixties, graying, slender, ruddy in complexion—speaks with an accent that is difficult to "place." He was born in Russia; his father, a lawyer, was a member of the first Duma (Czarist parliament) and editor of a liberal newspaper. But when the Communists came in 1919, the Nabokov's were forced to emigrate. Since then Vladimir has almost lived out of his bags, moving from Germany to France to the United States, with a short stay in England as a young student.

## Wanted Son to be in the US

"In 1935, my wife and I decided to go to America and live, since the language there was the language I wished to be near," he explains. "We had a little boy, too, and I wanted him there. And people began to translate my books in America. So the practical was associated with the metaphysical."

But the Nabokovs didn't get to America until 1940. Five years later, Mr. Nabokov became a naturalized American citizen. What does he think of the United States after twenty years?

"America is my home now. It is my country. The intellectual life suits me better there than any other country in the world. I have more friends there, more kindred souls than anywhere. I don't care for American food, mind you. Ice cream and milk are all right in their place. The American steak is a mistake. There's a pun for you.

"But these are material things, not important, really. No, there is something about American life and people and universities which keeps me perfectly and completely happy."

Mr. Nabokov's love for America has not always been returned in spades. Some of the critical reaction to his pet novel, *Lolita*—the story of a wild, comic, and touching affair between a middle-aged man and a young "nymphet"—was vehement.

"What bothered me most," recalls Mr. Nabokov, "was the belief that *Lolita* was a criticism of America. I think that's ridiculous. I don't see how anybody could find it in *Lolita*. I don't like people who see the book as an erotic phenomenon, either. Even more, I suppose, I don't like people who have not read *Lolita* and think it obscene."

The author believes too many critics overlooked the change that takes place in Humbert Humbert, the book's "hero," during the course of his affair with Lolita. "I don't think *Lolita* is a religious book," he says, "but I do think it is a moral one. And I do think that Humbert Humbert in his last stage is a moral man because he realizes that he loves Lolita like any woman should be loved. But it is too late; he has destroyed her childhood. There is certainly this kind of morality in it."

All the same, the critics can't be blamed entirely for their misreadings. Mr. Nabokov is a complex, eccentric writer. His novels abound with puns, stylistic tricks, sudden alterations of mood, and downright deception. In *Pale Fire*, for example, the narrator is plainly mad; in order to deduce the truth, the reader must discount almost everything Mr. Nabokov—through the narrator—tells him.

### There is No Teasing

Yet Mr. Nabokov denies that he sets out deliberately to mislead the reader. "I play with him, yes, but not as a cat with a mouse. I suppose there is a lot of shifting in my work, but that is natural to me. As one face or phrase passes, another takes over. But there is no teasing. I am very honest, actually."

For all his love of the oblique and the evasive, however, Mr. Nabokov is a man of blunt opinions—particularly about his fellow writers.

On Robert Frost: "Not everything he wrote was good. There is lots of trash. But I believe that rather obvious little poem on the woods ("Stopping by Woods on a Snowy Evening") is one of the greatest ever written."

On Ernest Hemingway: "Hemingway did some wonderful things. But those long novels—*For Whom the Bell Tolls* and the rest—I think they are abominable. He was, after all, a short story writer."

On William Faulkner: "I am completely deaf to Faulkner. I do not understand what people see in him. He has been invented. Surely, he was not a real person."

Mr. Nabokov writes in three languages—Russian, French, and English—and he speaks directly on this subject too. "At this point I write English better than the other two, and prefer it. I am appalled by the provincial inclinations and philistine thought of modern Russian."

What does he think of Russia today? "Lost country means to me lost childhood and abandoned language, little more. The idea of traveling to Moscow, where I've never been, seems as boring to me as that of visiting Belfast or Belgrade, where I've never been either."

It was not until the end of our conversation, when the last of the red wine had been downed, that Mr. Nabokov mentioned his latest work. "You have not asked about my labor of love. It is the great work of my life."

## A Russian "Don Juan"

This, of course, was *Onegin*. Pushkin first published it in Russian in 1824. It's an extravagant, bold poem, filled with jaded young aristocrats and bored damsels on their country estates—in brief, sort of a Russian *Don Juan*. Only a poet-translator could have brought this triumph of Russian romanticism alive for the English ear. And only a determined scholar could have annotated, interpreted, and restored it so completely.

All this says something about Mr. Nabokov. He is much more than the eccentric novelist of legend. He is a careful, precise thinker as well—even something of a pedant. Remember his own words: "It is the great work of my life." Add to them the concluding paragraph of the autobiography he wrote for the dust jacket of *Onegin*:

> He lectured on Russian literature at Wellesley (*1941–48*) and Cornell (*1948–58*) and has worked on Lepidoptera in the Museum of Comparative Zoology at Harvard (*1942–48*). He is also the author of several novels in English.

*He is also the author of several novels in English.* Undoubtedly, the playful Nabokov spirit is behind that sentence. But there is also a vein of honesty. Would Mr. Nabokov rather be remembered as the translator of Pushkin than the creator of *Lolita*? I am not sure, but I would not be surprised if he would.

# USA: The Novel—Vladimir Nabokov

## Robert Hughes / 1965

From National Educational Television, September 2, 1965. © Thirteen Productions LLC. Reprinted by permission of WNET.

**Vladimir Nabokov:** I'm not a good speaker, you see. When I start to speak I have immediately four—five lines of thought. Sort of roads, you know, trails, going various ways. I have to decide which trail I'm going to follow. And while I decide, this hawing and hemming begins and it may be very upsetting, but I do it myself. I can never understand those limpid, fluid speakers, as my father was, who just deliver perfect phrase, beautifully built, with an aphorism here and a metaphor there. I can't do it. I have to think it out. I have to take a pencil, I have to write it down laboriously, have it before me; do things like that. It's probably psychological. I can imagine what old Freud would have said, whom I heartily detest, as my readers know by now.

**Robert Hughes:** Mr. Nabokov, would you tell us why it is you detest Dr. Freud?
**VN:** I think he's crude. I think he's medieval and I don't want an elderly gentleman from Vienna with an umbrella inflicting his dreams upon me. I don't have the dreams that he discusses in his books. I don't see umbrellas in my dreams, or balloons.

**VN:** The first part of my life is marked by a rather pleasing chronological neatness. I spent my first twenty years in Russia.

**RH:** He began life in Saint Petersburg, eldest son of an aristocratic but liberal family. The author of *Lolita*, *Pale Fire*, *The Gift*, and *Speak, Memory* learned English from his governess before he learned Russian. At eighteen, the October Revolution destroyed his world, including his fortune.

**VN:** The next twenty, in Western Europe.

**RH:** A poet, a composer of chess problems, a deviser of crossword puzzles, after Cambridge University he lived as an exile in Berlin and Paris with his wife of forty years, Véra. Their son Dmitri is now an opera singer. Vladimir Nabokov eked out a living by tutoring, translating, coaching tennis, as well as by writing his eight novels in Russian.

**VN:** And the twenty years after that, from 1940 to 1960, in America.

**RH:** Here he taught literature at Cornell, Harvard, Wellesley, and Stanford. Before emigrating, he had translated two of his novels from Russian into English and written the first of his five English novels. His complete switch from Russian to English prose was exceedingly painful, but his lifelong love affair with the English language continues.

**VN:** I've been living in Europe again for five years now.

**RH:** Currently, in an elegant Swiss hotel overlooking Lake Geneva.

**VN:** But I cannot promise to stare down another fifteen, so I still retain the rhythm. Nor can I predict what new books I may write.

**RH:** But he soon told us of one of his many works in progress.

**VN:** I'm in the process of translating *Lolita* into Russian, which is like completing the circle of my creative life, or rather starting a new spiral. Shall I read three lines of this Russian version? Because, incredible as it may seem, perhaps not everybody remembers the way *Lolita* starts in English. So perhaps I should do the first five in English. First: *Lolita, light of my life, fire of my loins. My sin, my soul. Lo-lee-ta: the tip of the tongue taking a trip on three steps down the palate to tap, at three, on the teeth. Lo. Lee. Ta.* Now comes the Russian. Note by the way that the first syllable of her name sounds more like an 'R' sound than the 'O' sound. [Nabokov reads the opening in Russian.] I live in Montreux for certain family reasons. I have a sister in Geneva and a son not very far away [in] Milan, and also because I find the view so wonderfully soothing and exhilarating, according to my mood and the mood of the lake. Everything is bedaze when such formidable mediocrities as Galsworthy, Dreiser, Tagore, Maxim Gorky, Romain Rolland, and Thomas Mann were being accepted as geniuses. I have been perplexed and amused by fabricated notions about so-called "Great Books." That, for instance, Mann's asinine *Death in Venice* or Pasternak's melodramatic, vilely written *Doctor Zhivago* or Faulkner's corn-cobby chronicles can be considered masterpieces, or at least what journalists term "Great Books," is to me the sort of absurd delusion as when a hypnotized person makes love to a chair. My greatest masterpieces of twentieth century prose are, in this order, Joyce's *Ulysses*, Kafka's *Transformation*, Bely's *Petersburg*, and the first part of Proust's fairy tale *In Search of Lost Time.*

**RH:** I notice there are no American masterpieces on your list. What do you think of recent American writing? Who are the best of our writers since, say, forty-five?

**VN:** Seldom more than two or three really first-rate writers exist simultaneously in a given generation. I think that Salinger and Updike are, by far, the finest artists in recent years. Lots of Russian writers have strolled here [in Montreux]: Gogol, brewing here his *Dead Souls* and killing lizards with his cane, and Tolstoy, courting housemaids and meditating on social welfare and other exciting matters.

**RH:** Mr. Nabokov and his wife spent each of their twenty summers in America touring the country, collecting butterflies.

**VN:** It is really summers that are collected in my mind. They are a kind of rainbow, and they are really quite, quite wonderful.

**RH:** He came to know and love the United States and its minutest distinctions of style and landscape, and he talks of returning to America soon, for good. Since 1945, he has been a citizen.

**VN:** After all, that's the country where I have been happier than anywhere else.

**RH:** The American Museum of Natural History contains several butterflies first described by this lifelong lepidopterist. One is known as "Nabokov's Nymph," a unique specimen he named many years before giving our language the word "nymphet."

**VN:** Personally, I do not think in words. It is not a verbal process, it's just a sequence of, a blending of images. It can be something quite brief, quite short, a juxtaposition of two things in a brief composition or pattern. After that it will fall into words because I know that the words are there, no doubt as to where, behind the scene they are waiting to come out and the only difficulty is to find them. For me, what is called "inspiration" is a matter of recognition . . . These are index cards, which they call in France *fiche bristol*. I buy them at a shop here, one hundred, two hundred, every time. I use them not only to jot out notes and things which I want to remember, but actually to write the novel or story I am composing. Then I rearrange them in a given order because it doesn't matter, really, where I start. The thing is more or less in my mind. I just have to fill in the gaps. But it's a very convenient arrangement, a fashion, or method, that I acquired rather gradually. In the old days in Europe I remember writing in copy books.

**RH:** After you finish writing on the cards, do you type them out?
**VN:** I don't type, so when I finish with a card, and that means writing in pencil, arranging the card, rewriting it once or twice, then copying it out on another card or turning the card around and copying on the other side, and losing the card—I threw three cards away the other day like that. After that, my very kind and patient wife sits down at her typewriter and I dictate the matter of the cards to her, making some changes, and very often discussing this or that, "you can't say that; you can't say that; let's see, perhaps I can change it . . ." I start in the morning at eight, half past eight, and I start writing here [in his office] and correcting proofs. Today I've been cutting through proofs because I've got two sets at the same time. It's rather along the lines of the riddle of the sphinx, the ages of man . . . After lunch, I generally sit down after having rearranged my desk a little . . . it's often disorder here. After that, when I feel the heaviness of the evening weighing upon me, I go on the bed. That's where I end up. It's very funny though, sometimes after dinner I suddenly feel very, very fresh and full of inspiration, and I go back to the select chair and it starts all over again in a kind of cosmic arrangement. I like to correct proofs with this Florentine pencil my sister gave me. I have here a little note. I say here in the introduction [to the novel *Despair*] that, "The book has less White Russian appeal than have my other *émigré* novels." And there's an asterisk and a little note: "This did not prevent a communist reviewer (J.P. Sartre), who devoted in 1939 a remarkably silly article to the French translation of *Despair*, from saying that both the author and the main character are the victims of the war and the emigration." That's

wonderful, seeing the author and the protagonist on the same level. I have here some, not all, some of the editions of *Lolita*. [Nabokov shows various foreign editions of *Lolita*.] I have notes here in this copybook about the things I detest. For instance, italicized passages in a novel which are meant to represent the protagonist's cloudbursts of thought, background music, canned music, piped-in music, portable music, next-room music, inflicted music, concise dictionaries, bridge manuals, journalistic clichés: "the moment of truth." The moment of truth! "Senility"—splendid word . . . that kind of thing. These are the index cards of a new novel of mine.

**RH:** Have you given it a title?

**VN:** It's a kind of provisional title. It's called *The Texture of Time*. I'm not sure I'm going to use it. There's a book called *The Nature of Time*. Rather interferes with that title. But it's really about the texture of time, of the thing itself. It's very, very difficult to write. I find the more I speak about it, the vaguer it gets. The difficulty about it is that I have to devise an essay, a scholarly-looking essay, on time, and then gradually turn it into the story I have in mind. The metaphors start to live. The metaphors gradually turn into the story because it's very difficult to speak about time without using similes or metaphors. And my purpose is to have those metaphors breed. To form a story of their own, gradually, and then again to fall apart, and it will all end in this rather dry, though serious and well-meant, essay on time. It's proved so difficult I really don't know what to do about it. I think that the creative artist is an exile in his study, his bedroom, in the circle of his lamplight. He's quite alone there. He's the lone wolf. As soon as he gets together with someone else, he shares his secret, he shares his mystery, he shares his God with somebody else.

**RH:** You mentioned your tennis. We'd like to shoot you playing.

**VN:** No, no, no, no. It's out. First of all, I haven't played for three years. Three years ago I could still play a good game, but I wouldn't like to begin all of a sudden on a cold, autumn day. Anything might happen. It would make a beautiful picture: Death on the Tennis Court. But no, I think we'll play football, that's much better now.

**RH:** You mentioned a third sport.

**VN:** Chess is my third sport.

**RH:** Your indoor sport.

**VN:** Indoor. Strictly indoor. Very much so, yes.

**RH:** But we will be able to film you playing chess.

**VN:** Yes, if you like. It's not a very active kind of film. It's very quiet. It's still, really.

**RH:** Do you see any connection between composing chess problems and composing your novels?

**VN:** Actually, I think it's much the same thing. You also have the variations, the variance of which you have to choose. You also make false moves, and you make what chess problem composers call illusionary moves, deceitful moves. Sometimes a solution, a false solution, is prompted into the problem to mislead the solver, and the whole pleasure sometimes is in finding two or three false solutions, going through them, and coming at last to sometimes the very simple, actual solution of the problem. I think this kind of thing happens in my literary composition, too. Sometimes I don't actually plan them, but they are there—those illusions, those delusions, those little labyrinths which seem to be the right trail, the right path to my object, but actually lead the good reader astray.

**RH:** What is your greatest pleasure in writing?

**VN:** There is the first satisfaction of arranging it on a bit of paper after many false tries, false moves. Finally, you have the sentence that you recognize as the one you are looking for, the one you had lost somewhere, sometime, and it seems perfect to you. It doesn't mean that perhaps five years hence it won't look to you horrible. The next pleasure, in my case, is of reading it to [my] wife. She and I are my best audience. I should say my main audience. After that, when the thing is published, I do imagine a number of people whom I like, whom I admire, with whom I feel close kinship, it is nice to think that those people are reading that, perhaps at this very instant. But that's about all. I don't care about the general public. I am sometimes very much touched by the fan letters I get, especially by those that I get from remote parts of the States—from Kansas, from Texas; from South America, too. People writing to me to tell me how much they enjoyed the book, and picking up, deliberately or not, little things which show me that they not only understood the book, but that they liked it from the same point of view as I liked it when I was composing it. I think that's a great joy. That's another kind of joy that's much more human than this first thrill of diabolical pleasure in discovering that you have somehow cheated creation by creating something yourself. I think that takes care of your question.

# Nabokov

## Penelope Gilliatt / 1966

From *Vogue*, December, 1966. © The Estate of Penelope Gilliatt. Reprinted by permission.

"Is the Queen pregnant?" said Vladimir Nabokov.

"I don't believe so," I said.

"When I saw her on television at the World Cup watching football she kept making this gesture." He did a mime of smoothing a dress.

"She always does that."

"Oh, I see. A queenly movement. Permanently with child. With heir." He chuckled and looked interested.

We met in a distant part of Switzerland. I had said to him on the hotel telephone, sounding to myself ludicrously like a character in *Sherlock Holmes* but assuming that he wouldn't know it, that he could identify me downstairs in the lobby because I had red hair.

"I shall be carrying a copy of *Speak, Memory*," he had said back. (*Speak, Memory* is his autobiography.)

His ear for the idiom was instant and exact. It turned out later that his father had known Sherlock Holmes's creator, Sir Arthur Conan Doyle. ("Though Conan Doyle was much more proud of his intolerably boring books on South Africa.") Nabokov has a writer's passion for the physical details and likes Holmes's habit of passing half-a-crown through a chink in the cab to the cabdriver. He also has an intentness on the nuances of speech—Holmes's, mine, anyone's who uses English—that is made much more urgent by his exile from his own language.

Twenty-nine years ago he abandoned his "untrammelled, rich, and infinitely docile Russian tongue," which he had already used to write novels unpublishable in the Soviet Union and so not published at all, for an English that he learned first from governesses. Perhaps his command of it now is partly due to the obstacle, as a man will often think more swiftly who speaks with an impediment. Nabokov now writes a dulcet and raffish English that has found more of the secret springs of our language than most writers born to it can ever get under their fingers. For instance, he knows precisely the mechanism of an Anglo-Saxon use of bathos and rudeness, which will plant an anti-climactic word or a vernacular insult in a suave context where it goes off with a peculiar mixture of self-mockery and shabby bombast. For all that, his distress about losing Russian is obviously gnawing and will never be appeased. In the preface to *Lolita* he writes briefly about it as if he were an illusionist robbed of his luggage, performing on a stage where his plundered trickery has to be practiced without any of the apparatus of association.

It occurs to me that perhaps this is exactly what makes him write better about love than any other novelist in modern English. The afflictions of exile carry a taste of theft that is the pang of intimacy itself. The tricked focus in the experience of loving, the one that hideously connects rapture with mortality and causes lovers to hoard the present as though it were already gone, bestows a psychic foretaste of loss that is close to the one that gave the privileged Russian children of Nabokov's age a genius for recollection. They lived their Russian youth with the intensity of the grown-up in love, mysteriously already knowing too much about losing it. The ache that clings to good fortune or great accord is one of time's ugly gags, like the grasping housewife already secreted in the rapturous frame of little Lolita.

Humbert Humbert is in love with a booby trap. His whole situation hoaxes him. *Lolita* is an account of the passionate involvement of a man constantly ambushed by *dépaysement* and consigned to the plastic exile of motels. *De paysé*: de-countried: We need a word for it now in English far more than we need "deflowered." It isn't at all fully expressed by "alienation," or "rootlessness," for like the comic agony of love in *Lolita*, it is a concept of loss that includes the knowledge of what it can be to possess. Before I met Nabokov I had wondered sometimes how it was possible for a writer to live permanently in hotels, as he has done since 1960, mostly in Switzerland; but it was a stupid speculation about a great novelist of *dépaysement* who carries his country in his skull. His landscape isn't Russia, but Russian literature.

His permanent address now is a hotel in Montreux that he described as "a lovely Edwardian heap." We met in the Engadine, where he and his wife had come for the butterflies, in another Edwardian heap with spa baths in the basement. He is a tall, loping man whose gait and way of peering reminded me faintly of Jacques Tati's. "I am six foot," he said. "I have very thin bones. The rest is flesh." He picked at his arm as if it were a jacket.

In his autobiography he describes himself as having the Korff nose, passed on from his paternal grandmother's side: "A handsome Germanic organ with a boldly boned bridge and a slightly tilted, distinctly grooved, fleshy end." He wears spectacles, but switches to pince-nez after six to alter the ache in his nose. His accent is neither Russian nor American: I think it originates in the upper-class English undergraduate speech of immediately after the First World War, when he went to Cambridge. ("Cambridge, Cambridge, not Cambridge, Massachusetts," he said.) His French is delicate and pure. He hears it as dated: "The slang goes back to Maupassant." His Russian is the authentic sound of pre-Revolutionary St. Petersburg. He did a mischievously expressive example of the boneless accent of standard Pravda speech now. I don't suppose that either he or his wife can detect that their birth in itself is a distinct and commanding fact about them both; but then the upper-class people of Europe never do. It is only the rest who can see the difference, and the well-born truly believe themselves to be indistinguishable.

The Nabokovs think of going back to America to live, perhaps in California. They are looking for—what? A climate; and far more than that, a language. "We were in Italy, but we don't want to live there. I don't speak Italian. And the *scioperi* (strikes) . . . Véra found a chateau in France, but it would have cost a lot of money to convert it. It had drawbridges. It had its drawbridges and drawbacks." He has a habit of going back over what he has said and correcting it that is rather like the way he immediately uses an eraser on his notes. "I don't much care for de Gaulle. I fear things will happen there when he dies. I would go to Spain but I hate bullfights. Switzerland: lakes, charming people, stability. All my publishers pass through from one festival to another."

He had been up since six, as usual, and had a bath in the curative basement. "I discovered the secret of levitation," he said. "One puts the feet flat-braced against the end of the bath and rises, covered with bubbles like a fur. I felt like a bear. A memory of a former state."

We had a drink rather early in the morning. The whiskies looked small and he asked for soda. "Make the glass grow," he said, and then muttered: "The grass glow."

His books are written on index cards so that it is possible to start in the middle and insert scenes as he wants. He writes in 3B pencils that he says he sharpens compulsively. They have India rubbers on the ends which he uses to exorcise mistakes instead of simply crossing them out. My own error in writing with a pen struck him as technically cardinal. His pocket notebooks are made of paper squared like an arithmetic book. The formal pattern that might distract most people obviously stimulates him. I could understand this: it must be a little like seeing figments in the black and white tiles in public lavatories.

"Some of my best poems and chess problems have been composed in bathrooms looking at the floor," he said.

At some stage we started to play anagrams. I gave him "cart horse" (the solution is "orchestra"). He took the problem away on what was meant to be a nap, and came bounding into the bar two hours later with an expression that was a very Russian mixture of buoyancy and sheepishness. The tartanned paper of his little notepad was covered with methodically wrong steps. "Her actors," he said, in try-on triumph, eying me, and knowing perfectly well that the answer had to be one word. Then he started to laugh at his picture of the creature whose property the actors would be. Bossy women strike him as irresistibly comic: they trudge through his books, absurd, cruel, creatures of inane placidity who see everything in the world as a mirror of their womanliness and who will speak sharply about something like Bolshevism as though it were an obvious minor nuisance, like mosquitoes or the common cold. I believe his woman producer also amused him because he finds the theatre inherently funny when it is earnest: something to do with its thickness, I think, compared with the fine mesh of the novels he likes.

When he taught in America he lectured on *Anna Karenina*, Tolstoy's *The Death of Ivan Ilyitch*, *Ulysses*, Kafka's *The Metamorphosis*, and Jane Austen's *Mansfield Park*, which was suggested by Edmund Wilson. The precise butterfly-pinner discovered that Tolstoy made the two families in *Anna Karenina* age on a different timescale, so that more years have passed for one than for another. He also says that Joyce left out any reference to Bloom's coming back from the cemetery. "I know Dublin exactly. I could draw a map of it. I know the Liffey like the Moskva. I have never been to Dublin but I know it as well as Moscow. Also, I have never been to Moscow."

He and his wife both lived in St. Petersburg, but they met first in Berlin in exile. They could have met many times when they were children; at dancing class, perhaps; it bothers them and they go over it.

"Véra's coming down in a moment," he said. "She's lost something. A jacket, I think. When she loses things, it is always something very big." He started to shake again. His sense of humor is very Russian, and the sight of its taking him over is hugely pleasurable. There is a lot of the buffoon in it.

He is one of the few people I have seen who literally does sometimes nearly fall off his chair with laughing.

"Véra has been doing 'cart horse' as well," he said. "Eventually she suggested 'horse-cart.' She hadn't much hope."

In the lounge there was an Edwardian mural of naked lovers, except that they were not naked and seemed to have nothing much to do with loving. The woman was vulgarly draped and the man wore, as well as a tulle scarf across his groin, a vapourish example of early Maidenform around his chest. After days of looking at the picture Nabokov still found it mildly interesting. It happened to be a rather obvious demonstration of the intimacy in art between silliness and prudery. The high-flying philistinism of protected art tastes strikes him often as richly foolish. Long ago the Empress of Russia gave him pleasure by being an eager admirer of Ella Wheeler Wilcox. *Invitation to a Beheading*, one of his early Russian-language novels, has a sulphurous passage about an imaginary book considered to be "the acme of modern thought" in which world history is seen from the point of view of an elderly and apparently sagacious oak tree. Nabokov detests literature that has sweeping social pretentions. He also loathes prurience. The bad art of the past that has lost its power to bamboozle will often reveal that a large share of its badness consists in failing to go too far, which is the only course that is ever far enough in aesthetics. The streak of blue nerve in Nabokov's work is part of its quality. It has an effect that is close to the exhilaration of flair and courage in real conduct.

In the actual world, the vice for which Nabokov seems to have most loathing is brutality. He finds it in tank-shaped political bullies, "swine-toned radio music," the enjoyment of trained animals, the truisms of Freudianism, the abhorrence of Germany between the wars. (There is a German in one of his books who believes that "electrocution" is the root of "cute.") In the world of art his equivalent loathing is for mediocrity, which is perhaps only the aesthetic form of the same brutality. There are celebrated writers in whom he detects a naïveté that he obviously finds almost thuggish. He detests Zola, Stendhal, Balzac, Thomas Mann.

Nabokov spoke eagerly about the descriptions of the fish in Hemingway's *The Old Man and the Sea* and about the jungle passages and close physical descriptions in Graham Greene's *A Burnt-Out Case*. "The avant-garde French novels that I've read don't stir my artistic appetite. Only here and there. Even Shaw can do that." I asked him about Genet: "An interesting fairyland with good measurements." Ostrovsky, the Russian playwright, he described as having "a streak of poetry that he unfortunately put down because he was so intent on writing about the merchant class." Tin-eared translators torment him. "*Vive le pédant*," he writes defiantly in one of his prefaces, "and down with the simpletons who think that all is well if the spirit is rendered (while the words go away by themselves on a naïve and vulgar spree—in the suburbs of Moscow for instance—and Shakespeare is again reduced to play the king's ghost)."

The English translations of his Russian novels have been done by Nabokov himself, generally with his son, Dmitri, who is a racing driver and a singer. Nabokov has just finished doing a Russian translation of *Lolita*, typeset in New York. "To be smuggled in, dropped by parachute, floating down on the blurb." His attachment to words is urgent and moving. A copy of the unabridged *Webster's Dictionary* is carried about in the back of Nabokov's Lancia; in his hotel room on holiday it was opened among the M's, halfway through, which is the way he leaves it so as to save the spine. In his autobiography he speaks of turning even now to the last page of any new grammar to find "that promised land where, at last, words are meant to mean what they mean."

"In Massachusetts once I was ill with food poisoning," he said. "I was being wheeled along a corridor. They left the trolley by a bookcase and I drew out a big medical dictionary and in the ward I drew the curtains around myself and read. It wasn't allowed because it looked as if I were dying. They took the book away. In hospitals there is still something of the eighteenth century madhouse."

"Pasternak?" I asked. At once he talked very fast. "*Doctor Zhivago* is false, melodramatic, badly written. It is false to history and false to art. The people are dummies. That awful girl is absurd. It reminds me very much of novels written by Russians of, I am ashamed to say, the gentler sex. Pasternak is not a bad poet. But in *Zhivago* he is vulgar. Simple. If you take his beautiful metaphors, there is nothing behind them. Even in his poems: What is that line, Véra? 'To be a woman is a big step.' It is ridiculous." He laughed and looked stricken.

"This kind of thing recurs. Very typical of poems written in the Soviet era. A person of Zhivago's class and his set, he wouldn't stand in the snow and read about the Bolshevist regime and feel a tremendous glow. There was the *liberal* revolution at that time. Kerensky. If Kerensky had had more luck—but he was a liberal, you see, and he couldn't just clap the Bolsheviks into jail. It was not done. He was a very average man, I should say. The kind of person you might find in the Cabinet of any democratic country. He spoke very well, with his hand in his bosom like Napoleon because it had almost been broken by handshakes.

"Yet people like Edmund Wilson and Isaiah Berlin, they have to love *Zhivago* to prove that good writing can come out of Soviet Russia. They ignore that it is really a *bad book*. There are some absolutely ridiculous scenes. Scenes of eavesdropping, for instance. You know about eavesdropping. If it is not brought in as parody it is almost philistine. It is the mark of the amateur in literature. And that marvelous scene where he had to get rid of the little girl to let the characters make love, and he sends her out skating. In *Siberia*. To keep warm they gave her her mother's *scarf*. And then she sleeps deeply in a hut while there is all this going on. Obviously, Pasternak just didn't know what to do with her. He's like Galsworthy. Galsworthy, in one of his novels, gave a character a cane and a dog and simply didn't know how to get rid of them.

"And the metaphors. Unattached comparisons. Suppose I were to say 'as passionately adored and insulted as a barometer in a mountain hotel,'" he said, looking out at the rain. "It would be a beautiful metaphor. But who is it about? The image is top-heavy. There is nothing to attach it to. And there is a pseudo-religious strain in the book which almost shocks me. *Zhivago* is so feminine that I sometimes wonder if it might have been partly written by Pasternak's mistress.

"As a translator of Shakespeare he is very poor. He is considered great only by people who don't know Russian. An example." His wife helped him to remember a line of a Pasternak translation. "What he has turned it into in Russian is this: 'All covered with grease and keeps wiping the pig-iron.' You see. It is ridiculous. What would be the original?"

"Greasy Joan doth keel the pot?"

"Yes. 'Keeps wiping the pig-iron!'" He expostulated and looked genuinely angry. "Pasternak himself has been very much *helped* by translation. Sometimes when you translate a cliché—you know, a cloud has a silver lining—it can sound like Milton because it is in another language."

"Isn't that what happened to Pushkin?" said Véra.

"He had translated the French writers of his day. The small coin of drawing-room poets and the slightly larger coin of Racine. In Russian it became breathtaking." I remarked that someone had once said to me that the first man who compared a woman to a flower was a genius and the second, a fool. "And the third, a knave," said Nabokov.

We went for a drive in the new Lancia through the mountains. Mrs. Nabokov drove, rather fast, mostly in third gear on a tricky road, in the face of jibes from her husband about the sheer drops that she had chosen on other days as suitable places to turn.

"Sometimes my son wishes I wouldn't joke so much," he said with melancholy.

I sat on the backseat, which was still insulated in cellophane, and took off my shoes to keep the cover intact. A hat for butterfly-hunting and walks was on the back shelf.

"You could cover your toes with my hat," said Mr. Nabokov.

He looked for good meadows for butterfly-hunting and memorized promising paths off the road. His feeling about nature is communicable even to people who don't share it. He is the only man I have ever heard who responds to mention of Los Angeles not with abuse of the city but with glory in the vegetation. He wrote once that when he hunted butterflies it was his highest experience of timelessness, a way "to picket nature" and "to rebel against the void fore and aft." I think it is also an expression of the great writer's passion to define.

We had lemon tea and cream cakes in another hotel looking out across the mountains. He was charming to a waitress who had seemed not to have heard the order and said peacefully after a long wait: "I can tell by the nape of her neck that the cakes are coming." He has a comic affection for girls' bodies that is rather like his tenderness for gaffes, as though the naked toes or napes of girls absorbed by other things fall unknowingly into a category of farcical and touching blunders.

I asked him whether Lolita would have turned into a boy if his own real child had been a girl.

"Oh, yes," he said at once. "If I had had a daughter, Humbert Humbert would have been a pederast."

I thought perhaps that he might cherish a little hatred for *Lolita* now, as writers often do for books that have had more attention than anything else they have written, but his feelings seem not to have swerved. The book remains his favorite, though he says that *Pale Fire* was more difficult to write.

"I had written a short story with the same idea as *Lolita*. The man's name there is Arthur. They travel through France. I never published it. The little girl wasn't alive. She hardly spoke. Little by little I managed to give her some semblance of reality. I was on my way to the incinerator one day with half the manuscript to burn it, and Véra said wait a minute. And I came back meekly."

"I don't remember that. Did I?" said Mrs. Nabokov.

"What was most difficult was putting myself . . . I am a normal man, you see. I traveled in school buses to listen to the talk of schoolgirls. I went to school on the pretext of placing our daughter. We have no daughter. For Lolita, I took one arm of a little girl who used to come to see Dmitri, one kneecap of another."

He says in the preface that the book originated in a story in *Paris-Soir* of an ape that had been taught to draw: Its first drawing was of the bars of its cage. The brawl around *Lolita* and the fierce humor that stylizes all of his work often seems to obscure the extreme tenderness that impels it. His sensitivity to suffering and the exploited makes the attention paid to the plot facts of *Lolita* seem even more brutishly literal-minded than usual. When he was in Hollywood to do the script, the producers asked him to make Lolita and Humbert Humbert get married: Apparently, this would have pulled some knot of embarrassment for them. The idea of the book being classified as obscene—as it still is in Burma, for instance—is much more gross than anything in most pornography, for it is a book that extends exceptional gentleness to the yearning and the out of step. Elsewhere, in his *Laughter in the Dark*, a murderer thinks "impossible to kill while she was taking off her shoe"; it is a modern equivalent of the moment in *Hamlet* when a man cannot be murdered at prayer. In Nabokov's work sexuality stands for tenderness, and tenderness is the remaining sanctity.

In the car again, I asked him about something he had once written about the author of *Alice in Wonderland*.

"I always call him Lewis Carroll Carroll," he said, "because he was the first Humbert Humbert. Have you seen those photographs of him with little girls? He would make arrangements with aunts and mothers to take the children out. He was never caught, except by one girl who wrote about him when she was much older."

He started to answer something I was saying, and turned it into an imitation of Edmund Wilson saying, "Yes, yes." Nabokov and Edmund Wilson are old friends, but they have recently conducted a waspish public fight about Mr. Wilson's knowledge of Russian, involving claims that seem fairly foolish in the face of a Russian-speaker. Nabokov's private feelings seem affectionately caustic. The imitated "Yes" involved a head movement like a man trying to get down a pill when he is gagging on it. "Apparently, consent with him is so difficult he must make a convulsive effort," said Nabokov warmly enough, and came back to *Lolita*.

"It was a great pleasure to write, but it was also very painful. I had to read so many case histories. Most of it was written in a car to have complete quiet." He says in *Speak, Memory* that "in a first-rate work of fiction the real clash is not between the characters but between the author and world." This is the force of *Lolita*. The most unsparing love novel of our literature of glib and easy sex is about an obsession that is locally criminal, written by an alien attacking the numbness of a culture from the inside of the machine that best represents its numbness.

# The Artist in Pursuit of Butterflies

## Herbert Gold / 1967

From *The Saturday Evening Post*, February 11, 1967. © Herbert Gold, novelist and essayist. Reprinted by permission.

On the shore of Lake Geneva at Montreux, in an immense aging luxury hotel out of another time—all cuckoo-clock carved wood and space and silent, gliding service—lives Vladimir Nabokov, a sixty-eight-year old man with a booming laugh, who loves his wife, his son, and the interior landscape of his own mind. He enjoys good wines, good food, good company, but goes to bed early, since he rises at six A.M. He has a passion for butterflies and spends long periods chasing uphill and down dale with net and wife. In fact, he is a distinguished lepidopterist, but he is famous for another vocation.

More than a decade ago this reclusive White Russian *émigré*, who was then teaching literature at Cornell University, listened carefully to the speech of children on school buses, explored the spaces of America during vacation butterfly-collecting trips, marveled over the social complexities of the motel and composed an odyssey of the doomed love of the middle-aged Humbert Humbert for the adolescent Lolita Haze. Rejected by several American publishers, he finally sent the manuscript off to Paris, where it was published in 1955 by the Olympia Press. Admirers began importing the book, but American editors remained skittish. "I love it," said one of them. "It's a great book. Nabokov is a great writer. But I can't print it—you think I'm crazy?" Nevertheless, *Lolita* was finally published in the United States in 1958, and despite a few hostile reviews, the book earned an immense critical and popular success. And for good reasons. *Lolita* is a definitive guide to American roadside culture, and also a picture of the evolving teenager, and a metaphor for the eternal quest for innocence, and a case history of abnormal psychology, and an exercise of comic style and picaresque form and many other things besides—in short, a totally original work with the rough, undefined edges and mysteries of a masterpiece.

Through the curious fate of his darling "nymphet," who became both a household word and a movie, her author sustained an odd transmogrification. At last he is given his due as an authentic living master of the novel form, a great man of letters and also namer of the meat patties served at a San Francisco drive-in—"Lolitaburgers." He has made his mark at many levels.

*Lolita* aside, Vladimir Nabokov is a unique and remarkable party. He is presently supervising the translation of his early novels from Russian into English. He is planning the publication of his collected papers in lepidopterology. His particular specialty is the classification of butterflies; he has written twenty important articles; he still makes field trips; he has discovered and named several new species. As a man of many cultures, he has written eloquently about the problems of translation, and taken upon himself such duties as translation of the great Russian poet Pushkin into English and *Alice in Wonderland* into Russian. He moves from the creation of an immense zoo of jealous, nostalgic, obsessed, maddened wanderers and sticks-in-the-mud—in several collections of stories and poems, in some thirteen novels, in plays, in biographies, in his autobiography and his revision of his autobiography—toward the gradual revelation of an absolutely unique, perhaps both frightening and touching personality.

Does Vladimir Nabokov live, like others, in a world he never made? No, having suffered greater troubles than most, he has no pity for himself. He lives in a world he is continually remaking. "I travel through life in a space helmet," he says, roaring with laughter.

I was thinking to myself: Here I am in Europe—now what? I had arrived by ship, plane, train, and taxi on a hot day of Indian Summer. I checked in at that grand relic, the Montreux Palace, where Mrs. Nabokov had made a reservation for me, and decided to cool off in the pool before making contact with my friends. I was thinking, in the sight of these mountains and this lake where so many aristocratic Russians had taken the waters and the airs, of the irony of the cosmopolitan Nabokov finally bringing his intelligence, his humor, his nostalgia, his defiance, his art and his self to this traditional spa. While leaving thirty-five boxes of goods with Dean's Storage in Ithaca, New York. While leaving his childhood in Russia, his adolescence and early youth in Berlin and Paris, his young manhood in Cambridge (England and Massachusetts) and his fruitful middle years in Ithaca. And yet he knows who he is. The poet is a man with a child's needs and judgments. For Nabokov to remain a live poet, squalling and brawling, there had to be irony in his system. And steel. And Véra Nabokov watching over him.

I slumped into a beach chair for a bit of friendly, cross-culture study of the French, German, and Swiss poolside mini-flirts, and suddenly there were Véra and Vladimir Nabokov, bared to the sun, in lively conversation with some friends. Nabokov caught sight of me, seemed puzzled for a moment, and then burst into that deep, rich, Russian laughter. He accused me of dropping by parachute from the heavens. I was a secret agent. He had expected to meet a later train from Paris. There was jovial banter about the eight years passed since last we had met. How well I looked! How fit! How marvelously fit! But then the thoughtful Nabokov swerved: "You were a bit fattish, I think, last time."

One of our first occupations was for Nabokov to deny the truth of anecdotes which I had been telling about him since we had first known each other in 1958. For example, although he recalls his dislike of Pasternak's novel, he believes he never referred to it as "Doctor Van Cliburn." I did not check, for fear it might be denied, a conversation about a mutual friend. "Of course," said Nabokov, "he is a very nice fellow. Of course, do not lend him any money. Of course, he is completely untalented. Of course, he is a liar and a hypocrite. Of course, he is a pederast. Of course, isn't that good you know him, he's a *very nice fellow.*" But of course that was 1958, and I am quoting from memory, and Nabokov distrusts everyone's memory except his own. "You would like another orange squash?" he asked now.

He claims among his ancestors the first cave man who painted a mammoth, a medieval Tartar prince, a long line of German barons, an obscure Crusader, a well-known composer, the first President of the Russian Imperial Academy of Medicine, a Minister of Justice. His father was a noted liberal statesman, jurist and writer. Reading legal commentaries by his father, published over seventy years ago, he finds an eloquent denunciation of "crimes against young and tender girls by older men." Curious, he says. Lolita, he remarks dreamily. He likes to feel he is continuing a tradition.

He smiles at the thought that he is an avant-garde writer whose first work was printed more than fifty years ago. It was a pamphlet of poems and the place was St. Petersburg, and, in 1914, the poet was aged fifteen. His faraway childhood was rich in marvels. He learned English before he learned to read Russian. He also learned French. "I was a perfectly normal trilingual child," he says. He played chess, collected butterflies, loved soccer. After inheriting about two million dollars ("a lot of money in those days") and promptly losing it all in the revolution (a perfectly ordinary thing in those days), he studied at Cambridge, England, and then wrote in Russian in Berlin and Paris. The infusion of languages and cultures continued. He received about five dollars for his translation of *Alice in Wonderland*. He precariously survived by teaching boxing, tennis, languages, and by making the first Russian crossword puzzles. He wrote plays, poetry, novels. He was a part-time journalist. In his autobiography, *Speak, Memory,* he mentions a poor disappeared Russian *émigré* talent, V. Sirin, who is the writer of the period between the two wars whom he found most touching. V. Sirin was the pen name of Vladimir Nabokov.

There was the melodramatic shock—so like the events in his novels—of his father's murder. His father, a liberal, was killed at a meeting in Berlin by a fanatical Czarist who was aiming at someone else. Nabokov's father had thrown himself on one of the assassins when the other pumped bullets into him.

He fled the Nazis. He fled the communists. He fled the embittered White Russian fanatics. He married, he had a son, he wandered the face of Europe on a sickly refugee passport. He scrambled a step ahead of pauperdom. A life on continual beginnings and new starts, exiles and comebacks, except that he has never, despite several official invitations, gone back to Russia.

Arriving in the United States as Europe sank into war, he took up an academic career at Wellesley, where he taught Russian; at Harvard, where he did research in lepidopterology; and at Cornell, where he lectured on literature. He was hard on both students and colleagues and took a special delight in tormenting deans and administrators. Because he disliked department heads in particular, plus departments in general, he was made his own private department, given his courses, and assigned a Chairman of Nabokov to take care of paperwork. This was not so bad, he says with satisfaction. That's the way things ought to be.

He is now permanently an American, living in Switzerland on a merely temporary basis. He may dream of Russia, the spires and summer hazes of his childhood, but his heart is in Ithaca or Wyoming or Columbus or someplace. He admits that he is "not emotionally involved with Indian dances or pumpkin pie on a spiritual plane," but adds, "I am as American as April in Arizona."

Nabokov's main characteristic as a social person is a relaxed, detached affability. He likes jokes, particularly his own. He also can be impatient and sometimes brutal. A well-known writer tells of meeting Nabokov at a party and blurting out, "I love your book *Lolita*." Tall, twinkling, grave Nabokov gave him a cold eye and turned on his heel. Something in the tone had displeased him. He has said, "I don't fish, cook, dance, endorse books, sign declarations, eat oysters, get drunk, go to analysts, or take part in demonstrations. I'm a mild old gentleman. I'm very kind."

He telephoned mornings around nine o'clock, when his early writing was done, to make plans for our meetings that day—a swim, a walk, lunch, dinner. In the garden we talked about moths and butterflies. He is an expert on butterflies, not moths, he said. Adding an observation—"Did you know that the hawk moth can fly two or three hundred miles an hour? This was discovered by an airplane pilot who found the moths outdistancing him. He thought he was perhaps standing still or flying backwards."

He is a severe judge of other writers. A few years ago the names of Dostoyevsky, Freud, Thomas Mann, or Pasternak stimulated something like rage. They were interested in "ideas," "moral judgments," "doing good"; they were religious or they claimed to know something or they flattered the vulgar tastes of the half-educated and the theory-bound. Now it seemed that his contempt for them was adulterated with a small portion of the milk of human kindness. But this did not indicate any softening of the polemical spirit. During our six days of conversation he expressed fury at mistranslation, "creative" translation, doctors, Bolsheviks, critics of America. He looked younger and stronger than in 1958. Though he mentions neuralgia, insomnia and various other ills, he looks like a powerful middle-aged man, and his years are carried with elephantine grace.

He is planning a book of studies of Joyce, Proust and other writers.

He has a novel well under way, secreting it on his index cards and letting it grow. The central section is finished, he says.

He is still working on butterflies. He supervises translations of his work. He attends to his business.

There is a folk proverb which states: Behind every successful man there stands a surprised woman. Well, this is not true of Mrs. Nabokov. She is a calm, serious, and protective guardian of her husband's gifts; and not surprised. Clearly she has always believed utterly in his genius. She writes his letters, drives his car (he doesn't drive), criticizes his manuscripts, arranges his business matters, and signs hotel registers for them both (he does not give autographs). There is one lifelong friend to whom he occasionally writes a postcard. He is relaxed and easy, knowing that the way has been cleared for him. Occasionally she censors his conversation or interrupts an off-color story, but her steady regard expresses unshakeable approval of her husband.

Together they sometimes visit their thirty-two-year old son Dmitri, operatic bass and part-time racing driver, a tall, good-looking young man who has also translated some of his father's work from Russian into English. They keep a room for him in their set of suites at the Montreux Palace Hotel. They showed me an old passport photograph of Véra Nabokov with their child—an angelic little boy and a beautiful young woman with fine eyes and a strong, straight nose, traveling on French papers through the perils of Hitlerian Europe. Véra Nabokov does not like off-color jokes or jokes about Jews. She is Jewish, and one of the few social ills which seems to trouble this Russian aristocrat is racial or religious prejudice.

We stroll in the garden. Nabokov still recalls, with a lopsided grin, how he arrived at the scene of his father's murder just a few minutes after it happened. Smoke, confusion, horror. His father lay dead. An acquaintance with a flesh wound in the arm stopped him and wailed, "I was hurt too." This event, forty-five years gone now, made him rumble and hesitate as we paced on the shores of Lake Geneva. He commented on the man who showed his minor wound to a boy seeing his dead father: "He was a good man, not insensitive, just excited."

And the murderer? He was later employed by the Nazis, put in charge of Russian *émigré* affairs.

One of Nabokov's brothers was killed by the Germans in a concentration camp. He died of "inanition." The word fascinated him—"inanition." He has written about this brother in the recent revision of *Speak, Memory*.

Nabokov's books are melodramatic, filled with fantasies of violence and torture. He has lived with both the fantasies and the realities. Now, as they have been assimilated to his ironic, paradoxical mind, he is at peace with the demons. He almost enjoys their company. He has made his treaty with trouble, his own and history's.

Nabokov suffered all the usual childhood diseases, including the desire to write. He wanted to organize the strangeness of the world by the standards of words and classifications, poetry and arrangements of butterflies. He wanted to live by these measures and stylizations. He still makes up his own truths and is bewildered by the reluctance of others to see as clearly as he does. Sometimes Nabokov seems to have the quality he ascribes to Gogol: that of thoroughly planning his works *after* he has written and published them. But this after-the-fact reasoning is just as stubborn as the more usual kind of development. And Nabokov does not bother to explain his work; he *knows*, and demands that the reader know.

Here is how he describes the growth of a story by Gogol: "Mumble, mumble, mumble, lyrical wave, mumble, lyrical wave, mumble, lyrical wave, mumble, fantastic climax, mumble, mumble, and back into the chaos from which they all derived." This is also the fantastic way Nabokov's stories accumulate onto his magically shuffled index cards. And as he says of Gogol, he aims toward an appeal "to that secret depth of the human soul where the shadows of other worlds pass like the shadows of nameless and soundless ships."

When *The Gift*, one of Nabokov's early Russian novels, appeared in English, I noticed that one "Michael Scammell" was named as the translator. Never having heard of Michael Scammell, and being familiar with Nabokov's earnest playfulness, I decided that this was another of the master's hoaxes. Examining the name "Scammell," I derived a near anagram, Le Masc, which becomes Le Masque, which becomes, clearly, the Mask, for Nabokov. And so I wrote to accuse him of this ghostly behavior. My suspicions were confirmed by the sweet and evasive reply from Véra Nabokov: "My husband wishes to thank you for your recent very interesting communication . . ."

Epilogue to this story: It turns out that there really is a translator named Michael Scammell, though the Nabokov's did not find it necessary to disappoint me in my little discovery. This is an example of life turning into a Nabokov satire, Russian boxes within boxes, a phantom beckoning the pedantic friend into his hall of errors.

Each day we strolled in the dappled sunlight, avoiding the Swiss wet damp. He leaned forward with a scout's intensity to name and admire moths and butterflies. I noticed after a few days with him that I too saw butterflies everywhere. He destroyed thick headed critics and fake scholars. He asked who else besides him supports the President's policy in Vietnam. I told him that quite a few people do, according to the polls. With smiling generosity he tipped the waiters who brought us beer, orange squash, ice cream.

He reported that one night he dreamed a scene which he then wrote down and promptly afterward saw on Swiss television. He is sure that this is not clairvoyance or telepathy or any variety of seeing into the future; rather, it is remembering the future. Time does not move forward, tock tock tock, like the hand of a clock, he said.

We went into the *Chambre de Débarras*, the Room of Disorder, to see some of his stored books and materials—a Turkish translation of *Lolita*, tennis rackets, mountain climbing equipment, photographs, and a little American flag tilted at a crazy angle above the washbasin. "You recognize that?" he asked. "I love America," he said, "a great country." He is opposed to racial discrimination, but otherwise, as he says, "I approve of everything." He describes the American government as one of his "hobbies."

Now we spoke again about his conception of time, which is somewhat different from anyone else's. How to hold the instant without an object, without peopling it? He puzzles. The problems of Time contain the other great problems, Soul, Mortality, Art, a sense of life on earth. He has entitled a section of the novel he is writing "The Texture of Time."

Pause. He interrupts this train of thought to comment with a pleasant, mildly suffering sigh that a German television crew is coming to *do* him. Shake of heavy, much-imposed-upon head. Another sigh. He wonders why I don't ask more questions. "Ask some questions," he orders.

Taking my assigned role of Nabokov character (journalist, impertinent young fellow, poking around), I asked him about the movie of *Lolita*. Answer: He is a friend of James Mason's but never became a friend of Sue Lyon's. I decided to slip into the role of another Nabokov character (scholar, impertinent middle-aged fellow, poking around). We spoke of clairvoyance once more. Prophecy is the wit of the fool. He makes the judgment with a certain fierceness. No doubt it is connected with his notion of simultaneity, of Nabokovian time and of the irrelevance of most human projects. Intelligence is much too important to bother with such trivial matters as predicting the future.

The controversy buzzing around Nabokov's ambiguously affable head has not been calmed, despite his fame. The novelist and critic Mary McCarthy called *Pale Fire*, his last novel written in English, one of the great works of the twentieth century. But this strange tale of a New England scholar who may also be an exiled king, all cast in the form of a learned commentary on a long poem, represented yet another set of Russian boxes within boxes: a satire of a pastoral epic? A *real* pastoral epic? A parody of the pedant's habits? A parable about exile and isolation? The book was greeted by many of Nabokov's admirers with the sort of disarray which greeted James Joyce's *Finnegans Wake*. After we had grown accustomed to the elegant comic epic of *Lolita*, and the benign and touching bumbler *Pnin*, and the ironies and puns and the mad, pathetic, obsessed, nostalgic, and yet coherent monsters of so many other stories, what *was* this trickster genius doing in *Pale Fire*, what was this "crossword puzzle," as one flustered critic called it? Was he just putting everyone on, as some admirers insisted, or had he written, as others claimed, the ultimate novel?

And then there is his translation and commentary on the masterpiece of Russian poetry, Pushkin's *Eugene Onegin*. How is it possible that his old friend, Edmund Wilson, the dean of American criticism, can denounce him as a quirky and even incompetent translator? Surely their continuing bitter public controversy reads like a Nabokov novel—in fact, a little like *Pale Fire*. Who is who in this drama? After all, it is Nabokov who is a native Russian and Wilson who is mainly self-taught in the language. Can it be that Nabokov, who used to help Wilson with his grammar, has somehow lost his grip on his native language, and Wilson, the scholar from New England, can lecture him about the tenses of Russian verbs? . . . But again, we are in the worlds of Kinbote and John Shade, the shadowy fantasts of *Pale Fire*, dreaming of "Zembla, a distant northern land," where truth is really truth and reality can be defined.

May I now attempt a partial summary of the character and gifts of this triumphantly lonely spirit? (*Forgive me, friend far away in Montreux, if I sound like still another impertinent ghost from one of your novels.*) No, comes the answer, as sure as my real name is V. Sirin. Or rather, his answer would be: Irrelevant, foolish, like a German TV crew, like a moralist or a censor, like a true believer or a false believer.

*Nevertheless . . .*

Humor, an organized life and steady service by his brain helped Nabokov to keep his mysteries, his reserve, his private turf. If he doesn't understand the meaning of human life—most men don't—he at least knows what sort of map he has to the unknown country, and keeps in good repair his equipment for exploration and his sense of the treasure to be sought. "I travel through life in a space helmet." He does not get too close to earth; he does not judge or interpret a world. Rather, he finds and makes his own world, and makes himself the compassionate, ironic, horrified master in this made-up universe. He is absolutely self-confident. After navigating odder and harder paths than those which normally lie before a man, he has now gotten straight with himself. He has no need to fear putting on the wrong mask. He always has the right mask for himself and for others. Embarrassment exists only in the past, though the past endures.

"I would like to say something about time. The past is gone, the future is not here yet, and the present is slipping away at every instant—what is Time?" The gravity in his face is rare; he is allowing a part of the iceberg of his real thought to come to the surface. Once more he begins to speak of a dream in which he remembered something that had not yet occurred; he does not call it prediction, but memory of the future. This is not a joke to him. He notes that the blank abyss on one side of our lives—death—seems to frighten us more than the equally blank emptiness on the other side, when the world was there without us and the baby carriage sat empty in the photograph of the pregnant mother.

Capable of immediate tenderness and warmth, Nabokov is deeply suspicious of the human possibility of goodness. Discussion of it quickly
becomes, he intimates, "*poshlosty.*" ("Postlust" is a Russian word which he
defines as "vile vulgarity.") He has no illusions. He has built his spaceship
and he travels through life protected by it, secure in the knowledge that
when he walks out of it into space he can walk back, and if he cannot, well,
that was an amusing risk he was taking. Only an "S," as he says, makes the
difference between "cosmic" and "comic."

Near the hour of goodbyes we spoke about the future of this man who
has lived in hotels or taken rented lodgings ever since the Russian revolution. He insists on his American character despite his grand exile, like a
Russian aristocrat's, in Switzerland. He would like to live in Boston, New
York or California. But his wife doesn't like the Boston weather, and the
summers are very hot in New York, and California is very far away, though
there are some good butterflies nearby. And their son is studying music
again in Milan. And so, while waiting to find a permanent home, this odd
genius camps out in a hotel in Montreux, with boxes stored in Ithaca, with
relics spread all over the world, writing on his index cards, planning out
his terrible plans, secreting his criticisms, polemics, poems, stories, novels,
autobiography. To our great good fortune he both explains and conceals
himself with great skill.

So let us not examine him or his life too closely. Perhaps we should even
avoid the flood of dissertations which will soon engulf his privacy. Just ride
with the rhythm of his spirit. Let it glow.

As a farewell gift, Véra Nabokov gave me the bulletin of the Anti-Vivisec-
tion League. Certain passages were underlined. I am sure there was a reason
for this, but I lost it on the plane from Geneva, Switzerland, to Cleveland,
Ohio.

# An Interview with Vladimir Nabokov

## Alfred Appel Jr. / 1967

From *Wisconsin Studies in Contemporary Literature*, 8.2 (1967): 127–153 © 1967 by the Board of Regents of the University of Wisconsin System. Reproduced by permission of the University of Wisconsin Press.

**Alfred Appel Jr.:** For years bibliographers and literary journalists didn't know whether to group you under "Russian" or "American." Now that you're living in Switzerland there seems to be complete agreement that you're American. Do you find this kind of distinction at all important regarding your identity as a writer?

**Vladimir Nabokov:** I have always maintained, even as a schoolboy in Russia, that the nationality of a worthwhile writer is of secondary importance. The more distinctive an insect's aspect, the less apt is the taxonomist to glance first of all at the locality label under the pinned specimen in order to decide which of several vaguely described races it should be assigned to. The writer's art is his real passport. His identity should be immediately recognized by a special pattern or unique coloration. His habitat may confirm the correctness of the determination but should not lead to it. Locality labels are known to have been faked by unscrupulous insect dealers. Apart from these considerations, I think of myself today as an American writer who has once been a Russian one.

**AA:** The Russian writers you have translated and written about all precede the so-called "age of realism," which is more celebrated by English and American readers than is the earlier period. Would you say something about your temperamental or artistic affinities with the great writers of the 1830–40 era of masterpieces? Do you see your own work falling under such general rubrics as a tradition of Russian humor?

**VN:** The question of the affinities I may think I have or not have with nineteenth century Russian writers is a classificational, not a confessional matter. There is hardly a single Russian major writer of the past whom pigeonholers have not mentioned in connection with me. Pushkin's blood runs through the veins of modern Russian literature as inevitably as Shakespeare's through those of English literature.

**AA:** Many of the major Russian writers, such as Pushkin, Lermontov, and Bely, have distinguished themselves in both poetry and prose, an uncommon accomplishment in English and American literature. Does this signal fact have anything to do with the special nature of Russian literary culture, or are there technical or linguistic resources which make this kind of versatility more possible in Russian? And as a writer of both prose and poetry, what distinctions do you make between them?

**VN:** On the other hand, neither Gogol nor Tolstoy nor Chekhov were distinguished versificators. Moreover, the dividing line between prose and poetry in some of the greatest English or American novels is not easy to draw. I suppose you should have used the term "rhymed poetry" in your question, and then one might answer that Russian rhymes are incomparably more attractive and more abundant than English ones. No wonder a Russian prose writer frequents those beauties, especially in his youth.

**AA:** Who are the great American writers you most admire?

**VN:** When I was young I liked Poe, and I still love Melville, whom I did not read as a boy. My feelings towards James are rather complicated. I really dislike him intensely but now and then the figure in the phrase, the turn of the epithet, the screw of an absurd adverb, cause me a kind of electric tingle, as if some current of his was also passing through my own blood. Hawthorne is a splendid writer. Emerson's poetry is delightful.

**AA:** You have often said that you "don't belong to any club or group," and I wonder if the historical examples of the ways Russian writers have allowed ideology to determine, if not destroy, their art, culminating in the Socialist Realism of our own time, have not gone a long way in shaping your own skepticism and aversion to didacticism of any kind. Which "historical examples" have you been most conscious of?

**VN:** My aversion to groups is rather a matter of temperament than the fruit of information and thought. I was born that way and have despised ideological coercion instinctively all my life. Those "historical examples," by the way, are not as clear-cut and obvious as you seem to imply. The mystical didacticism of Gogol, or the utilitarian moralism of Tolstoy, or the reactionary journalism of Dostoyevsky, are of their own poor making and in the long run nobody really takes them seriously.

**AA:** Would you say something about the controversy surrounding the Chernyshevsky biography in *The Gift*? You have commented on this briefly before, but since its suppression in the thirties expresses such a transcendent irony and seems to justify the need for just such a parody, I think your readers would be most interested, especially since so little is known about the *émigré* communities, their magazines, and the role of intellectuals in these communities. If you would like to describe something of the writer's relationship to this world, please do.

**VN:** Everything that can be profitably said about Count Godunov-Cherdyntsev's biography of Chernyshevsky has been said by Koncheyev in *The Gift*. I can only add that I devoted as much honest labor to the task of gathering the material for the Chernyshevsky chapter as I did to the composing of Shade's poem for him. As to the suppression of that chapter by the editors of *Sovremennye zapiski*, it was indeed an unprecedented occurrence, quite out of keeping with their exceptional broadmindedness, for, generally speaking, in their acceptance or rejection of literary works they were guided exclusively by artistic standards. As to the latter part of your question, the revised Chapter Fourteen in *Speak, Memory* will provide additional information.

**AA:** Do you have any opinions about the Russian anti-utopian tradition (if it can be called this), from Odoyevsky's "The Last Suicide" and "A City Without a Name" in *Russian Nights* to Bryusov's *The Republic of the Southern Cross* and Zamyatin's *We* (to name only a few)?

**VN:** I am indifferent to those works.

**AA:** Is it fair to say that *Invitation to a Beheading* and *Bend Sinister* are cast as mock anti-utopian novels, with their ideological centers removed— the totalitarian state becoming an extreme and fantastic metaphor for the imprisonment of the mind, thus making consciousness, rather than politics, the subject of these novels?

**VN:** Yes, possibly.

**AA:** Speaking of ideology, you have often expressed your hostility to Freud, most noticeably in the forewords to your translated novels. Some readers have wondered which of Freud's works or theories you were most offended by and why. The parodies of Freud in *Lolita* and *Pale Fire* suggest a wider familiarity with the good doctor than you have ever publicly granted. Would you comment on this?

**VN:** Oh, I am not up to discussing again that figure of fun. He is not worthy of more attention than I have granted him in my novels and in *Speak, Memory*. Let the credulous and the vulgar continue to believe that all mental woes can be cured by a daily application of old Greek myths to their private parts. I really do not care.

**AA:** Your contempt for Freud's "standardized symbols" extends to the assumptions of a good many other theorizers. Do you think literary criticism is at all purposeful, and if so, what kind of criticism would you point to? *Pale Fire* makes it clear what sort you find gratuitous (at best).

**VN:** My advice to a budding literary critic would be as follows. Learn to distinguish banality. Remember that mediocrity thrives on "ideas." Beware of the modish message. Ask yourself if the symbol you have detected is not your own footprint. Ignore allegories. By all means place the "how" above the "what" but do not let it be confused with the "so what." Rely on the sudden erection of your small dorsal hairs. Do not drag in Freud at this point. All the rest depends on personal talent.

**AA:** As a writer, have you ever found criticism instructive—not so much the reviews of your own books, but any general criticism? From your own experiences do you think that an academic and a literary career nourish one another? Since many writers today know no other alternative than a life on campus, I'd be very interested in your feelings about this. Do you think that your own work in America was at all shaped by your being part of an academic community?

**VN:** I find criticism most instructive when an expert proves to me that my facts or my grammar are wrong. An academic career is especially helpful to writers in two ways: 1) easy access to magnificent libraries and 2) long vacations. There is, of course, the business of teaching, but old professors have young instructors to correct examination papers for them, and young instructors, authors in their own right, are followed by admiring glances along the corridors of Vanity Hall. Otherwise, our greatest rewards, such as the reverberations of our minds in such minds as vibrate responsively in later years, force novelist-teachers to nurse lucidity and honesty of style in their lectures.

**AA:** What are the possibilities of literary biography?

**VN:** They are great fun to write, generally less fun to read. Sometimes the thing becomes a kind of double paper chase: first, the biographer pursues his quarry through letters and diaries, and across the bogs of conjecture, and then a rival authority pursues the muddy biographer.

**AA:** Some critics may find the use of coincidence in a novel arch or contrived. I recall that you yourself at Cornell called Dostoyevsky's usage of coincidence crude.

**VN:** But in "real" life they do happen. Last night you were telling us at dinner a very funny story about the use of the title "Doctor" in Germany, and the very next moment, as my loud laughter was subsiding, I heard a person at the next table saying to her neighbor in clear French tones coming through the tinkling and shuffling sounds of a restaurant—[turning to his wife] just as you can hear at this moment the trilling of that little grebe on the lake through the sounds of the traffic—"Of course, you never know with the Germans if 'Doctor' means a dentist or a lawyer." Very often you meet with some person or some event in "real" life that would sound pat in a story. It is not the coincidence in the story that bothers us so much as the coincidence of coincidences in several stories by different writers, as, for instance, the recurrent eavesdropping device in nineteenth century Russian fiction.

**AA:** Could you tell us something about your work habits as a writer, and the way you compose your novels. Do you use an outline? Do you have a full sense of where a fiction is heading even while you are in the early stages of composition?

**VN:** In my twenties and early thirties, I used to write, dipping pen in ink and using a new nib every other day, in exercise books, crossing out, inserting, striking out again, crumpling the page, rewriting every page three or four times, then copying out the novel in a different ink and a neater hand, then revising the whole thing once more, recopying it with new corrections, and finally dictating it to my wife who has typed out all my stuff. Generally speaking, I am a slow writer, a snail carrying its house at the rate of two hundred pages of final copy per year (one spectacular exception was the Russian original of *Invitation to a Beheading*, the first draft of which I wrote in one fortnight of wonderful excitement and sustained inspiration). In those days and nights I generally followed the order of chapters when writing a novel; but even so, from the very first, I relied heavily on mental composition, constructing whole paragraphs in my mind as I walked in the streets, or sat in my bath, or lay in bed, although often deleting or rewriting them later. In the late thirties, beginning with *The Gift*, and perhaps under the influence of the many notes needed, I switched to another, physically more practical method—that of writing with an eraser-capped pencil on index cards. Since I always have at the very start a curiously clear preview of the entire novel before me or above me, I find cards especially convenient when not following the logical sequence of chapters but preparing instead this or that passage at any point of the novel and filling in the gaps in no special order. I am afraid to get mixed up with Plato, whom I do not care for, but I do think that in my case it is true that the entire book, before it is written, seems to be ready ideally in some other, now transparent, now dimming, dimension, and my job is to take down as much of it as I can make out and as precisely as I am humanly able to. The greatest happiness I experience in composing is when I feel I cannot understand, or rather catch myself not understanding (without the presupposition of an already existing creation), how or why that image or structural move has just come to me. It is sometimes rather amusing to find my readers trying to elucidate in a matter-of-fact way these wild workings of my not very efficient mind.

**AA:** One often hears from writers talk of how a character takes hold of them and in a sense dictates the course of the action. Has this ever been your experience?

**VN:** I have never experienced this. What a preposterous experience! Writers who have had it must be very minor or insane. No, the design of my novel is fixed in my imagination and every character follows the course I imagine for him. I am the perfect dictator in that private world insofar as I alone am responsible for its stability and truth. Whether I reproduce it as fully and faithfully as I would wish is another question. Some of my old works reveal dismal blurrings and blanks.

**AA:** *Pale Fire* appears to some readers to be in part a gloss on Plato's myth of the cave, and the constant play of Shades and Shadows throughout your work suggests a conscious Platonism. Would you care to comment on this possibility?

**VN:** As I have said, I am not particularly fond of Plato, nor would I survive very long under his Germanic regime of militarism and music. I do not think that this cave business has anything to do with my Shade and Shadows.

**AA:** Since we are mentioning philosophy *per se*, I wonder if we might talk about the philosophy of language that seems to unfold in your works, and whether or not you have consciously seen the similarities, say, between the language of Zemblan and what Wittgenstein had to say about a "private language." Your poet's sense of the limitations of language is startlingly similar to Wittgenstein's remark on the referential basis of language. While you were at Cambridge, did you have much contact with the philosophy faculty?

**VN:** No contact whatsoever. I am completely ignorant of Wittgenstein's works, and the first time I heard his name must have been in the fifties. In Cambridge I played football and wrote Russian verse.

**AA:** When in Canto Two John Shade describes himself, "I stand before the window and I pare/My fingernails," you are echoing Stephen Dedalus in *A Portrait of the Artist as a Young Man*, on the artist who "remains within or behind or beyond or above his handiwork, invisible, refined out of existence, indifferent, paring his fingernails." In almost all of your novels, especially in *Invitation to a Beheading*, *Bend Sinister*, *Pale Fire*, and *Pnin*—but even in *Lolita*, in the person of the seventh hunter in Quilty's play, and in several other phosphorescent glimmers which are visible to the careful reader—the creator is indeed behind or above his handiwork, but he is not invisible and surely not indifferent. To what extent are you consciously "answering" Joyce in *Pale Fire*, and what are your feelings about his esthetic stance, or alleged stance, because perhaps you may think that Stephen's remark doesn't apply to *Ulysses*?

**VN:** Neither Kinbote nor Shade, nor their maker, is answering Joyce in *Pale Fire*. Actually, I never liked *A Portrait of the Artist as a Young Man*. I find it a feeble and garrulous book. The phrase you quote is an unpleasant coincidence.

**AA:** You have granted that Pierre Delalande influenced you, and I would readily admit that influence-mongering can be reductive and deeply offensive if it tries to deny a writer's originality. But in the instance of yourself and Joyce, it seems to me that you've consciously profited from Joyce's example without imitating him—that you've realized the implications in *Ulysses* without having had recourse to obviously "Joycean" devices (stream-of-consciousness, the "collage" effects created out of the vast flotsam and jetsam of everyday life). Would you comment on what Joyce has meant to you as a writer, his importance in regard to his liberation and expansion of the novel form?

**VN:** My first real contact with *Ulysses*, after a leering glimpse in the early twenties, was in the thirties at a time when I was definitely formed as a writer and immune to any literary influence. I studied *Ulysses* seriously only much later, in the fifties, when preparing my Cornell courses. That was the best part of the education I received at Cornell. *Ulysses* towers over the rest of Joyce's writings, and in comparison to its noble originality and unique lucidity of thought and style the unfortunate *Finnegans Wake* is nothing but a formless and dull mass of phony folklore, a cold pudding of a book, a persistent snore in the next room, most aggravating to the insomniac I am. Moreover, I always detested regional literature full of quaint old-timers and imitated pronunciation. *Finnegans Wake*'s facade disguises a very conventional and drab tenement house, and only the infrequent snatches of heavenly intonations redeem it from utter insipidity. I know I am going to be excommunicated for this pronouncement.

**AA:** Although I cannot recall your mentioning the involuted structure of *Ulysses* when you lectured on Joyce, I do remember your insisting that the hallucinations in Nighttown are the author's and not Stephen's or Bloom's, which is one step away from a discussion of the involution. This is an aspect of *Ulysses* almost totally ignored by the Joyce Industry, and an aspect of Joyce which would seem to be of great interest to you. If Joyce's somewhat inconsistent involutions tend to be obscured by the vastness of his structures, it might be said that the structuring of your novels depends on the strategy of involution. Could you comment on this, or compare your sense of Joyce's presence in and above his works with your own intention—that is, Joyce's covert appearances in *Ulysses*; the whole Shakespeare-paternity theme which ultimately spirals into the idea of the "parentage" of *Ulysses* itself; Shakespeare's direct address to Joyce in Nighttown ("How my Oldfellow chokit his Thursday-momum," that being Bloomsday); and Molly's plea to Joyce, "O Jamesy let me up out of this"—all this as against the way the authorial voice—or what you call the "anthropomorphic deity impersonated by me"—again and again appears in your novels, most strikingly at the end.
**VN:** One of the reasons Bloom cannot be the active party in the Nighttown chapter (and if he is not, then the author is directly dreaming it up for him, and around him, with some real episodes inserted here and there) is that Bloom, a wilting male anyway, has been drained of his manhood earlier in the evening and thus would be quite unlikely to indulge in the violent sexual fancies of Nighttown. But I plan to publish my notes on *Ulysses*, and will not pursue the matter now.

**AA:** Ideally, how should a reader experience or react to "the end" of one of your novels, that moment when the vectors are removed and the fact of the fiction is underscored, the cast dismissed? What common assumptions about literature are you assaulting?

**VN:** The question is so charmingly phrased that I would love to answer it with equal elegance and eloquence, but I cannot say very much. I think that what I would welcome at the close of a book of mine is a sensation of its world receding in the distance and stopping somewhere there, suspended afar like a picture in a picture: *The Artist's Studio* by Van Bock.

**AA:** It may well be a failure of perception, but I've always been unsure of the very last sentences of *Lolita*, perhaps because the shift in voice at the close of your other books is so clear, but is one supposed to "hear" a different voice when the masked narrator says, "And do not pity C.Q. One had to choose between him and H. H., and one wanted H. H. . . ." and so forth? The return to the first person in the next sentence makes me think that the mask has not been lifted, but readers trained on *Invitation to a Beheading*, among other books, are always looking for the imprint of that "master thumb," to quote Franklin Lane in *Pale Fire*, "that made the whole involuted, boggling thing one beautiful straight line."

**VN:** No, I did not mean to introduce a different voice. I did want, however, to convey a constriction of the narrator's sick heart, a warning spasm causing him to abridge names and hasten to conclude his tale before it was too late. I am glad I managed to achieve this remoteness of tone at the end.

**AA:** Do Franklin Lane's *Letters* exist? I don't wish to appear like Mr. Goodman in *The Real Life of Sebastian Knight*, but I understand that Franklin Lane did exist.

**VN:** Frank Lane, his published letters and the passage cited by Kinbote certainly exist. Kinbote was rather struck by Lane's handsome melancholy face. And of course "lane" is the last word of Shade's poem. The latter has no significance.

**AA:** In which of your early works do you think you first begin to face the possibilities that are fully developed in *Invitation to a Beheading* and reach an apotheosis in the "involute abode" of *Pale Fire*?

**VN:** Possibly in *The Eye*, but *Invitation to Beheading* is on the whole a spontaneous generation.

**AA:** Are there other writers whose involuted effects you admire? Sterne? Pirandello's plays?

**VN:** I never cared for Pirandello. I love Sterne but had not read him in my Russian period.

**AA:** The Afterword to *Lolita* is significant, obviously, for many reasons. Is it included in all the translations which, I understand, number about twenty-five?

**VN:** Yes.

**AA:** You once told me after a class at Cornell that you'd been unable to read more than one hundred or so pages of *Finnegans Wake*. As it happens, on page 104 there begins a section very close in spirit to *Pale Fire*, and I wonder if you've ever read this, or seen the similarity. It is the history of all the editions and interpretations of Anna Livia Plurabelle's Letter (or "Mamafesta," text included). Among the three pages listing the various titles of ALP's letter, Joyce includes *Try our Taal on a Taub* (which we are already doing), and I wondered if you would comment on Swift's contribution to the literature about the corruption of learning and literature. Is it only a coincidence that Kinbote's "Foreword" to *Pale Fire* is dated "Oct. 19," which is the date of Swift's death?

**VN:** I finished *Finnegans Wake* eventually. It has no inner connection with *Pale Fire*. I think it is so nice that the day on which Kinbote committed suicide (and he certainly did after putting the last touches to his edition of the poem) happens to be both the anniversary of Pushkin's *Lyceum* and that of "poor old man Swift's" death, which is news to me (but see variant in note to line 231). In common with Pushkin, I am fascinated by fatidic dates. Moreover, when dating some special event in my novels I often choose a more or less familiar one as a *point de repère*, which helps to check a possible misprint in the proofs, as for instance "April 1" in the diary of Hermann in *Despair*.

**AA:** Mention of Swift moves me to ask about the genre of *Pale Fire*; as a "monstrous semblance of a novel," do you see it in terms of some tradition or form?

**VN:** The form of *Pale Fire* is specifically, if not generically, new. I would like to take this pleasant opportunity to correct the following misprints in the Putnam edition 1962, second impression: On page 137, end of note to line

143, "rustic" should be "rusty." On page 151, "Catskin Week" should be "Cat-kin Week." On page 223, the line number in the reference at the end of the first note should be not "550" but "549." On page 237, top, "For" should be "for." On page 241, the word "lines" after "*disent-prise*" should be "rhymes." And on page 294, the comma after "Arnold" should be replaced by an open parenthesis. Thank you.

**AA:** Do you make a clear distinction between satire and parody? I ask this because you have so often said you do not wish to be taken as a "moral satirist," and yet parody is so central to your vision.
**VN:** Satire is a lesson, parody is a game.

**AA:** Chapter Ten in *The Real Life of Sebastian Knight* contains a wonderful description of how parody functions in your own novels. But your sense of what "parody" means seems to stretch the usual definition, as when Cincinnatus in *Invitation to a Beheading* tells his mother, "You're still only a parody . . . Just like this spider, just like those bars, just like the striking of that clock." All art, then, or at least all attempts at a "realistic" art, would seem to produce a distortion, a "parody." Would you expand on what you mean by "parody" and why, as Fyodor says in *The Gift*, "The spirit of parody always goes along with genuine poetry?"
**VN:** When the poet Cincinnatus C., in my dreamiest and most poetical novel, accuses (not quite fairly) his mother of being a parody, he uses the word in its familiar sense of "grotesque imitation." When Fyodor, in *The Gift*, alludes to that "spirit of parody" which plays around the spray of genuine "serious" poetry, he is referring to parody in the sense of an essentially lighthearted, delicate, mockingbird game, such as Pushkin's parody of Derzhavin in *Exegi Monumentum*.

**AA:** What is your opinion of Joyce's parodies? Do you see any difference in the artistic effect of scenes such as the maternity hospital and the beach interlude with Gerty Macdowell? Are you familiar with the work of younger American writers who have been influenced by both you and Joyce, such as Thomas Pynchon (a Cornellian, Class of '59, who surely was in Literature 312), and do you have any opinion on the current ascendancy of the so-called parody-novel (John Barth, for instance)?
**VN:** The literary parodies in the Maternal Hospital chapter are on the whole jejunish. Joyce seems to have been hampered by the general sterilized tone

he chose for that chapter, and this somehow dulled and monotonized the inlaid skits. On the other hand, the frilly novelette parodies in the Masturbation scene are highly successful; and the sudden bursting of its clichés into the fireworks and tender sky of real poetry is a feat of genius. I am not familiar with the works of the two other writers you mention.

**AA:** Why, in *Pale Fire*, do you call parody the "last resort of wit?"
**VN:** This is Kinbote speaking. There are people whom parody upsets.

**AA:** Are the composition of *Lolita* and *Speak, Memory*, two very different books about the spell exerted by the past, at all connected in the way that the translations of *The Song of Igor's Campaign* and *Eugene Onegin* are related to *Pale Fire*? Had you finished all the notes to *Onegin* before you began *Pale Fire*?
**VN:** This is the kind of question that can be only answered by the interrogator himself. The task of pondering such juxtapositions and contrasts is above my capacities. Yes, I had finished all my notes to *Onegin* before I began *Pale Fire*. Flaubert speaks in one of his letters, in relation to a certain scene in *Madame Bovary*, about the difficulty of painting *couleur sur couleur*. This in a way is what I tried to do in re-twisting my own experience when inventing Kinbote. *Speak, Memory* is strictly autobiographic. There is nothing autobiographic in *Lolita*.

**AA:** Although self-parody seems to be a vital part of your work, you are a writer who believes passionately in the primacy of the imagination. Yet your novels are filled with little details that seem to have been purposely pulled from your own life, as a reading of *Speak, Memory* makes clear, not to mention the overriding patterns, such as the lepidopteral motif, which extend through so many books. They seem to partake of something other than the involuted voice, to suggest some clearly held idea about the interrelationship between self-knowledge and artistic creation, self-parody and identity. Would you comment on this, and the significance of autobiographical hints in works of art that are literally *not* autobiographical?
**VN:** I would say that imagination is a form of memory. Down, Plato, down, good dog. An image depends on the power of association, and association is supplied and prompted by memory. When we speak of a vivid individual recollection, we are paying a compliment not to our capacity of retention but to Mnemosyne's mysterious foresight in having stored up this or that

element which creative imagination may use when combining it with later recollections and inventions. In this sense, both memory and imagination are a negation of time.

**AA:** C. P. Snow has complained about the gulf between the "two cultures," the literary and scientific communities. As someone who has bridged this gulf, do you see the sciences and humanities as necessarily opposed? Have your experiences as a scientist influenced your performance as an artist? Is it fanciful to use the vocabulary of physics in describing the structures of some of your novels?

**VN:** I would have compared myself to a Colossus of Rhodes bestriding the gulf between the thermodynamics of Snow and the Laurentomania of Leavis, had that gulf not been a mere dimple of a ditch that a small frog could straddle. The terms "physics" and "egghead" as used nowadays evoke in me the dreary image of applied science, the knack of an electrician tinkering with bombs and other gadgets. One of those "Two Cultures" is really nothing but utilitarian technology; the other is B-grade novels, ideological fiction, popular art. Who cares if there exists a gap between such "physics" and such "humanities." Those eggheads are terrible philistines. A real good head is not oval but round.

My passion for lepidopterological research, in the field, in the laboratory, in the library, is even more pleasurable than the study and practice of literature, which is saying a good deal. Lepidopterists are obscure scientists. Not one is mentioned in *Webster*. But never mind. I have reworked the classification of various groups of butterflies, have described and figured several species and subspecies. My names for the microscopic organs that I have been the first to see and portray have safely found their way into the biological dictionaries (which is poorly matched by the wretched entry under "nymphet" in *Webster's* latest edition). The tactile delights of precise delineation, the silent paradise of the camera lucida, and the precision of poetry in taxonomic description represent the artistic side of the thrill that accumulation of new knowledge, absolutely useless to the layman, gives its first begetter. Science means to me above all natural science. Not the ability to repair a radio set; quite stubby fingers can do that. Apart from this basic consideration, I certainly welcome the free interchange of terminology between any branch of science and any raceme of art. There is no science without fancy, and no art without facts. Aphoristicism is a symptom of arteriosclerosis.

**AA:** In *Pale Fire*, Kinbote complains that "The coming of summer represented a problem in optics." *The Eye* is well-titled, since you plumb these problems throughout your fiction; the apprehension of "reality" is a miracle of vision, and consciousness is virtually an optical instrument in your work. Have you studied the science of optics at all, and would you say something about your own visual sense and how you feel it has served your fiction?

**VN:** I am afraid you are quoting this out of context. Kinbote was simply annoyed by the spreading foliage of summer interfering with his Tom-peeping. Otherwise, you are right in suggesting that I have good eyes. Doubting Tom should have worn spectacles. It is true, however, that even with the best of visions one must touch things to be *quite* sure of "reality."

**AA:** You have said that Alain Robbe-Grillet and Jorge Luis Borges are among your favorite contemporary writers. Do you find them to be at all similar? Do you think Robbe-Grillet's novels are as free of "psychology" as he claims?

**VN:** Robbe-Grillet's claims are preposterous. Those manifestos die with the dadas. His fiction is magnificently poetical and original, and the shifts of levels, the interpenetration of successive impressions and so forth belong of course to psychology—psychology at its best. Borges is also a man of infinite talent, but his miniature labyrinths and the roomy ones of Robbe-Grillet are quite differently built, and the lighting is not the same.

**AA:** I recall your humorous remarks at Cornell about two writers experiencing "telepathy" (I believe you were comparing Dickens and Flaubert). You and Borges were both born in 1899 (but so was Ernest Hemingway!). Your *Bend Sinister* and Borges' story *The Circular Ruins* are conceptually similar, but you do not read Spanish and that story was first translated into English in 1949, two years after *Bend Sinister*'s birth, just as in Borges' *The Secret Miracle*, Hladik has created a verse drama uncannily similar to your recently Englished play, *The Waltz Invention*, which precedes Borges' tale, but which he could not have read in Russian. When were you first aware of Borges' fictions, and have you and he had any kind of association or contact, other than telepathic?

**VN:** I read a Borges story for the first time three or four years ago. Up till then I had not been aware of his existence, nor do I believe he knew, or indeed knows, anything about me. That is not very grand in the way of telepathy. There are affinities between *Invitation to a Beheading* and *The*

*Castle*, but I had not yet read Kafka when I wrote my novel. As to Heming-way, I read him for the first time in the early forties, something about bells, balls, and bulls, and loathed it. Later, I read his admirable *The Killers* and the wonderful fish story which I was asked to translate into Russian but could not for some reason or other.

**AA:** As a matter of fact, Borges *does* know of your existence: he was sup-posed to contribute to the special issue of the French magazine *L'Arc* which was devoted to you but, for some reason, he did not. Your first book was a translation of Lewis Carroll into Russian. Do you see any affinities between Carroll's idea of "nonsense" and your bogus or "mongrel" languages in *Bend Sinister* and *Pale Fire*?

**VN:** In common with many other English children (I was an English child) I have been always very fond of Carroll. No, I do not think that his invented language shares any roots with mine. He has a pathetic affinity with H. H. but some odd scruple prevented me from alluding in *Lolita* to his wretched perversion and to those ambiguous photographs he took in dim rooms. He got away with it, as so many other Victorians got away with pederasty and nympholepsy. His were sad, scrawny little nymphets, bedraggled and half-undressed, or rather semi-undraped, as if participating in some dusty and dreadful charade.

**AA:** I thought that you *did* allude to Carroll in *Lolita* through what might be called "the photography theme"—Humbert cherishes his worn old pho-tograph of Annabel, has in a sense been living with this "still," tries to make Lolita conform to it, and often laments his failure to capture her on film. Quilty's hobby is announced as "photography," and the unspeakable films he produced at the Duk Duk Ranch would seem to answer Carroll's wildest needs.

**VN:** I did not consciously think of Carroll's hobby when I referred to the use of photography in *Lolita*.

**AA:** You have had wide experience as a translator and have made fictive use of translation. What basic problems of existence do you find implicit in the art and act of translation?

**VN:** There is a certain small Malayan bird of the thrush family which is said to sing only when tormented in an unspeakable way by a specially trained child at the annual Feast of Flowers. There is Casanova making love to a harlot while looking from a window at the nameless tortures inflicted on

Damiens. These are the visions that sicken me when I read the "poetical" translations from martyred Russian poets by some of my famous contemporaries. A tortured author and a deceived reader, this is the inevitable outcome of arty paraphrase. The only object and justification of translation is the conveying of the most exact information possible and this can be only achieved by a literal translation, with notes.

**AA:** Mention of translation brings me to one of the Kinbotian problems faced by critics who comment on your Russian novels in translation, but who themselves have no Russian. It has been said that translations such as *The Defense* and *Despair* must contain many stylistic revisions (certainly the puns), and moreover are in general much richer in language than *Laughter in the Dark*, written at about the same time but, unlike the others, translated in the thirties. Would you comment on this? If the style of *Laughter in the Dark* suggests it should have preceded *Despair*, perhaps it actually was written much earlier. In the BBC interview of four years ago, you said that you wrote *Laughter in the Dark* when you were twenty-six, which would have been 1925, thus making it your first novel. Did you actually write it this early, or is the reference to age a slip in memory, no doubt caused by the distracting presence of the BBC machinery.

**VN:** I touched up details here and there in those novels and reinstated a scene in *Despair*, as the Foreword explains. That "twenty-six" is certainly wrong. It is either a tele-scopation or I must have been thinking of *Mashenka* [*Mary*], my first novel written in 1925. The Russian original version (*Kamera Obskura*) of *Laughter in the Dark* was written in 1931, and an English translation by Winifried Roy, insufficiently revised by me, appeared in London in 1936. A year later, on the Riviera, I attempted—not quite successfully—to English the thing anew for Bobbs-Merrill, who published it in New York in 1938.

**AA:** There is a parenthetical remark in *Despair* about a "vulgar, mediocre Herzog." Is that a bit of added fun about a recent bestseller?
**VN:** Herzog means "Duke" in German and I was speaking of a conventional statue of a German Duke in a city square.

**AA:** Since the reissued edition of *Laughter in the Dark* is not graced by one of your informative forewords, would you tell us something about the book's inception and the circumstances under which you wrote it? Commentators are quick to suggest similarities between Margot and Lolita, but I'm much more interested in the kinship between Axel Rex and Quilty. Would you comment on this, and perhaps on the other perverters of the imagination one finds throughout your work, all of whom seem to share Rex's evil qualities.

**VN:** Yes, some affinities between Rex and Quilty exist, as they do between Margot and Lo. Actually, of course, Margot was a common young whore, not an unfortunate little Lolita. Anyway, I do not think that those recurrent sexual oddities and morbidities are of much interest or importance. My Lolita has been compared to Emmie in *Invitation*, to Mariette in *Bend Sinister*, and even to Colette in *Speak, Memory*—the last is especially ludicrous. But I think it might have been simply English jollity and leg-pulling.

**AA:** The *doppelgänger* motif figures prominently throughout your fiction; in *Pale Fire* one is tempted to call it a tripling (at least). Would you say that *Laughter in the Dark* is your earliest double fiction?

**VN:** I do not see any doubles in *Laughter in the Dark*. A lover can be viewed as the betrayed party's double but that is pointless.

**AA:** Would you care to comment on how the *doppelgänger* motif has been both used and abused from Poe, Hoffmann, Andersen, Dostoyevsky, Gogol, Stevenson, and Melville, down to Conrad and Mann? Which *doppelgänger* fictions would you single out for praise?

**VN:** The *doppelgänger* subject is a frightful bore.

**AA:** What are your feelings about Dostoyevsky's celebrated *The Double*; after all, Hermann in *Despair* considers it as a possible title for his manuscript.

**VN:** Dostoyevsky's *The Double* is his best work, though an obvious and shameless imitation of Gogol's *Nose*. Felix in *Despair* is really a *false* double.

**AA:** What are the criteria of identity which have made this theme so congenial to you? And what assumptions about identity have you reacted against in fashioning your own conception of the double?

**VN:** There are no "real" doubles in my novels.

**AA:** Speaking of doubles brings me to *Pnin*, which in my experience has proved to be one of your most popular novels and at the same time one of your most elusive to those readers who fail to see the relationship of the narrator and the characters (or who fail to even notice the narrator until

it's too late). Four of its seven chapters were published in *The New Yorker* over a considerable period (1953–57), but the all-important last chapter, in which the narrator takes control, is only in the book. I'd be most interested to know if the design of *Pnin* was complete while the separate sections were being published, or whether your full sense of its possibilities occurred later.
**VN:** Yes, the design of *Pnin* was complete in my mind when I composed the first chapter which, I believe, in this case was actually the first of the seven I physically set down on paper. Alas, there was to be an additional chapter, between Four (in which, incidentally, both the boy at St. Mark's and Pnin dream of a passage from my drafts of *Pale Fire*, the revolution in Zembla and the escape of the king—that is telepathy for you!) and Five (where Pnin drives a car). In that still un-inked chapter, which was beautifully clear in my mind down to the last curve, Pnin, recovering in the hospital from a sprained back, teaches himself to drive a car in bed by studying a 1935 manual of automobilism found in the hospital library and by manipulating the levers of his cot. Only one of his colleagues visits him there—Professor Blorenge. The chapter ended with Pnin's taking his driver's examination and pedantically arguing with the instructor who has to admit Pnin is right. A combination of chance circumstances in 1956 prevented me from actually writing that chapter, then other events intervened, and it is only a mummy now.

**AA:** In a television interview last year, you singled out Bely's *St. Petersburg*, along with works by Joyce, Kafka, and Proust, as one of the greatest achievements in twentieth century prose (an endorsement, by the way, which has prompted Grove Press to reissue *St. Petersburg*, with your statement across the front cover). I greatly admire this novel but, unhappily enough, it is relatively unknown in America. What are its qualities which you most admire? Bely and Joyce are sometimes compared; is the comparison a just one?
**VN:** *Petersburg* is a splendid fantasy, but this is a question I plan to answer in my essay on Joyce. There does exist some resemblance in manner between *Petersburg* and certain passages in *Ulysses*.

**AA:** Although I've never seen it discussed as such, the Ableukhov father-son relationship to me constitutes a doubling, making *Petersburg* one of the most interesting and fantastic permutations of the *doppelgänger* theme. Since this kind of doubling (if you would agree it is one) is surely the kind you'd find more congenial, say, than the use Mann makes of the motif in *Death in Venice*, would you comment on its implications?

**VN:** Those murky matters have no importance to me as a writer. Philosophically, I am an indivisible monist.

**AA:** Bely lived in Berlin in 1922–23. Did you know him there? You and Joyce lived in Paris at the same time. Did you ever meet him?

**VN:** Once, in 1921 or 1922, at a Berlin restaurant where I was dining with two girls. I happened to be sitting back to back with Andrei Bely who was dining with another writer, Aleksey Tolstoy, at the table behind me. Both writers were at the time frankly pro-Soviet (and on the point of returning to Russia), and a White Russian, which I still am in that particular sense, would certainly not wish to speak to a *bolshevizan* (fellow traveler). I was acquainted with Aleksey Tolstoy but of course ignored him. As to Joyce, I saw him a few times in Paris in the late thirties. Paul and Lucie Leon, close friends of his, were also old friends of mine. One night they brought him to a French lecture I had been asked to deliver on Pushkin under the auspices of Gabriel Marcel (it was later published in the *Nouvelle Revue Francaise*). I had happened to replace at the very last moment a Hungarian woman writer, very famous that winter, author of a bestselling novel, I remember its title, *La Rue du Chat qui Peche*, but not the lady's name. A number of personal friends of mine, fearing that the sudden illness of the lady and a sudden discourse on Pushkin might result in a suddenly empty house, had done their best to round up the kind of audience they knew I would like to have. The house had, however, a pied aspect since some confusion had occurred among the lady's fans. The Hungarian consul mistook me for her husband and, as I entered, dashed towards me with the froth of condolence on his lips. Some people left as soon as I started to speak. A source of unforgettable consolation was the sight of Joyce sitting, arms folded and glasses glinting, in the midst of the Hungarian football team. Another time my wife and I had dinner with him at the Leons' followed by a long friendly evening of talk. I do not recall one word of it but my wife remembers that Joyce asked about the exact ingredients of *myod*, the Russian "mead," and everybody gave him a different answer. In this connection, there is a marvelous howler in the standard English version of *The Brothers Karamazov*: a supper table at Zosima's abode is described with the translator hilariously misreading "Medoc" (in Russian transliteration in the original text), a French wine greatly appreciated in Russia, as *medok*, the diminutive of *myod* (mead). It would have been fun to recall that I spoke of this to Joyce, but unfortunately I came across this incarnation of *The Karamazovs* some ten years later.

**AA:** You mentioned Aleksey Tolstoy a moment ago. Would you say something about him?

**VN:** He was a writer of some talent and has two or three science fiction stories or novels which are memorable. But I wouldn't care to categorize writers, the only category being originality and talent. After all, if we start sticking group labels, we'll have to put *The Tempest* in the SF category, and of course thousands of other valuable works.

**AA:** Tolstoy was initially an anti-Bolshevik, and his early work precedes the Revolution. Are there any writers totally of the Soviet period whom you admire?

**VN:** There were a few writers who discovered that if they chose certain plots and certain characters they could get away with it in the political sense; in other words, they wouldn't be told what to write and how to finish the novel. Ilf and Petrov, two wonderfully gifted writers, decided that if they had a rascal adventurer as protagonist, whatever they wrote about his adventures could not be criticized from a political point of view, since a perfect rascal or a madman or a delinquent or any person who was outside Soviet society—in other words, any picaresque character—could not be accused either of being a bad Communist or not being a good Communist. Thus, Ilf and Petrov, Zoshchenko, and Olesha managed to publish some absolutely first-rate fiction under that standard of complete independence, since these characters, plots, and themes could not be treated as political ones. Until the early thirties they managed to get away with it. The poets had a parallel system. They thought, and they were right at first, that if they stuck to the garden—to pure poetry, to lyrical imitations, say, of gypsy songs, such as Ilya Selvinsky's—that then they were safe. Zabolotski found a third method of writing, as if the "I" of the poem were a perfect imbecile, crooning in a dream, distorting words, playing with words as a half-insane person would. All these people were enormously gifted but the regime finally caught up with them and they disappeared, one by one, in nameless camps.

**AA:** By my loose approximation, there remain three novels, some fifty stories, and six plays still in Russian. Are there any plans to translate these? What of *The Exploit*, written during what seems to have been your most fecund period as a "Russian writer"; would you tell us something, however briefly, about this book?

**VN:** Not all of that stuff is as good as I thought it was thirty years ago but some of it will probably be published in English by-and-by. My son is now working on the translation of *The Exploit*. It is the story of a Russian expatriate, a romantic young man of my set and time, a lover of adventure for adventure's sake, proud flaunter of peril, climber of unnecessary mountains, who merely for the pure thrill of it decides one day to cross illegally into Soviet Russia, and then cross back to exile. Its main theme is the overcoming of fear, the glory and rapture of that victory.

**AA:** I understand that *The Real Life of Sebastian Knight* was written in English in 1938. It is very dramatic to think of you bidding farewell to one language and embarking on a new life in another in this way. Why did you decide to write in English at this time, since you obviously could not have known for certain you would emigrate two years later? How much more writing in Russian did you do between *Sebastian Knight* and your emigration to America in 1940, and once there, did you ever compose in Russian again?
**VN:** Oh, I did know I would eventually land in America. I switched to English after convincing myself on the strength of my translation of *Despair* that I could use English as a wistful standby for Russian. I still feel the pangs of that substitution; they have not been allayed by the Russian poems (my best) that I wrote in New York, or the 1954 Russian version of *Speak, Memory*, or even my recent two-years-long work on the Russian translation of *Lolita*, which will be published sometime in 1967. I wrote *Sebastian Knight* in Paris, 1938. We had that year a charming flat on rue Saigon, between the Etoile and the Bois. It consisted of a huge handsome room (which served as parlor, bedroom and nursery) with a small kitchen on one side and a large sunny bathroom on the other. This apartment had been some bachelor's delight but was not meant to accommodate a family of three. Evening guests had to be entertained in the kitchen so as not to interfere with my future translator's sleep. And the bathroom doubled as my study. Here is the *doppelgänger* theme for you.

**AA:** Many people are surprised to learn that you have written seven plays, which is strange, since your novels are filled with "theatrical" effects that are patently un-novelistic. Is it just to say that your frequent allusions to Shakespeare are more than a matter of playful or respectful homage? What do you think of the drama as a form? What are the characteristics of Shakespeare's plays which you find most congenial to your own esthetic?
**VN:** The verbal poetical texture of Shakespeare is the greatest the world has known, and is immensely superior to the structure of his plays as plays. With Shakespeare it is the metaphor that is the thing, not the play. My most

ambitious venture in the domain of drama is a huge screenplay based on *Lolita*. I wrote it for Kubrick, who used only bits and shadows of it for his otherwise excellent film.

**AA:** When I was your student, you never mentioned the Homeric parallels in discussing Joyce's *Ulysses*. But you did supply "special information" in introducing many of the masterpieces: a map of Dublin for *Ulysses*, the arrangement of streets and lodgings in *Dr. Jekyll and Mr. Hyde*, a diagram of the interior of a railway coach on the Moscow-St. Petersburg express in *Anna Karenina*, and a floor plan of the Samsa's apartment in *The Metamorphosis* and an entomological drawing of Gregor. Would you be able to suggest some equivalent for your own readers?

**VN:** Joyce himself very soon realized with dismay that the harping on those essentially easy and vulgar "Homeric parallelisms" would only distract one's attention from the real beauty of his book. He soon dropped these pretentious chapter titles which already were "explaining" the book to nonreaders. In my lectures I tried to give factual data only. A map of three country estates with a winding river and a figure of the butterfly *Parnassius mnemosyne* for a cartographic cherub will be the endpaper in my revised edition of *Speak, Memory*.

**AA:** Incidentally, one of my colleagues came into my office recently with the breathless news that Gregor is *not* a cockroach (he had read an article to that effect). I told him I've known that for twelve years, and took out my notes to show him my drawing from what was for one day only Entomology 312. What kind of beetle, by the way, was Gregor?

**VN:** It was a domed beetle, a scarab beetle with wing-sheaths, and neither Gregor nor his maker realized that when the room was being made by the maid and the window was open, he could have flown out and escaped and joined the other happy dung beetles rolling the dung balls on rural paths.

**AA:** How are you progressing in your novel, *The Texture of Time*? Since the *donnée* for some of your novels seem to be present, however fleetingly, in earlier novels, would it be fair to suggest that Chapter Fourteen of *Bend Sinister* contains the germ for your latest venture?

**VN:** In a way, yes; but my *Texture of Time*, now almost half-ready, is only the central rose-web of a much ampler and richer novel, entitled *Ada*, about passionate, hopeless, rapturous sunset love, with swallows darting beyond the stained window and that radiant shiver . . .

**AA:** Speaking of *données*: At the end of *Pale Fire*, Kinbote says of Shade and his poem, "I even suggested to him a good title—the title of the book in me whose pages he was to cut: *Solus Rex*; instead of which I saw *Pale Fire*, which meant to me nothing." In 1940, *Sovremennye zapiski* published a long section from your "unfinished" novel, *Solus Rex*, under that title. Does *Pale Fire* represent the "cutting" of its pages? What is the relationship between it, the other un-translated fragment from *Solus Rex* ("Ultima Thule," published in *Novyy Journal*, New York, 1942) and *Pale Fire*?

**VN:** My *Solus Rex* might have disappointed Kinbote less than Shade's poem. The two countries, that of the Lone King and the Zembla land, belong to the same biological zone. Their subarctic bogs have much the same butterflies and berries. A sad and distant kingdom seems to have haunted my poetry and fiction since the twenties. It is not associated with my personal past. Unlike Northern Russia, both Zembla and Ultima Thule are mountainous, and their languages are of a phony Scandinavian type. If a cruel prankster kidnapped Kinbote and placed him, blindfolded, in the Ultima Thule countryside, Kinbote would not know—at least not immediately—by the sap smells and bird calls that he was not back in Zembla, but he would be tolerably sure that he was not on the banks of the Neva.

**AA:** This may be like asking a father to publicly declare which of his children is most loved, but do you have one novel towards which you feel the most affection, which you esteem over all others?

**VN:** The most affection, *Lolita*; the greatest esteem, *Priglashenie na kazn'* [*Invitation to a Beheading*].

**AA:** And as a closing question, sir, may I return to *Pale Fire*: Where, please, are the crown jewels hidden?

**VN:** In the ruins, Sir, of some old barracks near Kobaltana (*q.v.*); but do not tell it to the Russians.

# Vladimir Nabokov: The Art of Fiction XL

## Herbert Gold / 1967

From *The Paris Review*, Summer-Fall, 1967. © Herbert Gold, novelist and essayist. Reprinted by permission.

Vladimir Nabokov lives with his wife Véra in the Montreux Palace Hotel in Montreux, Switzerland, a resort city on Lake Geneva which was a favorite of Russian aristocrats of the last century. They dwell in a connected series of hotel rooms which, like their houses and apartments in the United States, seem impermanent, places of exile. Their rooms include one used for visits by their son Dmitri, and another, the *chambre de debarras*, where various items are deposited—Turkish and Japanese editions of *Lolita*, other books, sporting equipment, an American flag.

Nabokov arises early in the morning and works. He does his writing on filing cards, which are gradually copied, expanded, and rearranged until they become his novels. During the warm season in Montreux he likes to take the sun and swim at a pool in a garden near the hotel. His appearance at sixty-eight is heavy, slow, and powerful. He is easily turned to both amusement and annoyance, but prefers the former. His wife, an unequivocally devoted collaborator, is vigilant over him, writing his letters, taking care of business, occasionally even interrupting him when she feels he is saying the wrong thing. She is an exceptionally good-looking, trim, and sober-eyed woman. The Nabokovs still go off on frequent butterfly-hunting trips, though the distances they travel are limited by the fact that they dislike flying.

The interviewer had sent ahead a number of questions. When he arrived at the Montreux Palace, he found an envelope waiting for him. In accordance with Nabokov's wishes, all answers are given as he wrote them down. He claims that he needs to write his responses because of his unfamiliarity with English; this is a constant seriocomic form of teasing. He speaks with a dramatic Cambridge accent, very slightly nuanced by an occasional Russian pronunciation. Spoken English is, in fact, no hazard to him. Misquotation, however, is a menace. There is no doubt that Nabokov feels as a tragic loss the conspiracy of history which deprived him of his native Russia, and which brought him in middle life to doing his life's work in a language which is not that of his first dreams. However, his frequent apologies for his grasp of English clearly belong in the context of Nabokov's special mournful joking: he means it, he does not mean it, he is grieving for his loss, he is outraged if anyone criticizes his style, he pretends to be just a poor lonely foreigner, he is as American "as April in Arizona."

Nabokov is now at work on a long novel which explores the mysteries and ambiguities of time. When he speaks of this book, his voice and gaze are those of a delighted and bemused young poet eager to get to the task.

**Herbert Gold:** Good morning. Let me ask forty-odd questions.
**Vladimir Nabokov:** Good morning. I am ready.

**HG:** Your sense of the immorality of the relationship between Humbert Humbert and Lolita is very strong. In Hollywood and New York, however, relationships are frequent between men of forty and girls very little older than Lolita. They marry—to no particular public outrage; rather, public cooing.

**VN:** No, it is not *my* sense of the immorality of the Humbert Humbert— Lolita relationship that is strong; it is Humbert's sense. *He* cares, I do not. *I* do not give a damn for public morals, in America or elsewhere. And, anyway, cases of men in their forties marrying girls in their teens or early twenties have no bearing on *Lolita* whatever. Humbert was fond of "little girls"— not simply "young girls." Nymphets are girl-children, not starlets and "sex kittens." Lolita was twelve, not eighteen, when Humbert met her. You may remember that by the time she is fourteen, he refers to her as his "aging mistress."

**HG:** One critic (Pryce-Jones) has said about you that "his feelings are like no one else's." Does this make sense to you? Or does it mean that you know your feelings better than others know theirs? Or that you have discovered yourself at other levels? Or simply that your history is unique?

**VN:** I do not recall that article; but if a critic makes such a statement, it must surely mean that he has explored the feelings of literally millions of people, in at least three countries, before reaching his conclusion. If so, I am a rare fowl indeed. If, on the other hand, he has merely limited himself to quizzing members of his family or club, his statement cannot be discussed seriously.

**HG:** Another critic has written that your "worlds are static. They may become tense with obsession, but they do not break apart like the worlds of everyday reality." Do you agree? Is there a static quality in your view of things?

**VN:** Whose "reality?" "Everyday" where? Let me suggest that the very term "everyday reality" is utterly static since it presupposes a situation that is permanently observable, essentially objective and universally known. I suspect you have invented that expert on "everyday reality." Neither exists.

**HG:** *He* does [*names him*]. A third critic has said that you "diminish" your characters "to the point where they become ciphers in a cosmic farce." I disagree; Humbert, while comic, retains a touching and insistent quality—that of the spoiled artist.

**VN:** I would put it differently: Humbert Humbert is a vain and cruel wretch who manages to appear "touching." That epithet, in its true, tear-iridized sense, can only apply to my poor little girl. Besides, how can I "diminish" to the level of ciphers, et cetera, characters that I have invented myself? One can "diminish" a biographee, but not an eidolon.

**HG:** E. M. Forster speaks of his major characters sometimes taking over and dictating the course of his novels. Has this ever been a problem for you, or are you in complete command?

**VN:** My knowledge of Mr. Forster's works is limited to one novel, which I dislike; and anyway, it was not he who fathered that trite little whimsy about characters getting out of hand; it is as old as the quills, although, of course, one sympathizes with *his* people if they try to wriggle out of that trip to India or wherever he takes them. My characters are galley slaves.

**HG:** Clarence Brown of Princeton has pointed out striking similarities in your work. He refers to you as "extremely repetitious" and that in wildly different ways you are in essence saying the same thing. He speaks of fate being the "muse of Nabokov." Are you consciously aware of "repeating yourself," or to put it another way, that you strive for a conscious unity to your shelf of books?

**VN:** I do not think I have seen Clarence Brown's essay, but he may have something there. Derivative writers seem versatile because they imitate many others, past and present. Artistic originality has only its own self to copy.

**HG:** Do you think literary criticism is at all purposeful? Either in general, or specifically about your own books? Is it ever instructive?

**VN:** The purpose of a critique is to say something about a book the critic has or has not read. Criticism can be instructive in the sense that it gives readers, including the author of the book, some information about the critic's intelligence, or honesty, or both.

**HG:** And the function of the editor? Has one ever had literary advice to offer?

**VN:** By "editor" I suppose you mean proofreader. Among these I have known limpid creatures of limitless tact and tenderness who would discuss with me a semicolon as if it were a point of honor—which, indeed, a point of art often is. But I have also come across a few pompous avuncular brutes who would attempt to "make suggestions" which I countered with a thunderous "stet!"

**HG:** Are you a lepidopterist, stalking your victims? If so, doesn't your laughter startle them?

**VN:** On the contrary, it lulls them into the state of torpid security which an insect experiences when mimicking a dead leaf. Though by no means an avid reader of reviews dealing with my own stuff, I happen to remember the essay by a young lady who attempted to find entomological symbols in my fiction. The essay might have been amusing had she known something about Lepidoptera. Alas, she revealed complete ignorance, and the muddle of terms she employed proved to be only jarring and absurd.

**HG:** How would you define your alienation from the so-called White Russian refugees?

**VN:** Well, historically I am a "White Russian" myself since all Russians who left Russia as my family did in the first years of the Bolshevik tyranny because of their opposition to it were and remained White Russians in the large sense. But these refugees were split into as many social fractions and political factions as was the entire nation before the Bolshevist coup. I do not mix with "Black-Hundred" White Russians and do not mix with the so-called "bolshevizans," that is "pinks." On the other hand, I have friends among intellectual Constitutional Monarchists as well as among intellectual Social Revolutionaries. My father was an old-fashioned liberal, and I do not mind being labeled an old-fashioned liberal, too.

**HG:** How would you define your alienation from present-day Russia?

**VN:** As a deep distrust of the phony thaw now advertised. As a constant awareness of unredeemable iniquities. As a complete indifference to all that moves a patriotic *Sovietski* man of today. As the keen satisfaction of having discerned as early as 1918 the *meshchantsvo* (petty bourgeois smugness, philistine essence) of Leninism.

**HG:** How do you now regard the poets Blok and Mandelstam and others who were writing in the days before you left Russia?

**VN:** I read them in my boyhood, more than a half century ago. Ever since that time I have remained passionately fond of Blok's lyrics. His long pieces are weak, and the famous *The Twelve* is dreadful, self-consciously couched in a phony "primitive" tone, with a pink cardboard Jesus Christ glued on at the end. As to Mandelstamm, I also knew him by heart, but he gave me a less fervent pleasure. Today, through the prism of a tragic fate, his poetry seems greater than it actually is. I note, incidentally, that professors of literature still assign these two poets to different schools. There is only one school: that of talent.

**HG:** I know your work has been read and is attacked in the Soviet Union. How would you feel about a Soviet edition of your work?

**VN:** Oh, they are welcome to my work. As a matter of fact, the Editions Victor are bringing out my *Invitation to a Beheading* in a reprint of the original Russian of 1938, and a New York publisher (Phaedra) is printing my Russian translation of *Lolita*. I am sure the Soviet government will be happy to admit officially a novel that seems to contain a prophecy of Hitler's regime, and a novel that condemns bitterly the American system of motels.

**HG:** Have you ever had contact with Soviet citizens? Of what sort?

**VN:** I have practically no contact with them, though I did once agree, in the early thirties or late twenties, to meet—out of sheer curiosity—an agent from Bolshevist Russia who was trying hard to get *émigré* writers and artists to return to the fold. He had a double name, Lebedev something, and had written a novelette entitled *Chocolate*, and I thought I might have some sport with him. I asked him would I be permitted to write freely and would I be able to leave Russia if I did not like it there. He said that I would be so busy liking it there that I would have no time to dream of going abroad again. I would, he said, be perfectly free to choose any of the many themes

Soviet Russia bountifully allows a writer to use, such as farms, factories, forests in Fakistan—oh, lots of fascinating subjects. I said farms, et cetera, bored me, and my wretched seducer soon gave up. He had better luck with the composer Prokofiev.

**HG:** Do you consider yourself an American?

**VN:** Yes, I do. I am as American as April in Arizona. The flora, the fauna, the air of the western states, are my links with Asiatic and Arctic Russia. Of course, I owe too much to the Russian language and landscape to be emotionally involved in, say, American regional literature, or Indian dances, or pumpkin pie on a spiritual plane; but I do feel a suffusion of warm, light-hearted pride when I show my green USA passport at European frontiers. Crude criticism of American affairs offends and distresses me. In home politics I am strongly anti-segregationist. In foreign policy, I am definitely on the government's side. And when in doubt, I always follow the simple method of choosing that line of conduct which may be the most displeasing to the Reds and the Russells.

**HG:** Is there a community of which you consider yourself a part?

**VN:** Not really. I can mentally collect quite a large number of individuals whom I am fond of, but they would form a very disparate and discordant group if gathered in real life, on a real island. Otherwise, I would say that I am fairly comfortable in the company of American intellectuals who have read my books.

**HG:** What is your opinion of the academic world as a milieu for the creative writer? Could you speak specifically of the value or detriment of your teaching at Cornell?

**VN:** A first-rate college library with a comfortable campus around it is a fine milieu for a writer. There is, of course, the problem of educating the young. I remember how once, between terms, not at Cornell, a student brought a transistor set with him into the reading room. He managed to state that one, he was playing "classical" music; that two, he was doing it "softly"; and that three, "there were not many readers around in summer." I was there, a one-man multitude.

**HG:** Would you describe your relationship with the contemporary literary community? With Edmund Wilson, Mary McCarthy, your magazine editors and book publishers?

**VN:** The only time I ever collaborated with any writer was when I translated with Edmund Wilson Pushkin's *Mozart and Salieri* for *The New Republic* twenty-five years ago, a rather paradoxical recollection in view of his making such a fool of himself last year when he had the audacity of questioning my understanding of *Eugene Onegin*. Mary McCarthy, on the other hand, has been very kind to me recently in the same *New Republic*, although I do think she added quite a bit of her own angelica to the pale fire of Kinbote's plum pudding. I prefer not to mention here my relationship with Girodias, but I have answered in *Evergreen* his scurvy article in the *Olympia* anthology. Otherwise, I am on excellent terms with all my publishers. My warm friendship with Katharine White and Bill Maxwell of *The New Yorker* is something the most arrogant author cannot evoke without gratitude and delight.

**HG:** Could you say something of your work habits? Do you write to a pre-planned chart? Do you jump from one section to another, or do you move from the beginning through to the end?
**VN:** The pattern of the thing precedes the thing. I fill in the gaps of the crossword at any spot I happen to choose. These bits I write on index cards until the novel is done. My schedule is flexible, but I am rather particular about my instruments: lined Bristol cards and well sharpened, not too hard, pencils capped with erasers.

**HG:** Is there a particular picture of the world which you wish to develop? The past is very present for you, even in a novel of the "future," such as *Bend Sinister*. Are you a "nostalgist?" In what time would you prefer to live?
**VN:** In the coming days of silent planes and graceful aircycles, and cloudless silvery skies, and a universal system of padded underground roads to which trucks shall be relegated like Morlocks. As to the past, I would not mind retrieving from various corners of space-time certain lost comforts, such as baggy trousers and long, deep bathtubs.

**HG:** You know, you do not have to answer *all* my Kinbote-like questions.
**VN:** It would never do to start skipping the tricky ones. Let us continue.

**HG:** Besides writing novels, what do you, or would you, like most to do?
**VN:** Oh, hunting butterflies, of course, and studying them. The pleasures and rewards of literary inspiration are nothing beside the rapture of discovering a new organ under the microscope or an undescribed species on a mountainside in Iran or Peru. It is not improbable that had there been no

revolution in Russia, I would have devoted myself entirely to lepidopterology and never written any novels at all.

**HG:** What is most characteristic of "poshlust" in contemporary writing? Are there temptations for you in the sin of "poshlust?" Have you ever fallen?
**VN:** "Poshlust," or in a better transliteration "poshlost," has many nuances, and evidently I have not described them clearly enough in my little book on Gogol if you think one can ask anybody if he is tempted by "poshlost." Corny trash, vulgar clichés, philistinism in all its phases, imitations of imitations, bogus profundities, crude, moronic, and dishonest pseudo-literature—these are obvious examples. Now, if we want to pin down "poshlost" in contemporary writing, we must look for it in Freudian symbolism, moth-eaten mythologies, social comment, humanistic messages, political allegories, over-concern with class or race, and the journalistic generalities we all know. "Poshlost" speaks in such concepts as "America is no better than Russia" or "We all share in Germany's guilt." The flowers of "poshlost" bloom in such phrases and terms as "the moment of truth," "charisma," "existential" (used seriously), "dialogue" (as applied to political talks between nations), and "vocabulary" (as applied to a dauber). Listing in one breath Auschwitz, Hiroshima, and Vietnam is seditious "poshlost." Belonging to a very select club (which sports *one* Jewish name—that of the treasurer) is genteel "poshlost." Hack reviews are frequently "poshlost," but it also lurks in certain highbrow essays. "Poshlost" calls Mr. Blank a great poet and Mr. Bluff a great novelist. One of "poshlost's" favorite breeding places has always been the Art Exhibition; there it is produced by so-called sculptors working with the tools of wreckers, building crankshaft cretins of stainless steel, Zen stereos, polystyrene stinkbirds, objects trouvés in latrines, cannonballs, canned balls. There we admire the *gabinetti* wall patterns of so-called abstract artists, Freudian surrealism, roric smudges, and Rorschach blots—all of it as corny in its own right as the academic "September Morns" and "Florentine Flowergirls" of half a century ago. The list is long and, of course, everybody has his *bête noire*, his black pet, in the series. Mine is that airline ad: the snack served by an obsequious wench to a young couple—she eyeing ecstatically the cucumber canapé, he admiring wistfully the hostess. And, of course, *Death in Venice*. You see the range.

**HG:** Are there contemporary writers you follow with great pleasure?
**VN:** There are several such writers, but I shall not name them. Anonymous pleasure hurts nobody.

**HG:** Do you follow some with great pain?

**VN:** No. Many accepted authors simply do not exist for me. Their names are engraved on empty graves, their books are dummies, they are complete nonentities insofar as my taste in reading is concerned. Brecht, Faulkner, Camus, many others, mean absolutely nothing to me, and I must fight a suspicion of conspiracy against my brain when I see blandly accepted as "great literature" by critics and fellow authors Lady Chatterley's copulations or the pretentious nonsense of Mr. Pound, that total fake. I note he has replaced Dr. Schweitzer in some homes.

**HG:** As an admirer of Borges and Joyce you seem to share their pleasure in teasing the reader with tricks and puns and puzzles. What do you think the relationship should be between reader and author?

**VN:** I do not recollect any puns in Borges, but then I read him only in translation. Anyway, his delicate little tales and miniature Minotaurs have nothing in common with Joyce's great machines. Nor do I find many puzzles in that most lucid of novels, *Ulysses*. On the other hand, I detest *Punningans Wake* in which a cancerous growth of fancy word-tissue hardly redeems the dreadful joviality of the folklore and the easy, too easy, allegory.

**HG:** What have you learned from Joyce?

**VN:** Nothing.

**HG:** Oh, come.

**VN:** James Joyce has not influenced me in any manner whatsoever. My first brief contact with *Ulysses* was around 1920 at Cambridge University when a friend, Peter Mrozovski, who had brought a copy from Paris, chanced to read to me, as he stomped up and down my digs, one or two spicy passages from Molly's monologue, which, *entre nous soit dit*, is the weakest chapter in the book. Only fifteen years later, when I was already well formed as a writer and reluctant to learn or unlearn anything, I read *Ulysses* and liked it enormously. I am indifferent to *Finnegans Wake* as I am to all regional literature written in dialect—even if it be the dialect of genius.

**HG:** Aren't you doing a book about James Joyce?

**VN:** But not only about him. What I intend to do is publish a number of twenty-page essays on several works—*Ulysses*, *Madame Bovary*, Kafka's *Transformation*, *Don Quixote*, and others—all based on my Cornell and Harvard lectures. I remember with delight tearing apart *Don Quixote*, a cruel and crude old book, before six hundred students in Memorial Hall, much to the horror and embarrassment of some of my more conservative colleagues.

**HG:** What about other influences? Pushkin?
**VN:** In a way—no more than, say, Tolstoy or Turgenev were influenced by the pride and purity of Pushkin's art.

**HG:** Gogol?
**VN:** I was careful *not* to learn anything from him. As a teacher, he is dubious and dangerous. At his worst, as in his Ukrainian stuff, he is a worthless writer; at his best, he is incomparable and inimitable.

**HG:** Anyone else?
**VN:** H. G. Wells, a great artist, was my favorite writer when I was a boy. *The Passionate Friends, Ann Veronica, The Time Machine, The Country of the Blind*, all these stories are far better than anything Bennett or Conrad or, in fact, any of Wells's contemporaries could produce. His sociological cogitations can be safely ignored, of course, but his romances and fantasias are superb. There was an awful moment at dinner in our St. Petersburg house one night when Zinaïda Vengerov, his translator, informed Wells, with a toss of her head: "You know, *my* favorite work of yours is *The Lost World*." "She means the war the Martians lost," said my father quickly.

**HG:** Did you learn from your students at Cornell? Was the experience purely a financial one? Did teaching teach you anything valuable?
**VN:** My method of teaching precluded genuine contact with my students. At best, they regurgitated a few bits of my brain during examinations. Every lecture I delivered had been carefully, lovingly handwritten and typed out, and I leisurely read it out in class, sometimes stopping to rewrite a sentence and sometimes repeating a paragraph—a mnemonic prod which, however, seldom provoked any change in the rhythm of wrists taking it down. I welcomed the few shorthand experts in my audience, hoping they would communicate the information they stored to their less fortunate comrades. Vainly I tried to replace my appearances at the lectern by taped records to be played over the college radio. On the other hand, I deeply enjoyed the chuckle of appreciation in this or that warm spot of the lecture hall at this or that point of my lecture. My best reward comes from those former students

of mine who, ten or fifteen years later, write to me to say that they now understand what I wanted of them when I taught them to visualize Emma Bovary's mistranslated hairdo or the arrangement of rooms in the Samsa household or the two homosexuals in *Anna Karenina*. I do not know if I learned anything from teaching, but I know I amassed an invaluable amount of exciting information in analyzing a dozen novels for my students. My salary, as you happen to know, was not exactly a princely one.

**HG:** Is there anything you would care to say about the collaboration your wife has given you?

**VN:** She presided as adviser and judge over the making of my first fiction in the early twenties. I have read to her all my stories and novels at least twice; and she has reread them all when typing them and correcting proofs and checking translations into several languages. One day in 1950, at Ithaca, New York, she was responsible for stopping me and urging delay and second thoughts as, beset with technical difficulties and doubts, I was carrying the first chapters of *Lolita* to the garden incinerator.

**HG:** What is your relation to the translations of your books?

**VN:** In the case of languages my wife and I know or can read—English, Russian, French, and to a certain extent German and Italian—the system is a strict checking of every sentence. In the case of Japanese or Turkish versions, I try not to imagine the disasters that probably bespatter every page.

**HG:** What are your plans for future work?

**VN:** I am writing a new novel, but of this I cannot speak. Another project I have been nursing for some time is the publication of the complete screenplay of *Lolita* that I made for Kubrick. Although there are just enough borrowings from it in his version to justify my legal position as author of the script, the film is only a blurred skimpy glimpse of the marvelous picture I imagined and set down scene by scene during the six months I worked in a Los Angeles villa. I do not wish to imply that Kubrick's film is mediocre; in its own right, it is first-rate, but it is not what I wrote. A tinge of *poshlost* is often given by the cinema to the novel it distorts and coarsens in its crooked glass. Kubrick, I think, avoided this fault in his version, but I shall never understand why he did not follow my directions and dreams. It is a great pity; but at least I shall be able to have people read my *Lolita* play in its original form.

**HG:** If you had the choice of one and only one book by which you would be remembered, which one would it be?

**VN:** The one I am writing or rather dreaming of writing. Actually, I shall be remembered by *Lolita* and my work on *Eugene Onegin*.

**HG:** Do you feel you have any conspicuous or secret flaw as a writer?

**VN:** The absence of a natural vocabulary. An odd thing to confess, but it is true. Of the two instruments in my possession, one—my native tongue—I can no longer use, and this not only because I lack a Russian audience, but also because the excitement of verbal adventure in the Russian medium has faded away gradually after I turned to English in 1940. My English, this second instrument I have always had, is however a stiffish, artificial thing, which may be all right for describing a sunset or an insect, but which cannot conceal poverty of syntax and paucity of domestic diction when I need the shortest road between warehouse and shop. An old Rolls-Royce is not always preferable to a plain Jeep.

**HG:** What do you think about the contemporary competitive ranking of writers?

**VN:** Yes, I have noticed that in this respect our professional book reviewers are veritable bookmakers. Who's in, who's out, and where are the snows of yesteryear. All very amusing. I am a little sorry to be left out. Nobody can decide if I am a middle-aged American writer or an old Russian writer—or an ageless international freak.

**HG:** What is your great regret in your career?

**VN:** That I did not come earlier to America. I would have liked to have lived in New York in the thirties. Had my Russian novels been translated then, they might have provided a shock and a lesson for pro-Soviet enthusiasts.

**HG:** Are there significant disadvantages to your present fame?

**VN:** *Lolita* is famous, not I. I am an obscure, doubly obscure, novelist with an unpronounceable name.

# "To be Kind, to be Proud, to be Fearless"—Vladimir Nabokov in Conversation with James Mossman

## James Mossman / 1969

From *The Listener*, October 23, 1969. © The Estate of James Mossman. Reprinted by permission.

**Vladimir Nabokov:** I am a very poor speaker. I hope our audience won't mind my using notes.

**James Mossman:** What distinguishes us from animals?

**VN:** Being aware of being aware of being. In other words, if I not only know that I am but also know that I know it, then I belong to the human species. All the rest follows: the glory of thought, poetry, a vision of the universe. In that respect, the gap between ape and man is immeasurably greater than the one between amoeba and ape. The difference between an ape's memory and human memory is the difference between an ampersand and the British Museum library.

**JM:** As you recall a patch of time, its shapes, colors, and occupants, does this complete picture help combat time or offer any clue to its mysteries, or is it pleasure that it affords?

**VN:** Let me quote a paragraph in my book *Ada*: "Physiologically the sense of Time is a sense of continuous becoming . . . Philosophically, on the other hand, Time is but memory in the making. In every individual life there goes on from cradle to deathbed the gradual shaping and strengthening of that backbone of consciousness, which is the Time of the strong." This is Van speaking, Van Veen, the charming villain of my book. I have not decided yet if I agree with him in all his views on the texture of time. I suspect I don't.

**155**

**JM:** You have written of yourself as looking out "from my present ridge of remote, isolated, almost uninhabited time." Why uninhabited?

**VN:** Well, for the same reason that a desert island is a more deserving island than one with a footprint initialing its beach. Moreover, "uninhabited" makes direct sense here, since most of my former companions are gone.

**JM:** Does the aristocrat in you despise the fictionist, or is it only English aristocrats who feel queasy about men of letters?

**VN:** Pushkin, professional poet and Russian nobleman, used to shock the *beau monde* by declaring that he wrote for his own pleasure but published for the sake of money. I do likewise, but have never shocked anybody, except, perhaps, a former publisher of mine who used to counter my indignant requests by saying that I'm much too good a writer to need extravagant advances.

**JM:** Have you ever experienced hallucinations or heard voices or had visions, and, if so, have they been illuminating?

**VN:** When about to fall asleep after a good deal of writing or reading I often enjoy, if that is the right word, what some drug addicts experience: a continuous series of extraordinarily bright, fluidly changing pictures. Their type is different nightly, but on a given night it remains the same: one night it may be a banal kaleidoscope of endlessly recombined and reshaped stained-window designs; next time comes a subhuman or superhuman face with a formidably growing blue eye; or—and this is the most striking type—I see in realistic detail a long-dead friend turning toward me and melting into another remembered figure against the black velvet of my eyelid's inner side. As to voices, I have described in *Speak, Memory* the snatches of telephone talk which now and then vibrate in my pillowed ear. Reports on those enigmatic phenomena can be found in the case-histories collected by psychiatrists, but no satisfying interpretation has come my way. Freudians keep out, please.

**JM:** Is writing your novels pleasure or drudgery?

**VN:** Pleasure and agony while composing the book in my mind; harrowing irritation when struggling with my tools and viscera—the pencil that needs re-sharpening, the word that I always misspell and have to look up. Then the labor of reading the typescript prepared by a secretary, the correction of my major mistakes and her minor ones, transferring corrections to other copies, misplacing pages, trying to remember something that had to be crossed out or inserted. Repeating the process when proofreading. Unpacking the radiant, beautiful, plump advance copy, opening it, and discovering a stupid oversight committed by me, allowed by me to survive. After a month or so I get used to the book's final stage, to its having been weaned from my brain. I now regard it with a kind of amused tenderness, as a man regards, not his son, but the young wife of his son.

**JM:** You say you are not interested in what critics say, yet you got very angry with Edmund Wilson for commenting on you.
**VN:** I never retaliate when my works of art are concerned. Here the arrows of adverse criticism cannot scratch, let alone pierce, the shield of what disappointed archers call my "self-assurance." But I do reach for my heaviest dictionary when my scholarship is questioned, as was the case with my old friend Edmund Wilson, and I do get annoyed when people I have never met impinge on my privacy with false and vulgar assumptions—as, for example, Mr. Updike, who in an otherwise clever article absurdly suggests that my fictional character, bitchy and lewd Ada, is "in a dimension or two, Nabokov's wife."

**JM:** Do you see yourself sometimes as Nabokov the writer isolated from others, a flaming sword to scourge them, an entertainer, a drudge, a genius—which?
**VN:** The word "genius" is passed around rather generously, isn't it? At least in English, because its Russian counterpart, *geniy*, is a term brimming with a sort of throaty awe and is used only in the case of a very small number of writers—Shakespeare, Milton, Pushkin, Tolstoy. To such deeply beloved authors as Turgenev and Chekhov, Russians assign the thinner term, *talant*—talent, not genius. It is a bizarre example of semantic discrepancy—the same word being more substantial in one language than in another. Although my Russian and my English are practically coeval, I still feel appalled and puzzled at seeing "genius" applied to any important storyteller, such as Maupassant or Maugham. Genius still means to me, in my Russian fastidiousness and pride of phrase, a unique, dazzling gift—the genius of James Joyce, not the talent of Henry James.

**JM:** Can political ideas solve any of the big problems of an individual life?
**VN:** I have always marveled at the neatness of such solutions: ardent Stalinists transforming themselves into harmless socialists, socialists finding a sunset harbor in conservatism, and so forth. I suppose this must be rather

like religious conversion of which I know very little. I can only explain God's popularity by an atheist's panic.

JM: Great writers have had strong political and sociological ideas—Tolstoy was one. Does the presence of such ideas in his work make you think the less of him?

VN: I go by books, not by authors. I consider *Anna Karenina* the supreme masterpiece of nineteenth century literature; it is closely followed by *The Death of Ivan Ilyich.* I detest *Resurrection* and *The Kreutzer Sonata.* Tolstoy's publicistic forays are unreadable. *War and Peace,* though a little too long, is a rollicking historical novel written for that amorphic and limp creature known as "the general reader," and more specifically, for the young. In terms of artistic structure, it does not satisfy me. I derive no pleasure from its cumbersome message, from the didactic interludes, from the artificial coincidences with cool Prince Andrei turning up to witness this or that historical moment, this or that footnote in the sources used often uncritically by the author.

JM: Why do you dislike writers who go in for soul-searching and self-revelations in print? After all, do you not do it at another remove, behind a thicket of art?

VN: If you are alluding to Dostoyevsky's worst novels, then, indeed, I dislike intensely *The Brothers Karamazov* and the ghastly *Crime and Punishment* rigmarole. No, I do not object to soul-searching and self-revelation, but in those books the soul, and the sins, and the sentimentality, and the journalese, hardly warrant the tedious and muddled search.

JM: Is your attachment to childhood specially nostalgic and intense because you were abruptly banished by the Russian Revolution from the place where it evolved?

VN: Yes, that's right. But the stress is not on the Russian Revolution. It could have been anything—an earthquake, an individual departure prompted by a private disaster. The accent is on the abruptness of the change.

JM: Would you ever try to go back there?

VN: There's nothing to look at. New tenement houses and old churches do not interest me. The hotels there are terrible. I detest the Soviet theatre. Any palace in Italy is superior to the repainted abodes of the Czars. The village huts in the forbidden hinterland are as dismally poor as ever, and the wretched peasant flogs his wretched carthorse with the same wretched zest. As to my special northern landscape and the haunts of my childhood, well, I would not wish to spoil their images in my mind.

**JM:** How would you define your alienation from present-day Russia?
**VN:** I loathe and despise dictatorships.

**JM:** You called the revolution there "trite." Why?
**VN:** Because it followed the banal historical pattern of bloodshed, deceit and oppression, because it betrayed the democratic dream, and because all it can promise the Soviet citizen is the material article, secondhand philistine values, imitation of Western foods and gadgets, and, of course, caviar for the decorated general.

**JM:** Why do you live in hotels?
**VN:** It simplifies postal matters, it eliminates the nuisance of private ownership, it confirms me in my favorite habit—the habit of freedom.

**JM:** Did you sit up to watch the Americans land on the Moon? Were you impressed?
**VN:** "Impressed" is not the right word. Treating the soil of the Moon gives one, I imagine—or rather my projected self imagines—the most remarkable romantic thrill ever experienced in the history of discovery. Of course, I rented a television set to watch every moment of their marvelous adventure. That gentle little minuet that, despite their awkward suits, the two men danced with such grace to the tune of lunar gravity was a lovely sight. It was also a moment when a flag means to one more than a flag usually does. I am puzzled and pained by the fact that the English weeklies ignored the absolutely overwhelming excitement of the adventure, the strange, sensual exhilaration of palpating those precious pebbles, and of seeing our marbled globe in the black sky, and of feeling in one's spine the shiver and wonder of it. After all, Englishmen should understand this thrill, they who have been the greatest, the purest explorers. Why then drag in such irrelevant matters as wasted dollars and power politics?

**JM:** You parody the poet W.H. Auden in your novel *Ada*, I think. Why do you think so little of him?
**VN:** I do not parody Mr. Auden anywhere in *Ada*. I'm not sufficiently familiar with his poetry for that. I do know, however, a few of his translations,

and deplore the blunders he so lightheartedly permits himself. Robert Lowell, of course, is the greatest offender.

JM: Tolstoy said, so they say, that life was a "tartine de merde" which one was obliged to eat slowly. Do you agree?
VN: I've never heard that story. The old boy was sometimes rather disgusting, wasn't he? My own life is fresh bread with country butter and Alpine honey.

JM: Could you say how important your wife has been as a collaborator in your work?
VN: No, I could not.

JM: Does having a grown-up son help to make time less intolerable?
VN: My son is exactly half my age now: half-time, with his turn to face the sun. He is an opera singer with a magnificent bass voice.

JM: Which is the worst thing men do?
VN: To stink, to cheat, to torture.

JM: Which is the best?
VN: To be kind, to be proud, to be fearless.

# Nabokov: A Portrait

## Alfred Appel Jr. / 1971

From *The Atlantic Monthly*, September, 1971. © The Estate of Alfred Appel Jr. Reprinted by permission.

*They know that Hamlet and Lear are gay*
*Gaiety transfiguring all that dread.*
*-W.B. Yeats, "Lapis Lazuli"*

"I'm as American as apple pie," said Vladimir Nabokov as we walked through the main lobby of the Palace Hotel in Montreux, Switzerland. "You have a funny accent, Captain," I drawled, imitating Peter Sellers' impersonation of drunken and deranged Quilty being confronted by gun-toting Humbert Humbert in the film version of *Lolita*. Nabokov laughed, a full-bodied, very Russian laugh; his accent, however, is quite English, the language of his nursery and his university. He and his wife Véra have lived in the Montreux Palace since 1960. "Gogol began *Dead Souls* nearby, you know," said Nabokov, "and Tolstoy stayed here and risked his health by chasing chambermaids down these endless halls."

Montreux, says Nabokov, is "a rosy place for our riparian exile." Situated in the eastern corner of Lake Geneva, the little town is quiet save for the tourist season, when its main attraction is Byron's Castle of Chillon. "Our Alp," as Nabokov calls it, is visible from their window. The rococo Palace Hotel, erected in 1835, resembles the grand hotels at which Nabokov's family vacationed during his privileged childhood. There are personal and practical reasons, he says, for their staying there now; his sister, Elena, lives nearby in Geneva; their son, Dmitri, an opera singer, resides in Milan; and one of Nabokov's current works-in-progress, an illustrated history of the butterfly in art, "from Egyptian antiquity to the Renaissance," calls for research trips to various European museums. Montreux is not lonely, however, or without its social life. "There are the crested grebes of Lake Geneva," he says, "and we are always happy to see American intellectuals."

Nabokov's long absence from America is reflected in his work. *Lolita* (1955) and *Pnin* (1957) have American settings, but *Pale Fire* (1962), conceived in the States but completed in Europe, is only partly American in locale, and *Ada* (1969) is a fantasia that only in its final few pages touches ground, in Switzerland. "I can't use a contemporary American setting now," says Nabokov, "because I've lost touch with the slang." It is fitting that the last work he should have completed in America, after twenty years here (1940–1960), was his monumental translation of Pushkin's *Eugene Onegin*. If, as Nabokov says, "the writer's art is his real passport," then *Ada*, the first and only classic of Amerussian literature, makes it more difficult than ever for academic pigeonholers and census-takers to "place" him.

Vladimir Vladimirovich Nabokov was born in St. Petersburg on April 23, 1899, a birthday he shares with William Shakespeare and Shirley Temple, as he likes to point out, thereby defining the polar extremes of the vast areas of knowledge at his disposal as scholar and novelist. Widely read in three languages by the age of seventeen, when he inherited from his uncle a country estate and the equivalent of a few million dollars, Nabokov took with him into exile no legacy, but a mind filled with literature and memories of a loving and "harmonious world of perfect childhood," recreated with eloquence and elegance in his memoir, *Speak, Memory* (1951, revised edition, 1966). His was a truly distinguished as well as aristocratic family, with a long tradition of culture and public service. His father, Vladimir Dmitrievich, was an eminent jurist, the author of several books and thousands of articles, including "The Blood Bath of Kishinev," a famous protest against the 1903 pogrom in which hundreds of Jews were massacred. A leader of the prerevolutionary opposition party and a member of the first imperial parliament (Duma), he moved his family to the Crimea in 1917 (as Minister of Justice in the anti-Soviet government), and two years later, into exile in Berlin. His son noted that occasion with several poems, including one called "Hotel Room":

*Not quite a bed, not quite a bench*
*Wallpaper: a grim yellow*
*A pair of chairs. A squinty looking-glass*
*We enter—my shadow and I.*
*We open with a vibrant sound the window*
*the light's reflection slides down to the ground*
*The night is breathless. Distant dogs*

*with varied barks fracture the stillness*
*Stirless, I stand there at the window,*
*and in the black bowl by the sky*
*glows like a golden drop of honey*
*the mellow moon.*

Written shortly before his twentieth birthday in Sebastopol, "Hotel Metropole, room seven, April 8, 1919, a few days before leaving Russia," the poem provides the foreground frame for an infinite regress of rented rooms.

Nabokov's exile defines a state of mind and spirit and is not simply a matter of his being a so-called "White Russian." The figure of the exile embodies the human condition in our time, and it has become a commonplace to point out how many writers have either chosen this role or been cast literally in it: Joyce, Mann, Toller, Brecht, Beckett, Ionesco, and Russians too numerous to name, for they seem to have had all of modern history with which to contend. Nabokov's cousin and childhood playmate was killed by the Soviets in 1919; his brother died in a German concentration camp in 1945; and his father, age fifty-two, was shot at a political meeting in Berlin in 1922 as he was shielding a speaker from two Russian monarchist assassins. Under Hitler, Vladimir Dmitrievich's killer became chief of the Gestapo's *émigré* section.

The sorrows of exile were infinite: isolation, poverty, despair, disease, early death, suicide, or—if the *émigré* writer survived, languageless in some distant land—silence, obscurity, and the nightmare of nostalgia. "I haf nofing, I haf nofing," wails Pnin, and,

*Beyond the seas where I have lost a scepter,*
*I hear the neighing of my dappled nouns,*
*soft participles coming down the steps,*
*treading on leaves, trailing their rustling gowns*

writes Nabokov in "An Evening of Russian Poetry" (1945), the year he became an American citizen. Only the vulgar persist in believing that Nabokov scorns the Russian Revolution simply because it wiped out his wealth.

Nabokov graduated in 1922 from Trinity College, Cambridge, with a "first-class" (Honors) degree in foreign languages (French and Russian). From 1922 until 1937, except for many summers, he lived in Berlin where he wrote prolifically in Russian—numerous translations, fifty reviews and essays, hundreds of poems, nine plays, forty short stories, and nine novels—almost all under the pseudonym of "V. Sirin," which he adopted in 1920 so as to avoid confusion with his father, in whose newspaper, the liberal *émigré* publication *Rul'* (*The Rudder*), he often published.

One evening on her way back to their apartment, Véra Nabokov witnessed one of the first of the Berlin book-burnings, and the passage of time has not dulled her or her husband's memories. They have not revisited Germany since their return to Europe ten years ago; they cannot forget the crimes, or forgive a criminal, however hapless he may now seem. "It is always the year one," as one of his narrators says. Thus, the vehemence with which Nabokov noted the news coverage describing the return to Hamilton College in 1969 of a famous American poet whose activities as an Axis broadcaster are barely remembered: "That bit about Mr. E. Pound, a venerable mediocrity, making a 'sentimental visit' to his alma mater in Clinton, New York, and being given a standing ovation by the commencement audience—consisting, apparently, of morons and madmen."

Too many readers have taken Nabokov too literally when, in the prefaces issued from his present tower, he says he is not a political writer. He is no ideologue, to be sure, but *Invitation to a Beheading* (1935–1936) and *Bend Sinister* (1947) are in the best sense "political," and Nabokov's detractors should submit themselves to Adam Krug's anguish in *Bend Sinister* when he discovers that the State has murdered his young son by mistake, or the vision in *Pale Fire* of Obscene Gradus, the political assassin, fighting the effects of less-than-fresh *pommes frites* as he rushes to discharge his gun rather than his bowels.

Unable to obtain an academic job in England, which he visited during the winter of 1939, Nabokov, his wife and son, Dmitri, emigrated to America in May, 1940. On the Continent, Nabokov had supported his family by reading his works to Russian *émigré* audiences and by giving lessons in tennis and English. There was less demand for such services in America. During his first year here he wrote reviews on Russian subjects and received modest grants. The summer of 1940 was spent at the Vermont summer home of an old friend, Mikhail Karpovich, a professor at Harvard. One day at Karpovich's, the mail produced an invitation to contribute to the *New Republic*. The letter was signed by someone named Edmund Wilson, who also enclosed a copy of a book he had just published, *To the Finland Station*, thereby inaugurating a friendship that would last some twenty-five years. At about the same time, a telegram arrived from the Tolstoy Committee (an organization that, among other things, helped *émigrés* to resettle), advising Nabokov to return immediately to New York City; a job had been found for him in

publishing. Nabokov hurried back to the city. The Tolstoy Committee's secretary told him to present himself at the main desk of Scribner's Bookshop,
which is located below their editorial offices on Fifth Avenue. "And stand
up straight," she added, "you'll make a better impression." At Scribner's he
was received by a man named Wraden, whom he had known in Europe, and
who was somewhat nonplussed to see who had been sent over, since the
job opening was for a delivery boy on a bicycle. When young Dmitri regis-
tered at school, he wrote "tennis coach" in the blank space above "father's
occupation."

Nabokov's vocational identity was firmer by 1941. That summer he taught
Russian literature and a creative writing course at Stanford University, and
in the fall began teaching Russian grammar and literature at Wellesley College. The salary was in the neighborhood of two thousand dollars. "Not bad
for a beginning boy of forty-one," he says today, smiling slyly. There were
other upward turns. *The Real Life of Sebastian Knight*, which he had written
in English in Paris, was "bought for $150 in 1941 by New Directions." Lucie
Leon had gone over the manuscript in Paris; and now, still concerned with
what he calls "the fragility of my English at the time of my abandoning Russian in 1939," Nabokov "begged the late Agnes Perkins, the admirable head
of the English department at Wellesley, to assist me in reading the galley's
of the book." It was published just a few days after Pearl Harbor and did not
eclipse *The Song of Bernadette*, *The Robe*, or any of the other timely bestsell-
ers of the moment.

*The Real Life of Sebastian Knight* was not his first publication in English.
Gleb Struve, the *émigré* critic and scholar, had placed translations of Nabokov stories in *This Quartet*, an English-language little magazine based in
Montparnasse (1932), and in *Lovat Dickson's Magazine* in England (1934—
the misspelled byline read "V. Nabokov-Sirin"). An offer of further Nabokov
stories was rebuffed by a famous "liberal" magazine in London because it
was against their policy, during the worst years of Stalin's reign of terror,
to publish those reactionary "White Russians." Encouraged by the English
publication in 1936 of Winifred Roy's translation of *Laughter in the Dark*
(1932), Nabokov himself translated *Despair* (1934) at the end of 1936, and it
appeared in London the next year. "This was my first serious attempt," he
says, "to use English for what may be loosely termed an artistic purpose." It
sold badly, however, and the entire publisher's stock was destroyed by German bombs in 1940.

Publication in America continued to elude Nabokov. After Ivan Bunin
won the Nobel Prize for Literature in 1933, H.L. Mencken asked Albert

Parry (now chairman of the Russian department at Case-Western Reserve University) if there were any other *émigré* writers who deserved an American audience, and if he would write a piece on them for Mencken's *American Mercury*. Parry said there were, and his article, which also focused on Mark Aldanov and Nina Berberova, represents the first mention of Nabokov in America. It prompted the following letter to Parry from Slovo, the *émigré* publishing house in Berlin (dated September 1, 1933):

> *Dear Sir,*
> *We have had the pleasure of reading your fine article—"Belles-lettres among the Russian Émigrés"—in the July issue of the* American Mercury.
> *We are the publishers of Mr. Sirin's works and in this capacity highly appreciate your recognizing that author's great merits. You are right in supposing that Mr. Sirin's brilliant novels and short stories (with the only exception of one short story published in* The Quarter) *have not yet been translated either in America or in England. We should be very much obliged to you for any suggestion or advice you should care to give in regard to the chance of Mr. Sirin's works finding a publisher in America.*
> *We hope that you will kindly give your attention to this matter, and remain, dear, Sir,*
> > *Yours faithfully*
> > (*signed*)

Alfred A. Knopf, Bunin's publisher, saw Parry's article and invited him to his office to discuss Sirin, but nothing came of it; the economic realities of the Depression did not encourage Knopf to introduce another foreign author. But in 1938, Bobbs-Merrill published Miss Roy's rather flat translation of *Laughter in the Dark*, revised anew by the novelist, who at the time transliterated his name as "Nabokoff." While he was still living in Paris he also made his debut in an American magazine, the December, 1939, *Esquire*, wherein appeared Sirin's "The Potato Elf," a dark and haunting tale about a dwarf, quite out of place in a gala Christmas issue.

*Sebastian Knight* and *Laughter in the Dark* each had its American admirers, but only after "Hurricane Lolita" (to quote *Pale Fire*) did Nabokov's eight other Russian novels begin to appear here in English translations. In the mid-nineteen-forties, one of Dmitri's teachers asked him who his favorite Russian writers were. "Pushkin and my father," he answered, a piquant enough response, given the sudden disappearance of Sirin and the scant evidence in America that he had ever existed.

In addition to *The Real Life of Sebastian Knight*, 1941 saw the publication also of "Cloud, Castle, Lake" and "The Aurelian" in *The Atlantic Monthly*. Translations of short stories from the thirties, they were only the first of seven stories, both old and new, which Nabokov would contribute to that magazine in the forties; they made him visible. A novel, of course, is on its own, for better or worse, and *The Real Life of Sebastian Knight* and his next novel, *Bend Sinister* (1947), turned out to be lonely creatures indeed. *The Atlantic*, however, provided Nabokov with a body of readers large enough to call an audience, and these stories in turn formed the main content of *Nine Stories* (1947).

That first American audience included Professor Morris Bishop of Cornell University, who in 1947 found himself chairman of a committee searching for a new professor of Russian literature. Bishop sought out Nabokov, even though the latter had neither advanced degrees nor, worse yet, a record of academic publications. Nabokov liked Wellesley, especially since its proximity to Cambridge allowed him to work on Lepidoptera many hours every day (including Sundays) at the Harvard Museum of Comparative Zoology, but after seven years he still did not have tenure. He was invited to Cornell to present a paper and endure the customary "looking over," and shortly afterwards, in 1948, was offered an associate professorship, which he accepted—"though at heart," says Nabokov, "I have always remained a lean visiting lecturer."

The Bishops remember how Nabokov, seated in their living room before giving the paper, suddenly clasped his coat against his chest to see if his folded lecture was there, a heart-arresting gesture sufficiently reminiscent of Nabokov's own creation, the myopic and addlepated Professor Pnin. Lecturer Nabokov had his share of Pninian experiences. One letter of invitation from a department chairman was signed "Vladimir Nabokov." Only four people showed up for the resulting lecture; "I forgot to advertise," said the chairman, a genius of absentmindedness. As Nabokov began to speak, half of the audience, a mother and son, got up and left. They were in the wrong room. "Vladimir Vladimirovich, we are all Pnins," said an *émigré* colleague in the history department as they were walking across the snowbound Cornell campus shortly after one of the *Pnin* chapters had appeared in *The New Yorker*. "You know, he'd forgotten I'd written it," says Nabokov, fifteen years later, his disbelief firmly intact. But Nabokov is not Pnin. He did not take the wrong train to Cornell or arrive at the Bishops' a week too early, and the folded pages were in their place, as Morris Bishop fondly recalls.

Nabokov is one with Pnin, however, in his abhorrence of Soviet totalitarianism and "the philistine essence of Leninism." The decision to leave Wellesley had been hastened by the person in high authority there who had suggested to Nabokov that he tone down his classroom criticism of Soviet writers. "They are our allies, you know." Of the writers he met in this country, only Robert Frost seemed to share his opinion of Communism, but their fleeting political kinship was neutralized for Nabokov when Frost was gratuitously and excessively rude to their kind host. "My main regret," says Nabokov, is "that I didn't emigrate earlier to America." If he had lived in New York City in the thirties he might have offered "free lessons to pro-Soviet boosters." After receiving Edmund Wilson's presentation copy of *To The Finland Station*, Nabokov sent him an errata and a critique, which insisted, among other things, that the oft-repeated story about Lenin sparing a fox's life was both apocryphal and symbolically meaningless, considering certain facts and statistics.

Nabokov and Wilson met often thereafter, particularly in the forties, and exchanged "frank letters" for years. Wilson was kind in many ways, some of them professional—a long blurb for *Sebastian Knight*, a publisher for *Bend Sinister*—while Nabokov quietly aided and abetted Wilson backstage in his long struggle with the Russian language.

It would not be cheap or easy psychologizing to suggest that Wilson's famous 1965 assault on his old friend's *Eugene Onegin* translation was a monumental self-assertion dating back to their preceptorials in Russian. Wilson nevertheless sent the Nabokovs his customary Christmas card that year, enclosing a little wind-up paper butterfly. "It didn't work," complains Nabokov. "'Made in Japan.'"

Politics and pedagogy converge in Nabokov's view of the "student revolution." Lamenting the conformity of "group beards and group protests," he says that "rowdies are never true revolutionaries." Nabokov would be unhappy on today's campuses for more than one reason. "After all," he notes, "my method of teaching precluded genuine contact with my students," and it is, of course, that kind of contact which many students now demand.

Although Nabokov gave some seminars at Cornell—in Pushkin, for example—the subject matter and the catalogue description ("Prerequisite, proficiency in Russian") led no one to expect a rap session. Nabokov's other courses were conducted as lectures, even if the enrollment was modest, as in his survey of Russian literature. Few of his pre-*Lolita* students knew he was a writer. He was an immensely popular teacher, however, particularly in his Literature 311–312 course, "Masterpieces of European Fiction." The course was unique in the smallest of ways (witness the "bonus system" employed in examinations, allowing students two extra points per effort whenever they could garnish an answer with a substantial and accurate quotation—"a gem"—drawn from the text in question).

Carefully handwritten and then typed out, an artist-scientist's anatomical examination of the books he admired and adored, Nabokov's lectures ranged widely and wildly in mood, from the most moving to the most farcical of moments. "You cannot understand a writer if you cannot pronounce his name," he would say, introducing Gogol ("Gaw-gol, not Go-gal!"). He would then rehearse Gogol's death agonies, his head thrown back in pain and terror, nostrils distended, eyes shut, his beseechments filling the hushed lecture hall. Urging his students to become "creative readers," he would ask them to develop "the passion of the scientist and the precision of the artist"—double takes on the part of note-takers; didn't he mean the opposite?—and, digressing for the minute, Nabokov would toss brickbats at "Old Dusty" or "the Viennese quack," eliciting from the gallery as many gasps as laughs. He would conclude a lecture with a rhapsodic apostrophe to our writer's style: "Feel it in your spine; let us worship the spine—the upper spine, the vertebrate tipped at the head with a divine flame!" And then, as the hour ended, he would ask to see the students who had occupied seats 102 and 103 during the recent midterm examination: "I suspect mental telepathy!"

"My assistant," he always called her, with a decorous, businesslike impersonality, but everyone knew she was Véra Nabokov. Depending on the lecture room, she would sit either in the first row or at the end of the platform, her cool, steady gaze taking in the audience, one by one, it seemed. "My assistant has forgotten one label on the diagram . . . oh, it is a very important label," he said one day, rushing to the blackboard and picking up a piece of chalk. It was the only time anyone had seen her smile in class, even at one of his jokes, or, rather, *especially* at one of those jokes, since most of his funniest "asides" were in script, and, an experienced trouper, she had heard it all before, many times, and had no doubt typed it up. A woman of great dignity and natural elegance, Véra Nabokov has been a totally devoted collaborator, handling her husband's correspondence and business transactions, driving the car, grading thousands of examination papers, and running the household, such as it was. Fiercely intelligent, she is at once his ideal reader and only real editor. Since their marriage in Berlin in 1925, he has read to her all of his works at least twice, and she has reread them while typing them; *Ada* was the first manuscript to have been prepared by a professional secretary.

"Véra's Russian is stupendous," he says, and she learned Italian in order to be able to check the translations of his novels into that tongue. She reads widely in several languages and is very much "up" on contemporary American letters. "He has digested his Nabokov," she says of a well-known young novelist, genus Black Humor. "Trash," she says of another. Her memory may be better than her husband's. He does not remember Thomas Pynchon, a student in Literature 311–312, *circa* 1957, nor has he read *V.* ("Lovely title, lovely," says Nabokov), but she quickly responds, "Yes, I remember him, he had an unusual handwriting: half printing, half script." Nor is Véra Nabokov too shy to disagree with her husband, and their games of Scrabble (in English, and "Skrebl" in Russian) have the aura of an infinite series of good-natured rematches between Dempsey and Tunney. Inseparable, self-sufficient, they form a multitude of two.

Although he taught at major institutions, published in *Partisan Review* as well as *The New Yorker*, and had friends such as Edmund Wilson and Harvard's Harry Levin, Nabokov remained through his years at Cornell aloof from "literary circles" and naively unaware of their existence. One summer in the forties he taught at a writer's conference at the University of Salt Lake City. He remembers that the faculty included Wallace Stegner, Oscar Williams, and another man. "I don't remember his name," he says. "White-haired, eyeglasses, he wore a conservative suit and looked like a banker, yet wrote some extraordinary verse: 'Bells . . . Bells'—not Poe!—'Bells for John Whiteside's Daughter,' I liked particularly." The mystery faculty member was John Crowe Ransom, at that time one of the two or three most influential poet-critics in America and editor of the *Kenyon Review*. A well-known younger poet of that period who died in middle age sat next to Nabokov on a bus trip after they had both given readings. "He didn't want to talk about poetry," says Nabokov. "Only about the reputations of other poets." Nabokov also remembers how a distinguished professor of English at Cornell cut short a budding literary discussion at a cocktail party: "It's after five; no shop talk!" Nabokov laughs. "A strange man," he adds. But it is with no bemusement that he recalls the expert in linguistics who could not speak the language of the department he chaired, a phenomenon preserved in the pages of *Pnin*. Many of the most fantastic and grotesque perversions of learning in *Pnin* happen to be drawn from "real life" in the academy; it is the only novel he has ever written that bears the disclaimer, "All of the characters in this book are fictitious, and any resemblance to actual persons, living or dead, is purely coincidental."

Never once during his almost twenty years on campus did Nabokov write an academic article or attend a meeting of the Modern Language Association, but he did contribute continually to *Psyche* and other lepidopterological journals, and occasionally participated in scientific meetings. Once, at the American Museum of Natural History in New York where several of Nabokov's specimens are deposited, he met a rather stuffy old gentleman, a banker or businessman, who told Nabokov that he had recently caught a unique butterfly. As Nabokov recreates the scene in the museum, the man, eyes aglow, reached into his vest pocket and produced a little tin specimen box. He opened the box and, playing it close to the vest in the most literal sense of that cliché, he held it in his cupped palm, against his ample stomach, like a vendor of pornographic postcards in front of a church or school yard. Nabokov mimes his manner, and impersonating himself, leans over to see the proffered butterfly. Stolid and staid, the old gentleman had also experienced the quiet rapture of discovering an undescribed species, and like a long line of Nabokov's fictional creations, from Luzhin in *The Defense* to Humbert in *Lolita*, he too had pursued a secret life, an ardent desire, an obsessive quest.

Nabokov went butterfly-hunting every summer, and these adventures as a "lepist" carried him through two hundred motel rooms in forty-six states, along the same roads traveled by Humbert and Lolita. Though he had tenure at Cornell, the Nabokovs continued to rent, moving every year, sometimes every term—a mobility he bestowed on refugee Humbert. Morris Bishop, Nabokov's only close friend at Cornell, remembers visiting them after they had moved into the tastelessly furnished home of an absent professor. "I couldn't have lived in a place like that," says Bishop, "but it delighted him. He seemed to relish every awful detail." In a few years Bishop realized that these moves were a form of field research enabling Nabokov to study the natural habitat of Humbert's prey. *Lolita* was under way.

Nabokov usually has at least two works-in-progress at roughly the same time, and these literary companions often turn out to complement each other in extraordinary ways; this is most true of *Lolita* and *Speak, Memory* (or *Conclusive Evidence*, as its first, shorter edition was titled in 1951.)

In *Speak, Memory*, his fifth book in English, Nabokov became the master of a variegated and virtuoso prose; henceforth he would seek no further advice on English. *Speak, Memory* released him to write *Lolita*, and *Lolita* in her turn released him from the circumscribing spell of *Speak, Memory*, the cul-de-sac of nostalgia. It is no coincidence that after losing Lolita to

Quilty, it takes Humbert three years to find her again, the same number of years Nabokov spent writing *Speak, Memory*. "The past is the past," she tells him, after he has finally located but not recaptured his ineffable girl, now wan, veiny-armed, pregnant, a nymphet no more and badly in need of a few bucks.

The novel developed slowly as Nabokov faced technical problems and absorbed the necessary *couleur locale*—as Humbert might say—by renting Charlotte Haze's house, sampling teen-talk on school buses, reading case studies and movie magazines, observing, observing, wherever he went. Robert M. Adams, then in the English department at Cornell ("Ah, a duel!" Nabokov had exclaimed, when Adams appeared at the departmental office one morning with his newly broken arm in a sling), remembers a Monday morning in June, *circa* 1951, during the calm between commencement and summer session. A convocation of a youth group was to begin that day—the Young Lutherans or Future Farmers of America—and as Adams approached the wide bridge that separates the campus from the main dormitory area, he saw heading toward him, on the left side of the bridge, radiating the healthiness of a breakfast food ad, a seemingly endless swarm of blond and apple-cheeked junior-and senior-high-schoolers, and on the other side, walking alone in the opposite direction, his gaze taking them in, a man wearing hiking shoes, knee socks, baggy Bermuda shorts, a sporty cap, and carrying a butterfly net. As it crossed the bridge, the Norman Rockwell *tableau vivant* turned as one to stare in astonishment at *him*, since Nabokov was no doubt the first typical American college professor they had ever seen.

Written before class in Ithaca, or in a parked car on cloudy Colorado afternoons while butterflies slept, or at night in a motel after a long day of "lepping," *Lolita* was finally completed in the spring of 1954, surely no placid period for the Nabokovs. Back in 1950, when he had been discouraged, Véra Nabokov had prevented her husband from throwing the initial chapters into the garden incinerator, but now that the book was a reality she must have experienced some misgivings and anxieties about its publication and possible reception; even tenured professors are vulnerable. "But she had no doubts about *Lolita*," says Mrs. Bishop; "she knew it would be a classic." Véra Nabokov was absent from lecture the last two weeks of the term (typing the manuscript, no doubt), and one day Nabokov startled the class by appearing without tie or jacket, in old tennis shoes, clearly a distracted man. One friend urged Nabokov to issue the novel anonymously; another refused to publish it for fear that they'd both be imprisoned. With no fanfare whatsoever, the Paris-based Olympia Press brought out *Lolita* in 1955. Three years later it was published in America.

"A painful birth, a difficult baby, but a kind daughter," *Lolita* enabled Nabokov, at sixty, to resign his professorship. Part of the fortune lost in 1919 had been restored exactly forty years later, the rubles miraculously converted to dollars, and the Nabokovs soon moved again, first to Hollywood to script *Lolita*, and then to Switzerland in 1960.

Fifty years of renting furnished quarters has made Nabokov, along with Samuel Beckett, a laureate of the lonely room. He has learned to travel light, and his ambience at the Montreux Palace sustains this sense of him. The Palace is a grand hotel in the old tradition, with wide, spacious salons and lovely gardens, but there is nothing opulent about the Nabokov's apartment on the sixth floor, overlooking Lake Geneva. The living room, where they receive guests, is small, as are the other rooms. There is no TV; they rent a set for important events such as the moon landing and the World Cup soccer championship (Nabokov, who played goalie at Cambridge, notes that Brazil's spectacular player, Pele, "is powerful but has no style"). A card table next to the couch is stacked with books of recent vintage—mostly sent by publishers—which they are sampling and, in a few instances, reading. Nabokov recommends *The Godbotherers*, a novel by Philip Oakes, an Englishman, and is even more enthusiastic about *The Butterflies of Japan*. Paul McCartney, whom he has never met, has sent them his latest record album, the presentation note signed, "With love, Paul and Linda." A still life recently painted by Dmitri, his son's first try at oils, adds a genuine personal touch to the wall above the couch. Nabokov's study, in the next room, contains a lectern, a desk and chair, and a bed. Although he prefers to write standing up, he may use any of the three, depending on the hour and the pull of gravity. The walls are bare, but arranged along the top of the desk are a little family photograph, a framed butterfly, and postcard reproductions of a Picasso still life, *Pitcher, Candle, and Casserole*, and Fra Angelico's *Annunciation*, the radiant rainbow wings of the angel Gabriel easily outshining those of the framed specimen. A conspicuous presence in the room is a multivolume Russian dictionary and a well-worn *Webster's Unabridged*, second edition. Except for the back bedroom, which their part-time secretary has converted into an office, the Nabokov's apartment gives the impression that they could be packed and ready to leave on the shortest notice.

Nabokov rises at six A.M. and, armed with the discoveries of creative insomnia, begins to write immediately; *Transparent Things* is the title of the novel now in its early stages. By ten thirty, when he draws a hot bath, Nabokov has put in what many writers would call a full day's work. The fair-weather schedule he was following during my most recent visit (August, 1970) would next find him, at around eleven o'clock, walking down to the Montreux station to buy his three daily newspapers, *The Times* of London, *Le Monde*, and the Paris *Herald-Tribune*, where he follows, with determined loyalty and attention, the open-ended comic-strip adventures of Buzz Sawyer and Rex Morgan, M.D. Returning along the lakeside, Nabokov comments on its flora, fauna, and filth; Lake Geneva has not been immune to the waste that has so befouled America. "I saw it coming in the States twenty years ago, and would tell people that," says Nabokov, shaking his head, then deploring "the faddist aspects of the antipollution movement." He points out a ginkgo tree he is very fond of, and pauses to examine the venation of one of its butterfly-like leaves (a small wonder also marked in *Pale Fire*, note to line 49). Further on, he stops to watch some swans. "An overrated bird," he says, "the postures of its neck are grotesque, aesthetically absurd, and," he adds, "how can you respect or trust a creature that goes about with such a dirty neck?"

After lunch, there is coffee and conversation in the Nabokovs' apartment: the butterfly in art, the prosody of prose (Bely and Melville), the art of Keaton, Chaplin, the Marx Brothers, and his favorites, Laurel and Hardy. That subject leads logically to Nabokov's experiences in Hollywood while scripting *Lolita*: excellent "lepping" in the Hollywood hills and stimulating discussions with the film's producer, who wanted Humbert to marry Lolita, a small compromise Nabokov was unwilling to make.

The conversation turns to cannibalism. "It is not as uncommon as you'd think," Nabokov says, recalling a Belgian poet he had known in the nineteen-thirties. The poet's father had been a stationmaster. One day a terrible accident had severed a man's leg, and the poet, then a very young man, had helped himself to the limb, "prepared and waiting on the track."

"I never believed that story," says Véra Nabokov, with a tolerant smile.

"It happened, it happened!" insists her husband. "I couldn't make up such a story."

"I like people who have the gift of gab," says Nabokov, generalizing. "I mean 'good conversationalists,'" he adds, correcting himself, not wishing to hurt the feelings of anyone present. Nabokov clearly relishes good gab; gossip, anecdotes, and jokes pour forth from him, and he is one of those people whose laughter threatens to unseat them. To emphasize a point or underscore a punch line, he will often lower his head, wrinkle his brow, and peer over the top of his eyeglasses, a parody of a professor. His face, even at less animated moments, is very expressive, mobile; photographs reveal its protean qualities. "I've frequently been told I don't look like me," he says, pausing for a moment to enjoy the paradox. "Recently, a stranger, a tourist, approached me in the [hotel] garden, and said, 'I know you! You're . . . you're . . . *you're General MacArthur's brother!*'" Nabokov shakes with mirth, and dabs his eyes with a handkerchief, and catches his empty coffee cup and saucer as they are about to topple from his lap.

By three in the afternoon Nabokov retires for a rest and more work: the polishing of Dmitri's rendering into English of *Podvig* (1931)—*The Exploit*, now retitled *Glory*—the last of his untranslated Russian novels (Nabokov was delighted to find a forgotten passage in which the reverie of his fanta-sizing hero seems to anticipate Thurber's "The Secret Life of Walter Mitty," a story much admired by Nabokov). Then drinks and dinner, and more con-versation. Close students of the artist's metabolic patterns should note that Nabokov usually goes to bed by nine o'clock.

When Nabokov doesn't have visitors, he may spend the early afternoon reading in the hotel's poolside garden (always keeping notepaper by his side in case the Muse speaks unexpectedly), or else take long walks, sometimes for three or four hours, doing a lot of work in his head. In the spring, when the butterfly hunting is best, Nabokov may walk (and run) as many as fif-teen or twenty miles a day. It is not surprising that he is deeply tanned, firmly muscled, and looks considerably younger than his seventy-two years. Watching him kick around a soccer ball with Raffaello, one of the hotel's cabana boys, underscores the connection between his penchant for exercise and the enormous enthusiasm and creative energy which have resulted in, among many other things, three major works since his sixty-third birthday (*Pale Fire*, the four-volume *Onegin* translation, and *Ada*).

Wordplay is very much part of Nabokov's personal manner. He has a habit of repeating a phrase that he has just spoken, of spearing a word in midair and toying with the pieces. "No, tape recorders are out," he says. "No speaking off the Nabocuff. When I see one of those machines I start hemming and hawing . . . hemming and hawing. Hemingwaying all over the place."

When reviewers use the tag "Nabokovian," they are acknowledging that he is that rarest of artists—a man and a writer who discovers, defines, and expresses himself and his world in a voice that is consistently and uniquely his. Nabokov's voice is most vibrant and identifiable when he is describ-ing either his "passion for lepidopterological research" or his abhorrence of certain writers. "Had there been no Russian Revolution, I probably would have devoted myself solely to lepidopterology," says Nabokov, whose aesthetic of objectivity and precision is clearly that of a naturalist: "The use of symbols [is] hateful because it substitutes a dead general idea for a live specific impression . . . In high art and pure science detail is everything." His statements go far in helping to place in a quite reasonable context his remarks on other writers, remarks which are variously thought to be arrogant, eccentric, outrageous, indefensible, funny but frivolous. The zest with which he exorcises "bogeys and shams from the hall of false fame" and the verbs he favors ("detest," "loathe") are bound to set sensitive teeth on edge, while his inscrutable dismissals of famous works (*Death in Venice* is "asinine") rarely clarify his objections to them, or suggest the seriousness and consistency of his position or its source in the literary wars of Russia a hundred years ago. In the eighteen-sixties and-seventies, Nikolay Chernyshevsky and other influential radical polemicists insisted that literary artists be topical reporters and social commentators, and the proselytizing, ideological, and sociological nature of much nineteenth century Russian literature testifies to their success. Pushkin and Chekhov were attacked for their failure to be "relevant" and *engage* (to use today's trite terms), as Sirin would be in the nineteen-thirties, and today's Socialist Realism is the police state's transmutation of those earlier criteria and supposedly progressive principles. Beleaguered or not, Solzhenitsyn is in the main tradition of Russian literature, and the ironies are, of course, tragic.

When the first chapters of *The Defense* came out in 1929 in the leading *émigré* journal, the Paris-based *Sovremennye zapiski* (*Contemporary Annals*), Nina Berberova knew that "a great Russian writer, like a phoenix [had been] born from the fire and ashes of revolution and exile. Our existence from now on acquired a meaning. All my generation were justified. We were saved," she writes in her recent memoir (*The Italics are Mine*). She was not alone in her estimation of Nabokov, but a number of other *émigré* critics vilified him for being "un-Russian" in his concerns. So taken for granted were these assumptions about the writer's social responsibilities that the liberal editors of *Sovremennye zapiski*, not wishing to offend their readers, refused in 1937 to publish Nabokov's satirical biography of Chernyshevsky, now intact as Chapter Four of *The Gift*, which they were then in the process of serializing.

Living in Switzerland, writing in English, Nabokov is never more Russian than when offering to journalists and interviewers those seemingly fripperous remarks about writers he deems short on style and/or long on argument

and advice. Those remarks, hardly random, enable him to sustain his miraculous open-ended debate with Chernyshevsky, thereby fulfilling his own
polemical responsibilities as the embodiment of the other great Russian tradition: Pushkin, Chekhov, and the Tolstoy who wrote *Anna Karenina*, or at
least most of it. "Skip the hymn to the wheat," Nabokov would instruct his
students, referring to Tolstoy's Populist attitudes and Levin's day in the field.

Contrary to rumor, Nabokov is not totally ungenerous and has praised
in print many writers, from Shakespeare to Sirin. Of the famous moderns,
he most admires Joyce, Proust, Kafka, and H. G. Wells, his favorite boyhood
author. When Nabokov mentions his continued esteem for Wells, especially
his "romances"—*The Time Machine, The Invisible Man, The War of the
Worlds*—I ask him about Chapter Three of *Ada*, where he describes Aqua
Veen's private "War of the Worlds," and, in a haunting passage, her howling
disintegration. Did he have in mind, I wondered, the final pages of Wells's
fantasia, when the silence of devastated and darkened London is disturbed
by the terrible last lamentations of those mammoth invaders from Mars,
toppled by lowly bacteria?

"Yes," says Nabokov, "I can still hear those creatures," and the expression on his face and the tone of his voice remind me of two moments during other visits to Montreux. Late one afternoon in January, 1968, our conversation had turned to the dark days of the mid-nineteen-thirties, when
the Nabokovs were planning their permanent departure from Germany.
Because Véra Nabokov is Jewish, a future there seemed even more uncertain. Nabokov recalled Ivan Bunin's visit to Berlin in 1934. The most famous
of the *émigré* writers, Bunin had recently received the Nobel Prize and was
making a kind of triumphal tour. Nabokov attended the public ceremony
in Bunin's honor, and a few days later lunched with him at a Berlin restaurant. They were seated, Nabokov remembers, at the rear of a crowded room,
beneath a huge Nazi flag. When they met again shortly afterwards, in Paris,
Bunin told Nabokov and several others how on his departure from Berlin
he had been stopped by the Gestapo, ever on the alert for that most stable
of *émigré* commodities, a smuggled jewel or two. The handsome and erect
old gentleman was interrogated, searched, stripped, and searched again. An
empty bucket was placed behind the Nobel Laureate, who was then given a
strong and immensely successful dose of castor oil. The search of the naked
man was completed by the Gestapo agent who wiped him. As Nabokov finished the story, his forehead twisted into a tangle of lines, and he stared,
unblinking, at a point considerably distant from this small, nondescript
room in a Swiss hotel.

Late in the last evening of my September, 1966, visit we were talking about Soviet writers. Nabokov spoke contemptuously of "the literary double agents," "The party hacks," "The purveyors of works-to-order." Were there any writers of the Soviet period whom he admired? Yes, there were, and Nabokov spoke of several, concluding with Sinyavsky and Daniel, pacing back and forth across the living room as he talked, clasping and unclasping his hands behind his back as he summarized their strategems for survival. "All these people were enormously gifted," he said, softly, "but the regime finally caught up with them and they disappeared, one by one, in nameless camps." His voice trailed off, and for the first time he looked his age. It was eleven o'clock; late indeed for an early riser and insomniac who usually retires by nine. He stood by the open doorway of his small balcony; it was warm and muggy, the darkness over Lake Geneva was softened by a heavy mist, and he was the last free Russian writer.

"By the way, do you know how a dung beetle lays its eggs?" he asked, moments later, picking up an unresolved thread of conversation from earlier in the evening, when he had entomologically identified Kafka's metamorphosed Gregor Samsa. Since I had to confess that I did not know how a dung beetle laid its eggs, Nabokov imitated the process as best he could, bending his head toward his waist as he slowly walked away from the darkened doorway, making a dung-rolling motion with his hands until his head was buried in them and the eggs were laid.

*Laughter in the Dark* is clearly a resonant title. That it embodies the ample spirit of the man as well as his work is best illustrated for me by an incident at Cornell in 1953, when I was one of thirty or so students enrolled in Nabokov's Russian literature course. The class was held at the end of a long, dimly lit corridor in the basement of Goldwin Smith Hall. I was rushing to class one wintry morning, three or four minutes late, but slackened my stride when I noticed that Professor Nabokov was also late, and walking ahead of me halfway down the hall. He hurried into a classroom, and my heart sank as I realized it was one door too soon. I entered the class to find Nabokov several sentences into his lecture; not wanting to waste another minute, he was stooped over his notes, intently reading them to thirty stunned students, a shell-shocked platoon belonging to an even tardier don. Trying to be as transparent as possible, I approached the lectern and touched Nabokov on the sleeve. He turned and peered down at me over his eyeglasses, amazed. "Mr. Nabokov," I said very quietly, "you are in the wrong classroom." He readjusted his glasses on his nose, focused his gaze on the motionless figures seated before him, and calmly announced, "You

have just seen the 'Coming Attraction' for Literature 325. If you are interested, you may register next fall." Pnin no more, he closed his folder of notes
and moved one door down the hall. "A most extraordinary thing just happened, most extraordinary," he told the students of Literature 325, chuckling
to himself as he opened his folder once more and, not bothering to explain
what had happened, began to lecture.

# Understanding Vladimir Nabokov— A Red Autumn Leaf is a Red Autumn Leaf, Not a Deflowered Nymphet

## Alan Levy / 1971

From *The New York Times*, October 31, 1971. © The Estate of Alan Levy.
Reprinted by permission.

In the glassed-in greenhouse that lobbies for the Edwardian rococo Palace Hotel, a dozen Trumanesque tourists and their plum-pudding ladies are worrying one another about the weather—asking anxiously whether it will hold for their air-conditioned sightseeing excursion. Right in their midst, but clearly not part of them, a professional old gent is exulting: "It's been a wonderful summer for butterflies! Generally, their emergences are staggered. But this year, May and June were such bad months that the butterflies just waited—and then they all came out together!"

His enthusiasm cuts through the querulousness around him, and strangers eavesdrop. The most distinguished permanent resident of the Montreux Palace, Vladimir Nabokov, the author of *Lolita* and *Ada*, stands out in that crowd of transients not only because he is, at seventy-two, slightly older yet much sprier than the tour, but also because he dresses more like a tourist than the tourists: windbreaker over gold button-down sport shirt tucked into gray pin-striped shorts meshing with sun-textured freckled knees. Add to all this the gold-handled butterfly net (from an "entomological-instruments store on 33d Street") in his right hand, and the effect is septuagenarian Hulot—stooped a little by age, but the better to lean into the butterfly hunt that is looming. Now Hulot dons a white cap, and—*voila!*—instant Magoo!

The old magician tells stories, too, in a hale and hearty hiker's voice. My admiration for his "entomological instrument" elicits the tale of a lavishly equipped, heavily laden photographer who descended upon Nabokov recently: "I was curious about all the technology he carried, so he opened up his fancy camera case for me and there was his trouser belt! 'I've been looking for it all morning,' the man said, putting it on right then and there."

"Freud would have a field day with that," I remark. Nabokov (Na-BOA-koff) can be expected to snap at the bait, for he has penned and punned so vehemently and so often against "the Viennese witchdoctor," "quack" and "charlatan," against "Freudian voodooism" and "the lewd, ludicrous and vulgar . . . Signy-Mondieu analysts." Having vented his contempt (which, one recognizes from reading him, is based on a thorough familiarity with Freud), Nabokov can now afford to reply benignly: "A Freudian can have a field day with any object at hand." To demonstrate, in the public rooms of the Montreux Palace, Nabokov deftly manipulates his butterfly net like an outstretched umbrella, and it suddenly balloons to its full thirty-six inches. One of the Bess Truman ladies giggles, gasps, clucks and asks: "Who is that man? He's not one of *us*, is he?"

The Soviet Union's Short Literary Encyclopedia (Vol. V, 1968) answers the lady's question rather objectively—so much so, in fact, that the whole volume has been officially attacked for "objectivism." It says:

"Vladimir Vladimirovich Nabokov (1899-      )—Russian-American writer. Son of V. D. Nabokov, a leader of the Kadet Party. Finished the Tenishev School. Published his first collection of poetry in 1916. From 1919 he has been in emigration, where in 1922 he finished Trinity College (Cambridge). He achieved literary recognition after the publication of the novel *Mary* in 1926. N.'s works bear an extremely contradictory character. Among his most interesting works are the . . . long story *The Defense* (1929–30), which depicts the life tragedy of a phenomenal chess player, the novels *Laughter in the Dark* (1932–33), *Despair* (1934 . . . ), the stories . . . which reflect the process of spiritual bestialization of the *bourgeoisie* in Germany as it was becoming Fascist. In the novel, *The Gift* (1937 . . . ) N. presents a tendentiously distorted picture of N. G. Chernyshevsky. N.'s books are characterized by literary snobbism, replete with literary reminiscences. His style is marked by excessively refined 'estrangement' of devices and the frequent use of mystification. These same features are also characteristic of his lyrics. In N.'s prose the influence of F. Kafka and M. Proust can be felt; such as the novel *Invitation to a Beheading* (1935–36 . . . ) in which N. describes the nightmarish existence of a little man surrounded by the monstrous phantasms of the contemporary world. Such are the features which made possible the 'denationalization' of the work of N.—who in 1940 began to write in English. Since that time he has lived in the U.S.A., where for some time he taught literature in universities. Among his books of this period are

. . . the erotic bestseller *Lolita* (1955), the novel *Pnin* (1957). He translates Russian classical poetry into English. In 1964 he published a translation of A.S. Pushkin's *Eugene Onegin* in four volumes with extensive commentaries."

Aside from overlooking Nabokov's return to Europe in 1960, this Soviet listing is as complete as any. But his Russian chronologers take no note of his acclaim by serious critics as the "greatest living American novelist" and "most original writer and stylist since Joyce"; nor do they credit their fellow Slav with adding the improper nouns "nymphet" and "lolita" to the English language. And, for all their adventurousness, they could never begin to depict the *Hotelmensch* whose adult life has been spent camping in motels, cabins, furnished flats, sublet homes of professors on sabbatical; who calls the Montreux Palace "a rosy and opulent place for an exile," and who has never owned a home. "Nothing short of a replica of my childhood surroundings would have satisfied me," he says. "I would never manage to match my memories correctly, so why trouble with hopeless approximations?"

Nabokov is, says Alfred Kazin, a man with "no country but himself. He is the only refugee who could have turned statelessness into absolute strength." And in a 1969 cover story, *Time* magazine proclaimed him "an exile, a man who has triumphantly survived this century of the refugee, a man who has lost everything, yet transformed his losses through art and levity into a habitation of the mind."

Literary detection reveals that, living in Berlin in 1927, Nabokov was still "absolutely sure, with a number of other intelligent people, that sometime in the next decade, we would all be back in a hospitable, remorseful, racemose-blossoming Russia." But, with "the passing of years, I grew less and less interested in Russia and more and more indifferent to the once-harrowing thought that my books would remain banned there as long as my contempt for the police state and political oppression prevented me from entertaining the vaguest thought of return."

Through the late fifties and the sixties, while the Soviets were revising and rewriting their history, Nabokov was busily translating (often with his only child, Dmitri, an opera singer now thirty-seven) his earlier works from their original Russian and revising them. (The latest of these, his first novel, *Mary*, was issued in English last year.)

In his preface to the 1965 English rendition of *Despair*, he wrote:

"The ecstatic love of a young writer for the old writer he will be some day is ambition in its most laudable form. This love is not reciprocated by the older man in his larger library, for even if he does recall with regret a naked palate and a rheumless eye, he has nothing but an impatient shrug for the bungling apprentice of his youth."

No loss of ardor and no witty deceits have mellowed Nabokov's lifelong love for butterflies—a passion that has granted him immortality as the discoverer of finds that "will dwell in generations more numerous than editions." Some of his discoveries have been named after him, and he speaks with rapture of "that blessed black night in the Wasatch Range" when he boxed one of them, now classified as Nabokov's Pug (Eupithecia *nabokovi* McDunnough) "on a picture window of James Laughlin's Alta Lodge in Utah" in 1943.

From 1942 to 1948, while lecturing on literature at Wellesley, Nabokov was also a Harvard Research Fellow in Lepidoptera at the Museum of Comparative Zoology. "To know Nabokov at his best," a mutual friend told me, "is to know him when he's with butterflies." And thus was decreed the climax (though I hope not the end) of my friendship with the inventor of Humbert Humbert and Van Veen, Dolores Haze and Clare Quilty, Timofrey Pnin and Cincinnatus C, and Vivian Darkbloom, who once wrote under a pseudonym:

> "And the highest enjoyment of timelessness—in a landscape selected at random—is when I stand among rare butterflies and their food plants. This is ecstasy, and behind the ecstasy is something else, which is hard to explain. It is like a momentary vacuum into which rushes all that I love. A scene of oneness with sun and stone. A thrill of gratitude to whom it may concern—to the contrapuntal genius of human fate or to tender ghosts humoring a lucky mortal."

Prague, not the Ardors and Arbors of Ardis, is where this friendship of ours began, before we met, though its principal parts were staged in a dream-bright Switzerland. And Prague, stony and brooding, is where Nabokov's aristocratic mother lived in the nineteen-thirties on a small pension from the Czechoslovak government and where she died on the eve of World War II.

A year or so ago, toward the end of my own four-year stay as a correspondent in the Soviet-occupied city, I started hearing from a middle-aged Czech lady who worked for the trade union publishing house. She had met me just twice at parties, but now phoned sporadically to ask such bizarre questions as these: "What means in English when you say 'putty-buff-and-snuff' or 'engorged heart' or 'the gift of the menarche?'" She had been entrusted with the task of translating *Lolita* into Czech. While Nabokov is banned in his native Russia, his classic is known and even tolerated in some of the satellites. And while the lady's project was sometimes on and sometimes off the schedule ("It would be better," one of her newer bosses told me, "if this *Lolita* were about a worker"), she was plowing forward steadily but quietly on the Nabokovian assumption that, if nothing else, art would outlive politics.

When she called me with another list of queries last fall, I told her: "I'll be in Montreux on other business, but staying at the Palace Hotel where the Nabokovs live. I don't want to impose upon him, but if you'll write him a letter telling him when I'll be there, he can get in touch with me if he wants to."

The tweedy host who invited me down to the hotel's Green Room in November, 1970, for an eleven A.M. drink of "coffee, tea or grappa" (he chose grappa) was charming and marvelously preserved—even the red veins in his face seemed to glow. He took care of business right away by running down the Prague lady's list:

"Tell her that 'ululate' is not a dirty word. 'Lull' is a boy's name; at least, the only person I knew named Lull was a boy. 'Matted eyelash' means just that—not a pubic hair—and a 'red autumn leaf' is a red autumn leaf is a red autumn leaf, not a deflowered nymphet . . ."

Within ten minutes, Nabokov, having dissected *Lolita* and put her together intact for export to Prague, relaxed and chatted about himself, his health, and hotel living. His health was self-evident. I had just met Nabokov's uphill neighbor, Noel Coward, who is eight months the author's junior and was looking a good eight years older.

Speaking of Coward, whom he's never met, Nabokov said he was amused to be living in a community of Humbert Humberts. Coward had been offered the part in Stanley Kubrick's 1962 film of *Lolita* (Nabokov wrote the screenplay, and Kubrick used just enough of it to justify Nabokov's legal position as author of the script). Coward declined the part of Humbert because, he said, "We weren't able to finish reading the book." James Mason, who did play the part, lives five miles from Montreux and is a good friend of both Coward and Nabokov.

Nabokov does not number himself among the local Humberts, having once written: " . . . my creature Humbert is a foreigner and an anarchist, and there are many things, besides nymphets, in which I disagree with him." When I asked if he could give any instances of mistaken identity involving Humbert and himself and if he could list the most salient features they have in common, Nabokov replied: "Well, we both like tennis." Indeed, Nabokov once supported himself in Berlin by teaching tennis as well as English and Russian and by constructing crossword puzzles and chess problems.

Now we talked about a mutual ex-publisher in another country, and Nabokov said of him: "He's a rather astute man with a coarse streak right down the middle and—do you know?—I think it's his coarse part that kept me with him for so long. Each time I visited his city, he would take me home for dinner and—every single time—he would tell me, as we crossed his threshold, 'This is the house *Lolita* built.' Well, I've wrecked some lives in my time, but I also like to think that at least I made a house."

As he spoke, we were joined by a tall, regal, alabaster-skinned lady whom Nabokov introduced proudly as "the person to whom I've been married for forty-five years." Véra Evseevna Slonim Nabokov—daughter of a Jewish industrialist from St. Petersburg—is the Véra to whom all of his novels (six written in English and nine translated from Russian) published in English are dedicated. She is his confidante, proofreader, chief literary counselor and devoted audience as well as his partner at chess, Scrabble (often played in Russian), hiking, strolling, butterfly-hunting and business negotiating. "In wheeling and dealing," says a friend, "he is the silent partner. She does the arguing and he does the deciding."

From their *émigré* days together in Berlin (1925–37) and then Paris (1937–40) through academic days at Wellesley and then Cornell (1948–59) and onward into Alpine opulence, Mrs. Nabokov has always been the household manager and chauffeur. Despite his Humbert's climactic odyssey through the neon highways and motel courts of America, Nabokov does not pretend to be a driver. Much of *Lolita* was scrawled on index cards in a 1952 Buick during a transcontinental butterfly hunt with Véra at the wheel. Her husband was no help to her at all; he said in *Ada*, published in 1969: "There are people who can fold a road map. Not this writer."

Because Véra is fiercely protective of her man, outsiders tend to have more contact with her than with him, and there were those in Montreux who were willing to "assure" me that she ghostwrites him. "At the very least," said one such confidant, "they certainly must have collaborated on *Invitation to a Beheading*." They know Nabokov as the benign pedestrian who makes a point of buying *Time* and *Newsweek* and *The International Herald Tribune* at three different newsstands ("They're all good shops. It wouldn't be fair to give one of them all the business, would it?").

How could the theory that Mrs. Nabokov does the writing gain such currency in Montreux, particularly among tradesmen? Nabokov took that question in writing and supplied a written answer:

"The charm of that rumor is enhanced by the fact that what most Montreusiens seem to know of my work, or of its shadow, is the film *Lolita* (shown in Switzerland half-a-dozen years ago). My wife reads my stuff only after I have completed the fair copy in longhand on lined index cards, which I fill out while standing at my lectern or lolling in the garden. I am an uncommunicative toiler, and in the case of the longer novels my patient first reader awaits the unknown book with serenity for years and years. Formerly, that is before we could afford secretaries, she used to type all my works and correspondence. She continues to read, very carefully, typescripts and proofs, correcting my grotesque misspellings and sometimes querying an obscure or repetitious word. She also types my Russian letters. It may very well be that the observant and intelligent people who bring me fruit and wine, or come to repair radiators and radios, jump to wrong conclusions because they never see *me* sitting at a desk, let alone typing."

At first one is struck by Mrs. Nabokov's crowning glory, her snow-white hair. ("I still think of her hair whenever I hear the phrase 'White Russian,'" says one of her husband's former Cornell students.) Mrs. Nabokov sensed my admiration before I could express it and said matter-of-factly: "It started turning when I was twenty-five." Her husband added: "Véra was a pale blonde when I met her, but it didn't take me long to turn her hair white."

She apologized for joining us a little late; she had been upstairs searching for two trophies. Now she gave them to me for the translator in Prague. One was a bootleg edition of *Lolita*, translated by the author into his native Russian, "not because I wanted tourists to smuggle it in, but because I was more afraid some Moscow hack would do a translation and—well, for example, there's no such term as 'blue jeans' in the Russian language."

"I think there is now," I told Nabokov, who hasn't been back to Russia since fleeing the Bolsheviks with his family on a small and shoddy Greek ship carrying a cargo of dried fruit. "Behind the Iron Curtain these days, everyone wears one kind of blue jeans—made in East Germany, I think—with the brand name 'Super Rifle,' in English, sewn onto the right side of the seat."

Vladimir Nabokov loved that! He began to cackle—at the thought, he explained a minute later, of someone going through *Lolita* substituting "Super Rifle" for "blue jeans." "It would be a whole new book!" By Freud, no doubt.

The Slavonic words in his Russian *Lolita* (which was printed in New York and retails on the Leningrad black market for 20 rubles, or two "*Zhivagos*") would help his Czech translator with her work, he said. The Nabokovs' other trophy for her was a huge $5.95 paperback called *The Annotated Lolita*, edited by Prof. Alfred Appel Jr. of Northwestern University. Nabokov described Appel as "my pedant. A pedant straight out of *Pale Fire.* Every writer should have such a pedant. He was a student of mine at Cornell and later he married a girl I'd taught at another time, and I understand that I was their first shared passion." Looking positively cherubic, Nabokov paraphrased his earlier remark about wrecking some lives but making others.

Nabokov spends most of the year—except for business trips and one long butterfly-collecting expedition—in Montreux. The Palace Hotel, he said, provides adequate insulation, but enough uninvited callers still filter through. Some are doing Ph.D. dissertations on him or on a paragraph of his work; others are just admirers or social butterflies or would-be interviewers.

"Every Englishman, no matter what his title or credentials, turns out to be a journalist of some sort, but I enjoy talking with them. The Americans I seem to meet are often out to get more than they're here to give, so I tend to be wary. Not long ago, there was someone with an American name who kept leaving vague messages for me all over Montreux. I started leaving messages, too, that I was unavailable. Then I got one more message—a slip of paper that said, 'F— you.'

"Well, this was so much more explicit than the others that I asked the desk what kind of person had left this message. And the desk said: 'That wasn't a person, sir; that was two rather wild-looking American girls.' This intrigued me even more, so I looked at the slip of paper again. And there I found something at the end of the message which I hadn't noticed on my first reading: a question mark!"

Mrs. Nabokov changed the subject—even before our laughter died down—by asking me if I would "look in on Vladimir's younger sister, who still lives in Prague." It turned out that Nabokov's widowed sister, Olga, sixty-seven (to whom he sends fifty dollars a month), lived in the same district I did. Olga's late son married a Czech girl, and now it was Olga's devotion to her Czech grandson that, above all, kept her in Prague despite the discomforts of being a Russian living among Czechs, not to mention a Russian "of class origins" in what was now a Soviet colony held by the Red Army.

The lady who came to dinner in Prague one December Sunday had the same head, eyes and chin as her brother, plus a fairly thick crown of brown hair. "It's all my own!" she began, without waiting to be complimented. She talked with my family and me in Czech, French, and English—all with gargled "R's" and with the recurrent note of world-weary certainty that is the mark of *émigrés*, including (to a slighter degree) her brother. Though she had another married name, she wanted to be called "Nabokovová." She said: "Tell me, before I even take off my coat, what my brother is like!"

Her intense curiosity about the brother she hadn't seen for more than three decades barely lasted until we sat down in our living room. For Olga Nabokovová wanted to chat about *beaux-arts*. She had arrived a little out of breath from the official "Days of Soviet Culture," a month-long "festival" that most Czechs were boycotting. "How could I resist the show of Russian art from the Hermitage—from my own native city?" she demanded. Then she launched into a description of the exhibition and a discourse on Yugoslav religious wood carving.

The tide of talk swept to the dinner table, where I worked in the names of Nora Kaye and Margot Fonteyn. Olga Nabokovová suddenly said: "But, as for men dancers, it always strikes me as laughable when men go up on their toes." Here, she made a little finger ballet and both my children began to giggle. "Well," she went on, "it isn't at all masculine, is it?" Our guest was soon laughing so infectiously, as were my wife and children, that I found myself laughing, too, at the very idea of a man dancing!

"But that's incredible!" Nabokov exclaimed a few months later in Montreux when I told him about the conversation with his sister. "Because that's almost exactly what my mother used to say about 'male ballerinas.'" He stared into his gin and tonic, apparently unable to fathom why good things die while prejudices endure.

We were in the Green Room again, on a winter afternoon. Mrs. Nabokov said: "Olga wrote to us that you never invited her back, and she was very angry with you. But I wrote to her that you'd been expelled from Czechoslovakia soon after she saw you." Then Véra riveted me with the stare that precedes a pronouncement. "You are a bright young man," she said, "but you have one failing in perception: the places you've picked to live. First Prague, now Vienna. The Austrians were worse than the Germans. We never travel in those countries." (And Adolf Eichmann, given a copy of *Lolita* to read in prison, remarked: "That is quite an offensive book.")

Mrs. Nabokov's words were punctuated by a jolting thump from above. In the off-season, workmen were painting and pummeling the turreted façade of the Montreux Palace.

"Isn't that disgraceful!" she exclaimed. "The hotel shouldn't rent rooms when they're making this kind of noise."

"That last was not the noise of workmen, my dear," her husband interjected. "That was the noise of small American children."

"How do you know?" I asked.

"They run differently, they play differently and they fall differently from European children."

What does the author of *Lolita* think of little American children?

"I don't know any."

He did betray an opinion, though, when the conversation turned to his empire on the hotel's sixth floor. Mrs. Nabokov began to describe it: "Seven rooms, including two libraries, plus three bathrooms and four telephones, and we're starting to outgrow all that. The furniture is a joke . . ."

"Except for my marvelous wooden lectern," said Nabokov, referring to the living room rostrum at which he usually writes—on index cards while standing—from shortly after 5:30 A.M. until 3:30 P.M. "The hotel found the lectern somewhere and gave it to us soon after we moved in. It was used by Flaubert once."

"It's Louis Quinze or something," said Mrs. Nabokov, "but it's broken."

"It's very old and very shaky," her husband conceded, "but it's not broken."

"Well, there's a crack in the connecting wood between two legs," Véra argued.

"Let's just say that the legs are the weakest part," Nabokov suggested. "Looking at it, I can only guess that some Early American child came over to Europe and set about systematically kicking it to pieces."

She said: "As soon as it finally goes, I have the name of an excellent carpenter who made something like it for Mr. James Mason. But we hesitate to order it now."

"No need, no need," said he, and I think there was a glimmer of superstition behind his words.

Nabokov referred further questions about the way he works to a 1964 *Playboy* interview conducted by Alvin Toffler. In it, Nabokov, reading prepared answers from his index cards, said:

"I do not begin my novel at the beginning. I do not reach chapter three before I reach chapter four. I do not go dutifully from one page to the next, in consecutive order; no, I pick out a bit here and a bit there, till I have filled all the gaps on paper. That is why I like writing my stories and novels on index cards, numbering them later, when my whole set is complete. Every card is rewritten many times. About three cards make one typewritten page, and when finally I feel that the conceived picture has been copied by me as faithfully as physically possible—a few vacant lots always remain, alas—then I dictate the novel . . ."

Nabokov's initial reaction to the suggestion that I interview him for a profile had been one of casual indifference. "You know," he said, "if I'd ever wished to be a journalist, it would have been to cover Manson. That trial fascinates me. So much has been made of it."

"Yes," I said. "Even the President of the United States got into the act to pronounce him guilty."

"Well, he was absolutely right to do that!" Nabokov snapped. "If I were President, I'd have done it, too. Manson and those girls—they're cretins! They're not capable of thought." He mimicked their explanations: "We stuck the forks into her stomach so that her baby would never have to fight in the war." Then he asked, "What war?"

"The war in Vietnam," I guessed.

"Do you think those girls and Manson ever knew anything about the war in Vietnam? Yes, it exists, it's an idea to them, but it's hardly perceived. They talk about it, but they have no idea what they're talking about."

Inevitably, Manson generated a three-way argument. I spoke as a journalist, recognizing that our thirst for colorful copy creates "cretins" like Manson, and that the glory we grant them inspires a certain cult of "dumb intellectuals" who are quite ready to pass shallow judgments.

"Do you honestly believe that?" asked Mrs. Nabokov, impaling me again with her stare. "Only someone on drugs could be reached by a Manson. Why do you call them a cult? . . . I favor hanging them."

Her husband said he opposed capital punishment, but added: "If the aim of jail is rehabilitation, you cannot rehabilitate such people. Certainly, they should be caged for life."

"Then they'll be out in twelve years," said Mrs. Nabokov. "They're too dangerous. I was listening to the radio the other day and there was some baboon of a film producer in Paris saying, 'Manson expressed what a lot of us are feeling. We're all behind you, Charlie!"

"There!" I said. "Doesn't that indicate Manson's influence extends beyond his 'family,' and is spread by the media?"

"That baboon must have been on drugs, too," she answered.

"Even so," her husband pointed out, "we have friends to fit the description of 'dumb intellectuals.'" He whispered a name to his wife, then told her and me: "That couple is perfectly capable of coming out and saying something outrageous like 'We're all behind you, Charlie.'"

In a later, written exchange, I asked Nabokov why the Manson case fascinates him and why it made him wish to be a journalist. He replied:

"I have a taste for case histories, and it would have interested me greatly to look for one spark of remorse in that moronic monster and his moronic beast girls. I would also have been interested to find more about the cretins who 'admire' those brutes."

"As one American to another," I asked, "where do you stand on Vietnam?" He answered: "All I know is that I would not like S. Vietnam to turn into Sovietnam, and that blunders do not win wars."

Though it was winter when we spoke of Manson and Vietnam in Montreux, butterflies soon danced in the margin of our dialogue. I suggested that, when I rejoined Nabokov, it ought to be for butterfly-hunting. He took to the idea.

The day before he had played hooky from his writing to shop for shorts in Lausanne, fourteen miles away, in anticipation of the 1971 butterfly season. He had been looking for "something younger and narrower than heretofore," though not the "hot pants" the tailor dared to dandle before him. "The tailor and I talked for more than an hour, although we didn't settle everything. So I suppose I must make another trip to Lausanne before spring comes. Why, I talk about a trip to Lausanne the way others talk about a trip to Hawaii! Well, I only get over to Lausanne once or twice a year, though I go to New York or London or Rome oftener."

I asked about Nabokov's reading, his sources of information on the outside world, and mentioned Prof. Morris Bishop, who brought the author from Wellesley to Cornell and once recalled:

> "I was fascinated not only by the range and depth of Vladimir's knowledge but by his exclusions. He had small interest in politics, none in society's economic concerns. He cared nothing for problems of low-cost housing, school consolidation, bond issues for sewage-treatment plants. He got the news not from *The New York Times*, but from *The Daily News*, quivering with wickedness, lust and bloodshed. He subscribed for a time to Father Divine's periodical, revelatory of a lurid, exalted world. His study was rather of human behavior and misbehavior than the pratings of men in power."

"My old friend Morris Bishop is a great stylist," Nabokov wrote in reply, "and he has brought up the 'Father Divine's periodical' on a wave of style. I don't think I ever read it.

"Nowadays, in Switzerland, I dip into quite a number of periodicals: *The Herald Tribune, National Review, The New York Review of Books, Time,*

*Newsweek, The Saturday Review, The New Yorker, Playboy, Esquire, Encounter, The Listener, The Spectator, The New Statesman, Punch,* the London Sunday papers and so forth."

All spring, my questions and Nabokov's answers spilled through the mails between Vienna and Montreux as covering letters scheduled and rescheduled our butterfly hunt. A rendezvous in Sicily in late April or early May was canceled because of Italy's spring strikes. An early summer meeting in Lenzerheide, in the German-speaking part of Switzerland, was confirmed and reconfirmed; then all was undone when Véra Nabokov took sick. A bad reaction to antibiotics had put her into a Geneva hospital and, now that she was out, a fortnight of bedrest had left her with circulatory trouble in her feet. The Nabokovs' summer evenings were spent on their Montreux terrace as he read to her, in Russian, Aleksandr Solzhenitsyn's *August, 1914.* And who will deny that, from the Arbors of Ardis, there issued wild cackles of Laughter at the manly prose of this tragic, heroic political figure who would not risk going to Sweden to accept his Nobel Prize for fear Russia might force him into emigration?

Finally, though, the great day arrives, and—with Nabokov's chauffeur disabled and his auto garaged for repairs—I hire a taxicab for our butterfly expedition to the bird sanctuary at Grangette, six miles from Montreux. And an unwittingly jocose dispatcher sends us a Russian *émigré* cabbie, Mrs. Natalie Green-Skariatine, a Tartar who has "been out since 1920 and driving for thirty-nine years." The lady has driven the Nabokovs before, and today's conversation en route is in Russian.

When we arrive, Nabokov tells the driver where to wait and leads me to some underbrush that he calls "most tempting." He is looking for "a very interesting butterfly," the Purple Emperor. After calling for "silence, not total silence, but some silence," he describes "its beautiful violet sheen" and explains: "If you turn it this way and that way, the shimmer changes. It used to fly here until they asphalted this road. Now it's getting scarcer and scarcer. I saw one the other day up in Caux, but I couldn't look at it closer because it was flying higher and higher in such a hurry—*Ahhhh!*"

With a whooshing backhand swoop, Nabokov bags a lemonish yellow butterfly and holds his throbbing net up for inspection.

"A brimstone, not uncommon," he says. "This was supposed to be the first butterfly ever noticed; hence the name *butterfly.* Another version has it that the name was derived from 'flutter-by'—making it all a spoonerism!"

As Nabokov releases the butterfly I congratulate him on his backhand. "I'm glad you appreciated that," he says. "It's not easy to take a flying butterfly because it dodges. The best way is to wait for it to settle on a flower or on damp earth; it's quite easy to take." He confesses to "a little spring training in the room," more out of anticipation than necessity.

For the next quarter-hour the pickings are slim, and when the hunt bogs down in swampy underbrush Nabokov decides to go back to our starting point and take a different turn. Along the way, he mentions some of the hazards of butterfly hunting, including vipers ("Their bites are not fatal—unless you're ill or old or very young"), but dwells on bigger challenges:

> "I have walked among rattlesnakes. Yes, in Arizona, when I was writing the screenplay for *Lolita*. We would take my index cards in the morning and go out collecting and writing until lunch. And one day I remember killing an immense rattler that was just lying in wait for us when we came out toward the road. I was the first to hear its hysterical rattlings. Véra almost stepped on it, but I held her back. Then I picked up a piece of lead piping and smashed the thing. A moment later, I saw its female slithering away. Véra called me 'St. George' for quite a while after that."

From the perils of making the movie *Lolita* a decade ago, the talk shifts to the stage version, *Lolita, My Love*, a musical by Alan Jay Lerner and John Barry, that suffered grave personnel problems before it collapsed aborning last spring. Sight unseen ("but I have spies I incited to go see it") Nabokov announces: "Both girls—the one they fired and the one who replaced her— were awful; little bosomy girls, the wrong type altogether."

Does he retain any artistic control over such things?

"None whatsoever. I reason this way: If they're going to do it someday, they're going to do it. So I had better be around when they do it—not only to criticize the thing, but also to explain that I have nothing to do with it."

Dodging an occasional motorbike, we press on down the blacktopped road, then turn off as Nabokov announces: "The dimmer the place, the better the butterfly." Our walk ends suddenly with a lash of his net. "This one I will take," says Nabokov. "A lovely intergrade between the common Veined White and its cousin Bryony White."

The butterfly goes into a small glassine envelope that is secreted in an old Band-Aid box Nabokov keeps in his jacket pocket. "That envelope," he explains, "will hold the butterfly until I want to spread it. In there I can keep my butterflies for years and years, hundreds of years. When I am ready, I have only to relax them between wet towels and leave them overnight—and the next day pin them . . ."

"But the one in their now," I ask, "is it still alive?"

"Oh, you didn't see me pinching it under the net? That killed it, though sometimes I have to re-pinch them. When Véra's with me, she keeps an eagle eye on them. She hates to see half-dead butterflies."

With a "lovely intergrade" to take home to his ailing wife, Nabokov is soon willing to give up on his initial objective, the Purple Emperor. He admits that he was seeking it for sentimental reasons: "I just remember many places with it. As a boy, I hunted it in Bad Kissingen, in Bavaria."

Bearing his trophy, Nabokov returns to our waiting taxi, now pointed toward Montreux with the motor running.

"Was it a successful day?" the driver asks in English.

Gesturing knowingly toward me, Nabokov replies: "From *his* point of view, it was successful. From *mine*, well, I've had better days."

Later in the week, he will excuse himself to "go into hiding" and finish his new novel, *Transparent Things*, about which he will breathe not a word beyond the tentative title. But that will be merely an interlude. Rubbing his hands in anticipation, Vladimir Nabokov says: "*Transparent Things* is very nearly done, and then I have a rendezvous with The Butterfly on the Simplon on the fifteenth of the month."

# An Interview with Vladimir Nabokov

## Mati Laansoo / 1973

From the Canadian Broadcasting Corporation, March 20, 1973. © CBC.
Reprinted by permission.

**Mati Laansoo:** How do you regard the Nobel Prize for Literature? The people who have seriously read your works realize that you are indisputably
the greatest living author in the world. Given that, how do you explain the
lamentable omission of your works by the Nobel Prize Committee? Is it a
matter of geographic boundaries and ideological differences?

**Vladimir Nabokov:** Your first question is so precisely and pleasantly
phrased that I feel embarrassed by the display of vagueness with which I
must formulate my reply. Now and then, in the course of the last three or
four decades, I have caught myself idly reflecting on the attractive resemblance between the beginning of the name of that famous prize, and the
beginning of my own name: N,O,B, N,A,B, what a delightful recurrence of
letters! Alliteration, however, is a deceptive relationship. Its magic cannot
hope to establish the fortunate link between laurel and brow. On the other
hand, I do feel that as a writer I am not inferior to, say, Rabindranath Tagore
(1913) or Grazia Deledda (1926); but then, of course, quite a number of
uncrowned authors must exist, at this very moment, nursing the same for-
lorn feeling. In response to the conjecture at the end of your question, I can
only affirm my conviction that honest judges should not be prejudiced by
my geopolitical situation—that of a non-progressive American hailing from
a nonexistent Russia. The situation may look somewhat bizarre; it would be
absurd to call it hopeless. After all, let us not forget that another Russian,
in much the same position as I, did get that prize. His name is no doubt on
your lips. I am referring of course to Ivan Bunin (1933).

**ML:** One often hears the word "responsibility." How do you hold yourself
responsible to the children as an "elder," in the anthropological sense?

**VN:** I'm afraid that the little I know about anthropology as a science is limited to its taxonomic aspect dealing with the classification of various subspecies of *homo sapiens* and with problems relating to the skulls of ancestral forms of the creature. Otherwise, I find the subject of popular or "applied anthropology" tedious and even repulsive. The noun "elder," within that frame of reference, conjures up for me the image of a shaggy hermit all beads and beard with a more or less prehistoric cast of rugged features and a cave of sorts in the background. Tribal generalizations mean nothing to me. I prefer to use the term "responsibility" in its proper sense, linked with moral tradition, with principles of decency and personal honor deliberately passed from father to son. I can speak also of responsibility in the capacity of an educator, of the professor of literature which I taught for some twenty years in America. Here I was on my own, founding my own tradition, following my own taste, creating my own artistic values and trying to impress my own approach to art upon the minds of my students—or at least some of my students. I am responsible for having taught those best children of my time a method of appreciation based on the artistic and scholarly impact of literary fiction, but I never was directly concerned with the general ideas that they might derive from this or that great novel or the question how they would apply its more or less obvious ideas to their own life. That was the duty and choice of their actual, not metaphorical, elders.

**ML:** Having read your brief treatise on "Inspiration" in the *Saturday Review of the Arts*, I wonder, outside of your art, what tumbles your grimace from irritation to pain?
**VN:** The list of things, big and small, that I find utterly hateful is a long one. Pet hates are generally more banal than loves. Let me limit myself to a few obvious samples. Cruelty comes at the top, then dirt, drugs, nuisance by noise, coat hangers of wire, modish words (such as "charisma" or "hopefully"), quick quack art, breaking a finger nail with no scissors in sight, mislaying my spectacle case, finding that the current issue of my favorite weekly is suddenly devoted to Children's Books.

**ML:** At what portals has the burglar of laughter broken and entered into your edifices?
**VN:** Oh, laughter is not a burglar at all. Good old Laughter is a permanent lodger in every house I construct. He is in fact the built-in-roomer. He has the right to keep a mermaid in the bathtub. He is responsible for consigning Freud and Marx to the garbage can and destroying quite a few dictators.

He drives some of my silliest critics mad with helpless rage. To extend your metaphors—which I seem to be doing all the time—my books would be dreary and dingy edifices indeed had that little fellow not been around.

**ML:** Why do the Swiss make such good mercenaries and watches?
**VN:** I am the last person to be consulted on the subject of watches. I am apprehensive of watches as some people are of a coiled snake—and how abnormal it is to carry a watch around your wrist or keep one in your waist-coat pocket like a spare heart! Despite my terror of them, I love expensive watches—I shall always remember a very flat, thin, golden one of Swiss make that I had as a foppish boy sixty years ago, it lay on the palm of my hand like a pool of cold dew; yet watches detest me. I have never had one that was not fast or slow, and it takes at least a fortnight to have a Swiss watch repaired in the place where it was bought; and most terrible of all are the fake clocks of clock-makers' shop signs, which are set at a motionless and meaningless quarter to three to show how appealing they can spread their hands.

**ML:** The eggheads' endeavor involving the pressure-cooker blasted to the moon has hatched such rewards for mankind as Teflon, the five-year flash-light battery and the pocket mini-computer. How might the artist have hoped to improve on these dubious returns?
**VN:** The undescribable excitement and delight of reaching a celestial body, of palpating its pebbles, of sifting its dust, of seeing things and shadows of things never seen before—these are emotions of unique importance to a certain uniquely important variety of man. We are speaking of divine thrills, aren't we, not of comic-strip gadgets. Who cares for the practical benefits derived from the exploration of space! I shall not mind if more and more trillions of dollars are spent on visits to the moon or Mars. I would only recommend that our jaunty and fearless space sportsmen be accompanied by a few men of acute imagination, true scientists of Darwin's type, an artis-tic genius or two—even some gray octopus of a poet who might lose his mind in the process of gaining a new world, but what does it matter, it is the ecstasy that counts.

**ML:** Why did Fischer beat Spassky?
**VN:** Apart from the fact that Fischer showed himself to be the better player, there are psychological complications to be reckoned with. Fischer, when he played that match, was the free champion of a free country with no whims barred and no fear of retribution for a fatal blunder. Wretched Spassky, on

the other hand, always had a couple of stone-faced agents dogging him on an island with no escape or hiding place. He felt the presence and pressure of the Soviet police state all the time—and one wonders would Fischer have won had the roles been reversed and the eyes of those grim annotators followed *his* every move with the same governmental threat. The farcical little scene of the wife being flown over from Russia was, I thought, especially gruesome but also rather hilarious as a desperate hygienic measure revealing the peculiar animal stupidity that is in a way a redeeming feature of the most elaborate dictatorships.

**ML:** A Canadian artist has intimated that time is the thing that stops everything happening at once, and space is the thing that stops it happening all in the same place. Could you comment on this?

**VN:** That's very neatly put. But it is only an aphorism, only a flourish of wonderful wit. It suggests the way a timepiece and a piece of space work in relation to each other, but it tells us nothing of the texture of time or the substance of space. When composing my chapter about Time in *Ada*, I concluded—and am still leaning upon the gate of that conclusion—I concluded that Time has nothing to do with Space, and is not a "dimension" in the sense that Space is a dimension. Thought, for example, in order to breed properly, needs the broth of Time, no matter how scanty, but does not require Space. Yet, even when we speak about a "little" time or a "long" time we are not actually referring to size, and what we measure is not Time itself or the distance between two tangible points of Time (as we measure Space), but a stretch of our own existence between two recollections in a medium which our mind cannot really grasp. Everything in the nature of life is impossible to understand but some things are less possible to understand than others, and Time is among the most slippery ones.

**ML:** Is there anything that interests you about your audience, or, how would you interview your interviewer?

**VN:** In the first flush of my so-called fame, just before World War II, around, say, 1938, in Paris where my last novel written in Russian started to run in an *émigré* magazine, I used to visualize my audience, with tender irony, as a small group of my Russian *émigré* fans, each with one of my books held in his hands like a hymnal, all this in the rather subdued light of a backroom in a café. Ten years later, in my American transposition, the room of my fancy had grown as large as a comfortable auditorium. Still later, more and more people had to stand for want of seats. Then, in the sixties, after the appearance of *Lolita*, several new halls had to be built, both in the New World and in the Old. I have readers now not only in Brazil and Israel, but in the Soviet Union where factually my works are banned and every ghostly smuggler is equal to a hundred legitimate readers elsewhere. What interests me, or better say moves me, in regard to my present audience is that a figment of my fancy, not much more solid than an invented castle or cloud in one of my stories, has become an actual event. I am a shy, retiring person. I feel stupidly confused to have my books provoke such attention and ask so much of my readers, whose eyesight in some cases is not too good (as their nice letters, with stamps enclosed, tell me) and whose fathers or children happen to be hospitalized with some terrible terminal illness which a simple autograph from me would certainly cure. "Dear Vladimir Nabokov," some say, "excuse me for using a page of my exercise book, but teacher has assigned all your books—and I am only a high school kid"—all this in the handwriting of an old professional collector of autographs. I am an old collector too, but of butterflies, not autographs, and it is my entomological hunts in Canada that come to my mind as my voice is being projected onto Canadian air. One of my favorite spots remains a ravine smothered in flowers, near Fernie, three miles east of Elko, British Columbia, where on a summer day in 1958 I collected specimens of a very local little blue butterfly (*Lycaeides idas ferniensis*) which I badly wanted for the Cornell University Museum. Your curiosity about audiences has produced, as you see, quite a bit of digressive response, so let me now have your tenth and last question.

**ML:** How does your wife Véra Nabokov puzzle you?

**VN:** I am puzzled by many things about her: by her inability to keep figures and dates in her head, by the disorder on her desk, by her gift of tracking down a needed item that is the more precious the more complicated the search in the maze. I marvel at the way she can quote by heart old Russian sayings and ditties—sometimes quite new to me after almost half-a-century of shared life. I find fascinating the accuracy with which she picks out the best book in the batch that publishers send me every month or so with their compliments and hopes. I am filled with wonder every time that my random thought or actual sentence is simultaneously voiced by her in those flashes of domestic telepathy whose mystery is only enhanced by their frequency. And I also find enigmatic the stroke of miraculous intuition that makes her find the right words of consolation to give me when something awful, such as a misprint somehow left uncorrected by me in a recent novel, causes me to plunge into a torrent of Russian despair.

# Checking in with Vladimir Nabokov

## Gerald Clarke / 1975

From *Esquire*, July, 1975. © Gerald Clarke. Reprinted by permission.

Vladimir Nabokov spreads his hands around the bulge of his stomach like a pregnant woman who, long past the time for such things, cannot quite believe what God and man have done to her. "My dear fellow," he tells me, "I am *gorged* with questions."

Nabokov does not generally pride himself on his modesty, but he is, in fact, only telling the simple truth. Sometimes it seems he draws more people to Switzerland than do the Alps and secret bank accounts. Interviewers from both hemispheres badger him for audiences, and doctoral candidates in English literature, who have made Nabokov studies a growth industry in the graduate schools—just beneath the Big Three: Joyce, James, Eliot—write, call, and make the pilgrimage to Montreux in search of a blessing from the Master. Even ordinary tourists, who probably know only that he once wrote a dirty book called *Lolita*, have picked up the scent of Aging Literary Genius. During the season, they try to surprise Nabokov with their Nikons and Instamatics as he goes to buy the English and American papers or as he and his wife Véra take their customary constitutional along the promenade bordering Lake Léman. "One man even left a letter at the desk for us," Véra told me crossly. "'I have just bought an expensive camera,' the letter said, 'and I have waited three days to catch you unawares. But I haven't seen you. When can I photograph you?'"

For the first two thirds of his life, despite a steady outpouring of brilliance in Russian and English, which he learned simultaneously as a child, fame eluded Nabokov like one of those butterflies he is always chasing. Its shimmering wings were always fluttering, with bright, airy arrogance, just out of reach, half a step ahead. Now, though he has violated all the accepted rules of the literary hype, fame lights on his shoulder, takes its ease on his nose and throws its wing dust on his pince-nez as it dances before his eyes.

Instinctively and with low cunning, the amateur paparazzi, the journalists, and the importuning graduate students have stumbled on a certain, but rarely advertised, truth: in an age in which everything is rated, novelists—like pitchers, boxers, racehorses, and French poodles—are numbered on a chart, and every five years the professors and the critics bring it out for revision. And today, as he has been for the last half decade or so, Nabokov, a semi-reclusive Russian who lives in Switzerland but claims that he is as American as April in Arizona, is No. 1 on the Quality Lit. Ladder, with no serious challenger in sight. Writers as unalike as Mary McCarthy, George Steiner, Joyce Carol Oates and John Updike have strewn his path with critical roses: Oates—not overlooking Homer, Shakespeare, and Norman Mailer—has written that Nabokov is "as exciting as any writer who has ever lived," and I have seen such a disparate pair as Gore Vidal and John Barth grow positively misty-eyed, or as misty-eyed as these cool gentlemen ever get, when they talk about Nabokov's work.

For some people, respect is tempered by fear, and when he becomes angry, Nabokov, his critical powers undiminished at seventy-six, hurls such high-voltage thunderbolts from his Montreux mountainside that Jupiter himself might snatch up his toga in alarm and scurry for shelter with the rest. The ink still stings from his epical exchange in the mid-sixties with his onetime friend Edmund Wilson, who dared to denigrate Nabokov's four-volume translation of Pushkin's *Eugene Onegin*. Lesser figures who disturb Nabokov's Alpine calm are crushed as well, and of course journalists writing about him have suffered from his ire. One reporter who talked with him a few years ago was so unstrung at the prospect of actually shaking hands with such a fearsome monument, let alone risking its wrath, that he stopped several times during the hour-long drive from Geneva, each time to vomit from nervousness into Lake Léman; and an editor who had business with Nabokov came close to turning around half a dozen times and calling in sick. Both visitors, I should add, were treated, as I was, with extreme, elaborate courtesy.

My own experience was that the Master of Montreux is more fearsome in prospect than in person—but not so many managed the chance to make that judgment. Like everyone else who interviews Nabokov, I first had to negotiate with Véra, who handles all such matters. He would sit down with me, she wrote briskly, only if I agreed to several conditions: I would have to state my questions in writing; I would have to ascribe to Nabokov only what he would actually say; and I would have to pledge to show him my finished story and make "whatever alterations he requests." The first two conditions were easy enough. I had not, of course, planned to misquote him anyway and, having learned his habits from *Strong Opinions*, a compendium of his likes and dislikes, I had anticipated, however reluctantly, being required to submit written questions. Nabokov, after all, looks at everything he writes or says with a magnifying glass over his eye, like a jeweler inspecting the insides of a watch; he visibly squirms at the possibility, however unlikely, of a verbal accident, an inappropriate adjective set bawling before a strange noun or an innocent participle left dangling atop an ungrammatical chasm. "I admire people who can speak and it all comes out in well-ordered, beautifully rounded sentences," he later told me. "I cannot do that. I can't speak that way. I am an idiot in conversation."

The third stipulation, however, that I submit the story for approval and possible changes, was one I could not agree to, and I told Véra so. She gracefully relented in the next mail, explaining, somewhat apologetically, that her husband had had a bad experience not long before with someone who had then tried to psychoanalyze him in print. Psychoanalyze Nabokov! Next to the Bolsheviks, he hates no one so much as the Freudians. Probably nothing could be more distasteful to him than a session with a shrink, amateur or otherwise. In almost every book, he mounts a harsh slap or two at the analytic profession, and he has described poor Sigmund himself as everything from that "figure of fun" to the "Viennese quack." For my part, I promised Véra that I would not play analyst with my typewriter. The interview, finally, was arranged, and in mid-September I arrived in Montreux.

To say that Montreux is mummified would be an overstatement, but not much of one. Situated between Vevey and Chillon, whose castle Byron immortalized ("Chillon! thy prison is a holy place"), it really has only two streets, one high, one low, running parallel to Lake Léman. The Montreux Palace Hotel, where the Nabokovs have lived for more than a decade, is Montreux's best, one of those vast piles in which Henry James' rich, young American heroines used to stay with their mothers while taking the waters, falling in love, catching consumption. The hotel now caters to summer vacationers, conventioneers, and a score or more elderly residents like the Nabokovs, all of whom nod and bob in friendly, old-fashioned formality as they pass. In an effort to get with it, the management has recently modernized, and it now brings guests into the lobby from the street in an all-glass elevator, greeting them with piped-in music—rock and Johnny Cash—several decibels too loud. Fortunately for Nabokov, who abhors strange sounds assaulting him from hidden places, modernization has not yet penetrated into the hotel's annex, where he and Véra have a suite of small rooms, with an office across the hall and a space in the attic for excess books. A Spanish cook, who can prepare four simple dishes very well, according to Véra, makes all their meals, and only when visitors like me appear do the Nabokov's venture down to the hotel's grand dining room.

The concierge was expecting me when I checked in, and he immediately handed me an envelope. "I shall be down in five minutes," Nabokov's letter began, "giving you time to look through my replies to your questions. Please tell *Esquire* that work on these writings takes me such a long time (first a draft is laboriously composed, then my wife corrects the slips of my pencil, and then my secretary types the Q's and A's in their final form) that I would expect *Esquire* to pay me for my contributions—or at least to airmail me a free copy of every issue of the magazine in the future." When I had finished the letter, the concierge then sent me to a lounge down the hall, where I followed directions, sat down, and read Nabokov's answers to my questions:

**Gerald Clarke:** What are you working on now, or preparing to write?
**Vladimir Nabokov:** At the moment I'm basking in the afterglow of a novel I have just completed, *Look at the Harlequins!* (do not drop the exclamation mark). This stage of retrospective sunbathing is a very short, very private affair, unconnected with any awareness of impending publication, etc. It includes a mental rereading of the thing in spectral script. My next task is a meticulous checking of the French translation of *Ada*—a huge bedraggled tome typed on anemic paper. The preparation of an interview for the German TV and the examining of an English translation of yet another collection of my old Russian stories will fill up the intervals between the next chapters of Fayard's adventures with Ada. And after that, or still somewhere in between, I shall go on accumulating the bones and flints of a new novel—a rather paleontological kind of research in reverse, so to speak. According to some of my criticasters, the unfortunate readers of my books have to look up words like "paleontological."

**GC:** Could you describe a typical day in the life of V. N.? Do you have any habits or devices that get you started writing, like sharpening pencils or filling pens? Schiller was supposedly comforted by the odor of rotting apples in his desk, while Balzac (or was it Hugo?) would put on a monk's robe before writing the first sentence each day. Do you have any similar spur to the imagination?
**VN:** Friends would sigh and foes grind their teeth if I relisted for the

hundredth time my daily habits to an innocent interviewer. It is all in my *Strong Opinions*, you know. All I care to repeat is that the first sentence of the day is composed in my morning bath.

**GC:** Which modern writers do you read for pleasure? Are there any living writers you particularly admire? Or particularly dislike?

**VN:** I find morbidly fascinating the leisurely letters in which English authors of a former age praise at length contemporaneous writers (mostly their correspondents) or revile in detail writers belonging to other so-called "groups" or "schools" of the time. And mind you, those epistolarians' professional output was a tomb-slab-thick novel per year. My personal letters are rare and brief. Though anything but a prolix novelist, I fear squandering the energy reserved for my novels. On the other hand, I am happy to report that my library of modern literature, which is housed in an attic kindly allotted to me by the hotel, is growing steadily owing to contributions from publishers. A great number of those volumes are ephemeral—you know the type— romances all slaughter and semen or collections of essays by pretentious hacks—but when I think of the care that went into every detail of the jacket, into this or that pathetic little touch of the printer's art, I feel disinclined to ridicule the dream between the covers.

**GC:** Your life has been divided into geographic segments—Europe, America, and now Europe again—yet you are an American citizen. Do you still consider yourself American? Do you think that your writing has an American accent?

**VN:** I have spent nineteen years in Russia, three in England, sixteen in Germany, four in France, twenty in America, thirteen in Switzerland. Of these the longest time segment is the American one. I am American.

**GC:** Someone has described you, with some admiration, as "a brilliant monster." Would you care to comment? Do you feel very monstrous?

**VN:** I guess you've invented that "someone" but it is a plausible invention. One of the definitions that my dictionary gives under "monster" is "a person of unnatural excellence." Of course, I'm aware of my unnatural excellence. I am aware of it, however, only in certain domains (too obvious to be mentioned); but I also am aware of my hopeless ineptitude in other matters such as technology, finance, music and go-getting, to name a few. The epithet "brilliant" is a little redundant. Most monsters have shining appendages or eyes.

**GC:** In its concern for memory and the recollection of specific detail, your writing reminds me of Prousts.' Do you see any resemblance?

**VN:** I see no resemblance whatever. Proust *imagined* a person (the "Marcel" of his long fairy tale *In Search of Lost Time*) who had a Bergsonian concept of past time and was thrilled by its sensual resurrection in sudden juxtapositions pertaining to the present. I am *not* an imaginary person and my memories are direct rays deliberately trained, not sparks or spangles.

**GC:** You are now in your mid-seventies. How do you feel as you look back at your life? Have you accomplished all or most of the things you hoped to accomplish, or has some goal eluded you?

**VN:** The literary line of my fate from 1920 to 1940 is what I expected at nineteen. I have written in Russian the kind of books I wanted to write. The English ones that followed in the next thirty-four years are a rare recompense for the trouble I took over my first compositions in my native language. If any goal has eluded me, it must be sought in another domain, that of lepidopterology. At the middle point of my life (1940–48), I used to devote many hours daily, including Sundays, to the working out of taxonomic problems in the laboratories of two great museums. Since my years at the Museum of Comparative Zoology in Harvard, I have not touched a microscope, knowing that if I did, I would drown again in its bright well. Thus I have not, and probably never shall, accomplish the greater part of the entrancing research work I had imagined in my young mirages, such as "a monograph of the Eurasian and American *machaon* group," or "The *Eupisthecia* of the World." Gratitude for other pleasures leaves, really, no room in my mind for that ghost of regret.

**GC:** Are you still an insomniac?

**VN:** I have lately started jogging before turning in. Delightful! Keeping it up for a couple of hours, in the deepening dusk, along lakeside lanes, is both exhilarating and soothing. Except for a few pairs of lovers disentangling themselves to watch my passage, there is nobody to notice me. I wear tennis shorts and a heavy sweater which I usually shed after the first hour. I'm afraid I've made up this story *in toto* but it shows how desperate I am beginning to be in my fight with insomnia. Harmless pills have ceased to affect me, and I decline to rely on brutal barbiturates. My afternoon siesta has stretched to almost three hours, and my night's sleep has dwindled to about the same length of time. At least two kind strangers have suggested a little warm milk with a spoonful of honey at bedtime.

**GC:** Which of your books do you remember with the greatest pleasure? Of which character are you fondest?

**VN:** Oh, the *The Gift* and *Lolita*, of course, and also the novels I wrote in the sixties and seventies. And the four volumes of my work on *Eugene Onegin*. I am inordinately fond of those old books. (My weakest is certainly *Laughter in the Dark*, by the way.) As to the characters in them, I cannot love them separately, they are on a par with the fantasy and the fun and the moth on the mottled tree trunk.

**GC:** If you had had a choice, what language would you have preferred to have been born with?

**VN:** Russian.

On that emphatic note, the author himself appeared, with Véra at his side. Others, who have known them longer, say that both Nabokovs have aged markedly in the last couple of years. I can only guess that, until recently, they must then have looked younger than they were because, for their ages, both seemed to me exceedingly fit and healthy. Nabokov was more stooped than I had expected, but, in his walking shorts and long socks, he was all ruddy alertness, a testament to Swiss air and mountain water—he even boasts in *Strong Opinions* that he can still walk fifteen miles a day. Véra, who has had snowy white hair since she was twenty-five, seems at this point almost ageless, as if, by giving up then her youthful color, she had made a compromise with time all those years ago and plans to insist as long as she lives on the exact terms of the contract. A compatriot of theirs who saw them both at *émigré* gatherings in Paris in the thirties, admiringly describes Véra as having been "quick, very quick, with great personal charm." And so she still is.

As he sat down, Nabokov was as amiable as he had been unamiable in the letter, written that day, that had come with his answers. He offered me a drink—"A gin and tonic perhaps?"—and professed amazement, shock and incomprehension when I wanted instead a local Swiss beer, the agreeable but slightly acidic Feldschlossen.

"Feldschlossen!" he snorted, waking up the lounge, which seemed, like the rest of the hotel in that off-season, to be in a hibernating doze. "Feldschlossen is for field mice! Try a German beer."

"Maybe he likes light beer," Véra gently suggested.

"It's not a question of light or dark. It's a question of good or bad," Nabokov argued, pointing out the aesthetic issue involved. We met halfway, on a neutral bottle of Danish Carlsberg, and moved on. He corrected my handy copy of *Look at the Harlequins!*, in which a misprint on page eight, particularly annoying because it was not obvious, had turned a "confirmed madman" into a "confined madman," and he happily accepted my gift of Gore Vidal's *Myron*. The latest volume of Vidal's *Forsyte Saga*, in modern drag, had recently come out in the United States, and I thought that it might make Nabokov's celebrated insomnia bearable for an hour or two—or else, depending on his taste, cure it entirely. Besides that, I knew that Vidal had had an apartment in Switzerland and that, though they have never met, the two authors enjoy exchanging polite barbs from time to time through a mutual woman friend. "Vidal calls my husband the Black Swan of Lake Léman," Véra told me. "But he is so witty you can't get angry."

By way of conversation, I reminded Nabokov that another writer, Thomas Pynchon, had attended his course at Cornell in the late fifties, and I asked him if he remembered his most celebrated student. He did not—though Véra, who had helped him grade student exams, did.

"My wife remembers him by his handwriting," Nabokov said. "It was very good."

"No," she corrected him. "It was very bad, half written, half printed." He had tried to read *Gravity's Rainbow*, Pynchon's newest, biggest, and best novel, Nabokov added somewhat dolefully, but he could not understand it and gave it up. It was a charming confession, I thought, to have come from the author of *Ada*, that vast metaphorical mansion with trompe l'oeil doors, helical hallways, and booby-traps even for the very wary.

Later, over dinner in the hotel dining room, with the maître d' and his staff circling around like nervous destroyers protecting their flagship, the Nabokovs became friendlier still. Nabokov, who had abandoned knee socks and cardigan for a grey suit, grey V-neck sweater, and grey tie, with a pince-nez for the menu, was by turns a superb, funny storyteller, whose eyes would water at his own elegant, elongated punchlines, and a dogged interviewer, with as many questions for me as I had for him.

Both he and Véra were extremely curious about life in America, which they had left in 1960 to be nearer to their only child, Dmitri, who was then launching a career as an opera singer in Italy. (Dmitri, now forty-one and unmarried, is still singing, and the Nabokovs, who obviously adore him, still remain nearby. At six feet five, Dmitri towers above old dad, loves to ski, pilot speedboats and drive fast cars; he has translated his father's old Russian novels into English, and a novel in English, *Transparent Things*, into Italian.) They lighted on Montreux, a place that, for reasons I can scarcely fathom, has historically attracted writers. "Shelley and Byron were both here with their two girls," Nabokov told me. "Later there were the Russians. It was here that Gogol came and beat the lizards with his stick because in Russia they are meant to represent the devil with their naked tails. And then, of course, there was Tolstoy."

The Nabokovs had both been happy in America, however, which provided them with much, including security and comfort, that revolutionary Russia had taken away. They enjoyed life at Cornell, in Ithaca, New York, and they would travel thousands of miles through the West each summer vacation in search of butterflies, particularly the blues Nabokov so much admires. *Lolita* was written in the course of those trips, Véra driving their '52 Buick across plain and prairie while Nabokov scribbled endlessly on his ever-present three-by-five index cards. (*Ada*, his longest book, was written on 2500 such cards.) Nabokov, in fact, has expressed the regret that they had not gone to the United States even earlier than they did, and he and Véra are as stoutly protective of their adopted country as any American Gothic Republican with a flagpin in the lapel. "The Germans are usually quite right when they hate Germany," said Véra, who is Jewish. "The Americans are *never* right when they hate America." At another time she complained about criticism of the C.I.A., whose role in subverting the Allende government in Chile had just been found out. "Why shouldn't the United States try to stop governments it disagrees with?" she demanded. "The Communists certainly do." Because of its radical politics, she told me, she and her husband call *The New York Review of Books* the "Barbarous Review."

"Will you ever return to America?" I asked her husband. "I think so," he answered. "At first we came here for certain family reasons. Then we stayed on. But it is so hard in America to find a place that is not terribly expensive."

"I don't think you will find any place in America as expensive as it is right here," I suggested. The Nabokovs seemed surprised to hear me say so—and more than a little interested. There is a widespread impression that Nabokov is, like a mountain Prospero, above thinking about money in his protected aerie. "Nabokov is beyond money," Norman Mailer recently told an interviewer from *Rolling Stone*, as if he were merely repeating something so obvious and so well-known that it did not need amplification. But while Nabokov's temperament is antipodal to his fellow writers in so many other ways, it is exactly the same when it comes to the folding green. He does care about money, as his publisher at G.P. Putnam's Sons, who offhandedly said much the same thing as Mailer, found out when Nabokov packed up his books and his prestige for a better deal at McGraw-Hill. Born into an immensely rich St. Petersburg family—he inherited the equivalent of two million dollars from an uncle when he was still in his teens—he lost almost everything to the Bolsheviks and was too poor too long not to watch every penny now.

"If you ever do go back," I continued, "where will you live?"

"California," he said, without a moment's reflection. "California is one of my favorite states. I like the climate, the flora and the fauna—the butterfly fauna. And it's close to Mexico and Alaska. I have never been to Alaska, unfortunately. It is the best place for butterflies."

"Which part of California would you go to?"

"I like it all. I love Los Angeles, where we lived while I was writing the screenplay of *Lolita*. I had never seen jacaranda trees before, at least in bloom." He turned to his wife. "Do you remember, darling? There was a whole street lined with jacarandas." Still, despite the jacarandas and the Alaskan butterflies, I doubt they will ever return to America, at least to live, and my impression was that the Nabokovs feel the United States has become a dangerous shoot-em-up jungle in the decade and half since they left. On their trips through the West, Véra used to hide a Browning hand-gun in a glove compartment of their Buick. But she would probably not be so quick on the draw nowadays. They asked me where it is safe in America, quizzing me about their favorite spots in the West. Nabokov finally ended his list in Colorado, asking me earnestly if a place like Colorado Springs, so beautiful, so serene, so safe when they knew it, were still acceptable.

Celebrating their fiftieth anniversary this year, the Nabokovs seem to have refined their marriage into a work of art, the structure of which is, like one of those complicated Spenserian sonnets, nimble and formal at the same time. While Nabokov spins his arachnoid tales across his little index cards, Véra manages all of his business, negotiates with people who want to see him, and generally tries to keep distant the niggling, nagging problems that bedevil so many other writers. Edmund Wilson, in *Upstate*, thought that she was too protective, an opinion that further evoked Nabokov's outrage. But most people feel that the Nabokovs' is a totally admirable partnership. Most of his books are dedicated simply, "To Véra," and she seems the model for the last, perfect wife of the narrator in *Look at the Harlequins!*, his autumnal and in many ways his most personal novel so far. "They have always had an ideal marriage," one of their acquaintances, not otherwise an admirer, told me. "There has never even been a hint of anyone else."

Their conversation, to return to the sonnet comparison, often has a kind of formulary, interlocking rhyme. One will begin a story, and the other will correct it, add to it, or give it a twist the originator had ignored or forgotten. I asked Nabokov, for example, whether he had anything to do with a fellow *émigré*, Solzhenitsyn, across the Alps in Zurich. Yes, he replied, he was very friendly with Solzhenitsyn. "Just by letter," Véra interjected. "You've never met him." Well, Nabokov said, looking a little abashed, their letters had been very friendly. "He just replied to one of yours," she told him. At another point, I asked Nabokov if he were read in the Soviet Union. "Yes, very much so," he said proudly. "My books are constantly smuggled into Russia. They consider me to be a Russian writer who has been kidnapped by the United States and forced to write in English." To which Véra, referring to the presumably jocular part about kidnapping, appended quietly for my sake: "You can take that with a grain of salt." These interchanges were like a good-humored duet, like Hermione Gingold reminding Maurice Chevalier in the movie *Gigi* that she had worn blue, not white, and that the sky had been clear, not rainy, the night they had parted.

One of Nabokov's funniest stories was on himself, and he told it with considerable pleasure. Before he was hired by Cornell, he said, he was invited up to Dartmouth to give a lecture and to be looked over in the process. Everything went perfectly. The friend who had issued the invitation met him and Véra when they arrived, brought together a small, congenial group for dinner before the lecture, then escorted the party to the auditorium—where there was an audience of three. This friend had remembered all of the duties of host but had forgotten to announce the lecture. "At least," the fellow said, looking at the room's little trio, 'they are well distributed.'" Nabokov repeated the punch line with glee, then added half a one of his own. "The only interesting thing that happened was during the dinner beforehand, when one of the guests kicked his wife under the table." Véra, following his invisible and seemingly unintentional cue, finished the line. "Not under the table, dear. It was out in the open. *That* is what made it interesting." Turning to me, she added: "She was flirting with my husband, and her husband didn't like it." Nabokov chuckled, admitting the point. "They had been studying wolves in the Arctic for two years, and she needed intellectual stimulation."

The Nabokovs' gentle play of point-counterpoint works both ways, however. Scarcely had Véra started her own anecdote about "four beautiful women" than Nabokov interrupted her. "No, darling," he said patiently. "They were not beautiful women. They were men dressed as women. *That* is the point of that story."

After dinner we went back to the lounge where we had begun our conversation in the afternoon and now continued it over some glasses of grappa. Once again we turned to writers and writing.

"When I last saw my good friend Edmund Wilson, who was sitting in your chair, I asked him who the best writer in America was," Nabokov began. "He said there was only one—James Baldwin." He smiled and sat back in his chair like a prosecuting attorney who had just concluded a triumphant case, Baldwin obviously not being one of Nabokov's favorites.

"Wilson was a smart man," I said. "He should have known better."

"He was not a smart man," Nabokov insisted. "He had many soft spots. He would turn up with a worthless story by Gogol and say that it was the best thing in Russian literature. It was all rather endearing."

"Whom do *you* most admire," I asked, repeating one of the questions I had sent him, without getting, as his written reply shows, a very explicit response.

"Edmund White. He wrote *Forgetting Elena*. He's a marvelous writer. I'm also a great admirer of John Updike—the up, up, up Updike. J. D. Salinger is another writer I admire tremendously. Beautiful stuff! He's a real writer. I like some of Truman Capote's stuff, particularly *In Cold Blood*. Except for that impossible end, so sentimental, so false. But there are scenes in which he writes with true appetite, and he presents them very well."

Over our second glass of grappa, Nabokov looked at his watch and began his goodbyes. "Oh, my goodness," he said. "It is way past my bedtime. Why, it is almost dawn!"

It was ten minutes after ten.

# Vladimir Nabokov on the Loose

## Hugh A. Mulligan / 1977

From *The Washington Star*, January 16, 1977. © The Estate of Hugh A. Mulligan. Reprinted by permission.

Vladimir Nabokov, the dazzling stylist whom John Updike, among other critics, regards as the greatest living American writer, admits to being a kept man these past twenty-five years.

Since 1952, when he first studied her gum-chewing charms and "drip" and "goon"-strewn slang on bus rides around Ithaca, New York, the reclusive novelist has lived off Lolita. The tantalizing, shocking, "disgustingly conventional" American adolescent whose subspecies he classified under the word "nymphet," adding a new erotic noun to the language, has made him more famous than the moth and two butterflies named for him as a world-renowned lepidopterist.

"Between the age limits of nine and fourteen," Nabokov's stricken hero, Humbert Humbert, describes the species, "there occur maidens who, to certain bewitched travelers twice or many times older than they, reveal their true nature which is not human, but nymphic (this is, demoniac) and these chosen creatures I propose to designate as 'nymphets.'"

Although the film was only a minor success and the musical by Alan J. Lerner went nowhere, Nabokov is pleased as any parent that his little girl has behaved so well in translation and paperback and hardcover and as a rapidly accepted noun herself—"Lolita: a sexually attractive young girl" (*Webster's*)—in the English language.

There have since been other novels, *Pale Fire* and *Ada*, and a brilliant autobiography, *Speak, Memory*, to bolster his reputation as the most original English prose stylist since Joyce. As a Russian novelist he is measured with Pasternak (whom he abhors) and Solzhenitsyn (whom he greatly admires), but Lolita has been faithful in her fabulous fashion.

"Lolita is famous, not I. I am an obscure, doubly obscure novelist with an unpronounceable name," says Nabokov, who will be seventy-eight in April and has lived in lonely luxury in a deluxe hotel suite overlooking Lake Geneva since 1961, but with characteristic alliteration regards himself as "American as April in Arizona."

Proudly, with a patrician glare around the surrounding Alps at his film star neighbors, he proclaims that he is not a tax exile.

"I pay US income taxes on every cent I earn at home and abroad," he says with patriotic ardor, admitting that at times the tax bill is "so high as to obscure the view from my easy chair." He has not yet computed what the new law reducing exemptions for Americans abroad will do to his royalty statements.

Driven out of Imperial Russia by the Bolsheviks and from Berlin and Paris by the Nazis, leaving behind a fortune, his beloved native language and, on each occasion, priceless butterfly collections, Nabokov loves America with an immigrant's fervor and forgiveness.

America, he says, "is the only country where I feel mentally and emotionally at home."

He broke the glacial silence of his Alpine retreat to rent a television set and watch the astronauts land on the moon. "That gentle little minuet that, despite their awkward suits, the two men danced with such grace to the tune of lunar gravity was a lovely sight," he exulted. "It was also a moment when a flag means more to one than a flag usually means."

In a rare response to the critics, whom he dismisses as "hacks and hicks," he issued a thunderbolt from his six-room atelier on the top floor of the Montreux Palace Hotel here: "Whether or not the critics think that in *Lolita* I am ridiculing human folly leaves me supremely indifferent, but I am annoyed when the glad news is spread that I am ridiculing America."

A half century ago in a debate at Cambridge University, Nabokov gave his last political speech, denouncing the Russian police state, to which he never has returned. But he lost the day to the "Soviet apologist on *The Guardian*."

His political outlook has "remained as bleak and changeless as an old gray rock. It is classical to the point of triteness. Freedom of speech, freedom of thought, freedom of art. The social or economic structure of the ideal state is of little concern to me. My desires are modest. Portraits of heads of government should not exceed postage stamp size. No torture and no executions. With the passing of years I grow less and less interested in Russia and more and more indifferent to the once-harrowing thought that my books would remain banned there as long as my contempt for the police state and political oppression prevented me from entertaining the vaguest thought of return."

But he takes sly delight in the knowledge that *Lolita*, which he himself translated into Russian, has been smuggled in for the decadence of the comrades.

Aloof as Byron's *Prisoner of Chillon*, who lived just down the road, and sharing the same social circle of "tufted ducks and crested globes on Geneva's lake," Nabokov is content with the company of his books and Véra, his wife of fifty years, to whom all his novels are dedicated. It was Véra who rescued the manuscript of *Lolita* from a backyard incinerator in faculty row at Cornell University, where he was a funny, flamboyant lecturer teaching a course in masterpieces of European fiction that the football players who flocked to it called "Dirty Lit."

After the novel's success, the professor resigned, choosing Switzerland for its "exquisite postal service, no bothersome demonstrations, also butterflies and fabulous sunsets."

The *émigré* novelist who wrote his first book "on the moth-eaten couch of a German boarding house" and has been living the semi-permanent life of an exile ever since in motels, hotels, furnished flats and homes rented from professors on sabbatical, now prefers the transient glories of one of Europe's poshest hotels because "it simplifies postal matters, it eliminates the nuisance of private ownership and confirms me in my favorite habit, freedom."

Or, as he explained on another occasion, "I propelled myself out of Russia with such indignant force that I have been rolling madly on ever since."

Nabokov was born on a country estate fifty miles from St. Petersburg in 1899, the same year as Hemingway. His first novel in Russian, *Mashenka* [*Mary*], was published in 1926, the same year as Hemingway's first novel, *The Sun Also Rises*. His father, a jurist, liberal politician and member of the first Russian parliament, was ruined by the revolution, went into exile in 1919 and was assassinated in Berlin "by fascist thugs while trying to shield his friend, Professor Milyukin." Osip, his father's valet, was shot "by the Bolshevik's for appropriating the family bicycles instead of turning them over to the state."

Bilingual in English and Russian from his earliest infancy and adding French at five, Nabokov was educated by a series of tutors who taught him chess, boxing, tennis and encouraged his demon: butterfly hunting. His first published works were in English, a poem called "Remembrance," in the 1919 issue of the Trinity College, Cambridge, literary magazine, and in the same year a learned paper on Crimean butterflies.

Nine novels in Russian under the pseudonym V. Sirin followed before, at forty-one, he came to America and resumed writing in English, which he found "exceedingly painful, like learning anew to handle things after losing seven or eight fingers in an explosion."

He fondly recalls the "blessed day in 1939" when a fellow *émigré* writer in Berlin asked him to take his place lecturing on Slavic languages at Stanford University. Sergei Rachmaninoff sent him off with a carton of old clothes. Nabokov moved east to lecture on literature at Wellesley and take a part-time job as a lepidopterist at Harvard's Museum of Comparative Zoology. Meticulous about his English, as he remains to this day—he still hates to "speak off the Nabocuff"—he wrote out and read one hundred lectures on novelists from Jane Austen to James Joyce and one hundred on Russian Literature. He used the same technique at Cornell, where his classes had an enrollment of more than four hundred and Véra corrected his examination papers.

A chess master, whose hobbies include composing chess problems, making up crossword puzzles in Russian and playing "Skrebl," which is Scrabble in a Cyrillac alphabet, the *émigré* professor never could understand the intricacies of American football.

"I don't belong to any club or group," Nabokov once described himself to a BBC interviewer. "I don't fish, cook, dance, endorse books, co-sign declarations, eat oysters, get drunk, go to church, go to analysts or take part in demonstrations."

He doesn't drive, either.

Véra was at the wheel for the nationwide butterfly hunts that led to the discovery of Nabokov's pug, "a little American moth named after me," on the window of a Utah hunting lodge. Those hunts also netted the splendid details of motels and roadside cafes for Humbert Humbert's cross-country debauch with Lolita. The book passed through his Cornell days like a dream. He still remembers the innocent coeds coming up asking him to autograph gift copies for their fathers and grandfathers.

Shunned by shocked American publishers, *Lolita* ignominiously came to print in Paris at the hands of the Olympia Press, whose titles included *White Thighs* and *The Sex Life of Robinson Crusoe*. Graham Greene discovered it, called it one of the three best books he had read all year and *Lolita* was on her way. Still among the most sensuous, illicit stories ever told, the book does not have a single four-letter word.

Nabokov, a gentle, benign man of Olympian opinions, dismisses D. H. Lawrence as "a pornographer," prefers Hemingway to Conrad (with whom to his horror he is often compared as the master of a second language) and has "the deepest admiration for H. G. Wells."

He speaks of "not quite first-rate Eliot and definitely second-rate Pound." His list of "formidable mediocrities" includes Camus, Lorca, Gorky, Faulkner, Balzac, Brecht, Stendhal, Galsworthy, Thomas Wolfe, and E. M. Forster.

He detests "the four doctors: Dr. Freud, Dr. Zhivago, Dr. Schweitzer, and Dr. Castro, but the first takes the fig." Freud to Nabokov is always "the Viennese quack."

Nabokov cherishes Tolstoy, Pushkin, and Chekhov, against whom his writings in Russian often are measured. He likes Proust, Kafka, Poe, Melville, Hawthorne, Keats, Browning, J. D. Salinger, and John Updike. As "an English child brought up by governesses," he has an abiding affection for Lewis Carroll—"He has a pathetic affinity to Humbert Humbert"—and translated *Alice in Wonderland* into Russian.

Nabokov does all his writing in pencil on large index cards while standing at a lectern "which faces a bright corner of the room instead of the bright audiences of my professorial days." *Ada* covered 2,500 cards.

Recovering from a five-month bout with bronchial pneumonia, he has done most of his recent writing in bed, which has slowed down the start of his new novel, *The Original of Laura*. He is also getting together a volume of correspondence with Edmund Wilson, another early champion.

"Generally," he says, "I am a slow writer, a snail carrying its house at the rate of two hundred pages of final copy a year."

Nabokov likes sunbaths on the hotel lawn, walking along the lake, a "triangular gulp of canned beer," and keeping up with American slang through the flocks of magazines, newspapers, and book reviews that flutter into his pigeonhole in the hotel lobby.

Sadly, he has not gone butterfly hunting since July, 1975, when he skidded on wet grass in an Alpine valley near Davos and had to suffer jeers and laughter from the passengers in a passing cable car when he called for help. He still dreams about the incident and his injuries and the memory of an uncle who died at Davos.

On the day of this rare interview, Nabokov was in high spirits. Winter was drawing a white shade down the bleak mountains as the snow line approached the lake, and his son, Dmitri, a professional opera singer with a powerful bass voice, was singing *Figaro* in the bathroom. He was surprised that Carter had won the election but didn't think life would change much in his beloved America. Russia, he mused, was the same as he had left it, the same muzhik flailing the same horse, all bones, with the same whip.

"Nobody can decide," he once said, "if I am a middle-aged American writer or an old Russian writer or an ageless intellectual freak."

Then with typical gusto, he summed up himself: "I am an American writer, born in Russia and educated in England where I studied French literature before spending fifteen years in Germany."

## Vladimir Off the Nabocuff

**Hugh A. Mulligan:** What is the Nabokov diet these days, both literary and caloric?

**Vladimir Nabokov:** My caloric diet usually consists of bread and butter, transparent honey, wine, roast duck with red whortleberry jam, and similar plain fare. (Whortleberries are a kind of wild cranberry, also known as Lingonberries.) My literary regime is more fancy, but two hours of meditation, between two A.M. and four A.M. (when the effect of a first sleeping pill evaporates and that of a second one has not begun) and a spell of writing in the afternoon, are about all my new novel needs.

**HAM:** Somewhere I read that you have never flown across the Atlantic. Do long distance flights frighten or bore you, and does the phasing out of the passenger liners account for your fewer trips to America?

**VN:** The first ascent I made took place in a small cheap plane over Margate, Kent, in 1920. Nowadays my flights are limited to delightful hops from Montreux to Nice and back again. I shall certainly enjoy flying across the Atlantic when the last luxurious liner is extinct.

**HAM:** There was, I believe, a recent exchange of letters between you and Solzhenitsyn. What was the gist of them?

**VN:** I praised the freedom and happiness of the West; he deplored the fact of his children not being able to get a Russian education abroad.

**HAM:** You have said, "America is the only country in which I feel mentally and emotionally at home." After the jolts and flaws of lost Vietnam and the self-flagellating Watergate, do you worry about the future of America?

**VN:** Political squabbles and awkward wars will soon be forgotten. Let us prepare new weapons and whistle softly as we work. Let me write my new novel in peace. This is my work, my duty. America does not need my worrying about her. The jitters I leave to other countries, and the worse they are the better.

**HAM:** On the tenth anniversary of the Bolshevik Revolution you wrote *An Anniversary*, proclaiming ten years of contempt for the Soviet police state and celebrating ten years of freedom from it. The sixtieth anniversary is at hand this year. In the intervening half-century, has your contempt diminished? Is there less freedom outside Russia to celebrate?

**VN:** My contempt for tyranny shall last forever. Things hidden from tourists—the terrible backwoods, the jails, the concentration camps—cannot be compensated by a few more motor cars, stale sugar buns in redecorated shops, or the new fad—artificial caviar. And thus it will remain until that dreary and diabolical regime is destroyed.

**HAM:** Steam shovels, according to an A.P. report, are biting into Peking's Square of Heavenly Peace for a mausoleum to Mao Tse-Tung. What is your opinion of the late chairman as a person and a poet? I take it that you did not share the reported world grief at his passing?

**VN:** Epitaph:

> *Not a thing do I know about him*
> *I'm not even sure he could swim*

**HAM:** Lillian Hellman's *Scoundrel Time* has been both praised for her courage in standing up to (Sen. Joseph) McCarthy and criticized for its myopia toward the evils of Soviet Communism. When you were at Cornell did you come under any pressure from the McCarthy committee or was there equal pressure to conform with the leftist academics?

**VN:** Throughout my ten years' stay in Cornell I was never subjected to any pressure either from left or right.

(At both Harvard and Cornell, however, Nabokov resolutely refused to sign any faculty resolutions or join any demonstrations regardless of the cause.)

**HAM:** You once gave your preference for celestial neighbors—Shakespeare laughing ribaldly at frying Freud. Does this indicate a belief in the hereafter and an insight into or resumption of your own future booking arrangements?

**VN:** No. An infinite comic strip would soon become a dreadful bore.

**HAM:** I am in the process of polishing, dusting and perhaps even demolishing some of the statuary in my personal pantheon. Would you assist, please, with some pumice or a hammer for Willa Cather, Fitzgerald, Waugh, Mauriac, and Capote?

**VN:** Mauriac has written some wonderful stuff (e.g. *Le Noeud de Viperes*). Are we sure you have not confused him with the execrable Malraux? Waugh had talent. The scene of the murder in Capote is great. You must have invented Willa Cather and I don't remember anything of Fitzgerald's writings.

(Nabokov administered the hammer to Miss Cather with an innocent smile, claiming honestly never to have heard of her. His wife and lifelong proofreader gently rebuked his lapse, and he could not be drawn into mitigating sentence on Fitzgerald.)

**HAM:** Will the new US income tax law for Americans living and working abroad drive you up the wall and out of Switzerland? (Nabokov has always made it his patriotic duty to pay full US income taxes on all his earnings at home and abroad.)

**VN:** I have not yet tried to compute what the new tax law in all its glory will cost me.

# A Blush of Color—Nabokov in Montreux

### Robert Robinson / 1977

From *The Listener*, March 24, 1977. © Immediate Media Co. Reprinted by permission.

**Robert Robinson:** First, sir, to spare you irritation, I wonder if you will instruct me in the pronunciation of your name.

**Vladimir Nabokov:** Let me put it this way. There exists a number of deceptively simple-looking Russian names whose spelling and pronunciation present the foreigner with strange traps. The name Suvarov took a couple of centuries to lose the preposterous middle "a"—it should be Suvorov. American autograph-seekers, while professing a knowledge of all my books—prudently not mentioning their titles—re-juggle the vowels of my name in all the ways allowed by mathematics. "Nabakav" is especially touching for the "a"s. Pronunciation problems fall into a less erratic pattern. On the playing-fields of Cambridge, my football team used to hail me as "Nabkov" or facetiously, "Macnab." New Yorkers reveal their tendency of turning "o" into "ah" by pronouncing my name "Nabarkov." The aberration, "Nabokov," is a favorite one of postal officials; now the correct Russian way would take too much time to explain, and so I've settled for the euphonious "Nabokov," with the middle syllable accented and rhyming with "smoke." Would you like to try?

**RR:** Mr. NabOkov.

**VN:** That's right.

**RR:** You grant interviews on the understanding that they shall not be spontaneous. This admirable method ensures there will be no dull patches. Can you tell me why and when you decided upon it?

**VN:** I'm not a dull speaker, I'm a bad speaker, I'm a wretched speaker. The tape of my unprepared speech differs from my written prose as much as the worm differs from the perfect insect—or, as I once put it, I think like a genius, I write like a distinguished author, and I speak like a child.

**RR:** You've been a writer all your life. Can you evoke for us the earliest stirring of the impulse?

**VN:** I was a boy of fifteen, the lilacs were in full bloom; I had read Pushkin and Keats; I was madly in love with a girl of my age; I had a new bicycle (an Enfield, I remember) with reversible handlebars that could turn it into a racer. My first poems were awful, but then I reversed those handlebars, and things improved. It took me, however, ten more years to realize that my true instrument was prose—poetic prose, in the special sense that it depended on comparisons and metaphors to say what it wanted to say. I spent the years 1925 to 1940 in Berlin, Paris, and the Riviera, after which I took off for America. I cannot complain of neglect on the part of any great critics, although as always and everywhere there was an odd rascal or two badgering me. What has amused me in recent years is that those old novels and stories, published in English in the sixties and seventies, were appreciated much more warmly than they had been in Russian thirty years ago.

**RR:** Has your satisfaction in the act of writing ever fluctuated? I mean, is it keener now or less keen than once it was?

**VN:** Keener.

**RR:** Why?

**VN:** Because the ice of experience now mingles with the fire of inspiration.

**RR:** Apart from the pleasure it brings, what do you conceive your task as a writer to be?

**VN:** This writer's task is the purely subjective one of reproducing as closely as possible the image of the book he has in his mind. The reader need not know, or, indeed, cannot know, what the image is, and so cannot tell how closely the book has conformed to its image in the author's mind. In other words, the reader has no business bothering about the author's intentions, nor has the author any business trying to learn whether the consumer likes what he consumes.

**RR:** Of course, the author works harder than the reader does; but I wonder whether it augments his—this is to say, your—pleasure that he makes the reader work hard, too.

VN: The author is perfectly indifferent to the capacity and condition of the reader's brain.

RR: Could you give us some idea of the pattern of your working day?
VN: This pattern has lately become blurry and inconstant. At the peak of the book, I worked all day, cursing the tricks that objects play upon me, the mislaid spectacles, the spilled wine. I also find talking of my working day far less entertaining than I formerly did.

RR: The conventional view of an hotel is as of a temporary shelter—one brings one's own luggage, after all—yet you choose to make it permanent.
VN: I have toyed on and off with the idea of buying a villa. I can imagine the comfortable furniture, the efficient burglar alarms, but I am unable to visualize an adequate staff. Old retainers require time to get old, and I wonder how much of it there still is at my disposal.

RR: You once entertained the possibility of returning to the United States. I wonder if you will.
VN: I will certainly return to the United States at the first opportunity. I'm indolent, I'm sluggish, but I'm sure I'll go back with tenderness. The thrill with which I think of certain trails in the Rockies is only matched by visions of my Russian woods, which I will never revisit.

RR: Is Switzerland a place with positive advantages for you, or is it simply a place without positive disadvantages?
VN: The winters can be pretty dismal here, and my old borzoi has developed feuds with lots of local dogs, but otherwise it's all right.

RR: You think and write in three languages—which would be the preferred one?
VN: Yes, I write in three languages, but I think in images. The matter of preference does not really arise. Images are mute, yet presently the silent cinema begins to talk and I recognize its language. During the second part of my life, it was generally English, my own brand of English—not the Cambridge variety, but still English.

RR: At any point do you invite your wife to comment on work in progress?
VN: When the book is quite finished, and its fair copy is still warm and wet,

my wife goes carefully through it. Her comments are usually few but invariably to the point.

**RR:** Do you find that you reread your own earlier work, and if you do, with what feelings?

**VN:** Rereading my own works is a purely utilitarian business. I have to do it when correcting a paperback edition riddled with misprints or controlling a translation, but there are some rewards. In certain species—this is going to be a metaphor—in certain species, the wings of the pupated butterfly begin to show in exquisite miniature through the wing-cases of the chrysalis a few days before emergence. It is the pathetic sight of an iridescent future transpiring through the shell of the past, something of the kind I experience when dipping into my books written in the twenties. Suddenly, through a drab photograph, a blush of color, an outline of form seems to be distinguishable. I'm saying this with absolute scientific modesty, not with the smugness of aging art.

**RR:** Which writers are you currently reading with pleasure?

**VN:** I'm rereading Rimbaud, his marvelous verse and his pathetic correspondence in the Pléiade edition. I am also dipping into a collection of unbelievably stupid Soviet jokes.

**RR:** Your praise for Joyce and Wells has been high. Could you identify briefly the quality in each which sets them apart?

**VN:** Joyce's *Ulysses* is set apart from all modern literature, not only by the force of his genius, but also by the novelty of his form. Wells is a great writer, but there are many writers as great as he.

**RR:** Your distaste for the theories of Freud has sometimes sounded to me like the agony of one betrayed, as though the old magus had once fooled you with his famous three-card trick. Were you ever a fan?

**VN:** What a bizarre notion! Actually, I always loathed the Viennese quack. I used to stalk him down dark alleys of thought, and now we shall never forget the sight of old, flustered Freud seeking to unlock his door with the point of his umbrella.

**RR:** The world knows that you are also a lepidopterist but may not know what that involves. In the collection of butterflies, could you describe the process from pursuit to display?

**VN:** Only common butterflies, showy moths from the tropics, are put on display in a dusty case between a primitive mask and a vulgar abstract picture. The rare, precious stuff is kept in the glazed drawers of museum cabinets. As for pursuit, it is, of course, ecstasy to follow an undescribed beauty skimming over the rocks of its habitat, but it is also great fun to locate a new species among the broken insects in an old biscuit tin sent over by a sailor from some remote island.

**RR:** One can always induce a mild vertigo by recalling that Joyce might not have existed as the writer but as the tenor. Have you any sense of having narrowly missed some other role? What substitute could you endure?
**VN:** Oh, yes, I have always had a number of parts lined up in case the muse failed. A lepidopterist exploring famous jungles came first, then there was the chess grand master, then the tennis ace with an unreturnable service, then the goalie saving a historic shot, and finally, finally, the author of a pile of unknown writings—*Pale Fire, Lolita, Ada*—which my heirs discover and publish.

**RR:** Alberto Moravia told me of his conviction that each writer writes only of one thing—has but a single obsession he continually develops. Can you agree?
**VN:** I have not read Alberto Moravia but the pronouncement you quote is certainly wrong in my case. The circus tiger is not obsessed by his torturer, my characters cringe as I come near with my whip. I have seen a whole avenue of imagined trees losing their leaves at the threat of my passage. If I do have any obsessions I'm careful not to reveal them in fictional form.

**RR:** Mr. Nabokov, thank you.
**VN:** You're welcome, as we say in my adopted country.

# VN—RIP

## William F. Buckley Jr. / 1977

From *National Review*, July 22, 1977. © 1977 National Review, Inc. Reprinted by permission.

The cover of this magazine had gone to press when word came in that Vladimir Nabokov was dead. I am sorry—not for the impiety; sorry that VN will not see the cover, or read the verse, which he'd have enjoyed. He'd have seen this issue days ahead of most Americans because he received *National Review* by airmail, and had done so for several years. And when we would meet, which was every year for lunch or dinner, he never failed to express pleasure with the magazine. In February, when I last saw him, he came down in the elevator, big, hunched, with his cane, carefully observed by Véra, white-haired, with the ivory skin and delicate features and beautiful face. VN was carrying a book, which he tendered me with some embarrassment—because it was inscribed. In one of his books, a collection of interviews and random fare, given over not insubstantially to the celebration of his favorite crotchets, he had said that one of the things he *never* did was inscribe books.

Last year, called back unexpectedly to New York, I missed our annual reunion. Since then I had sent him my two most recent books, and about these he now expressed hospitable enthusiasm as we sat down at his table in the corner of the elegant dining room of the most adamantly unchanged hotel in Europe: I cannot imagine, for all its recent architectural modernization, that the Montreux Palace was any different before the Russian revolution.

He had been very ill, he said, and was saved by the dogged intervention of his son, Dmitri, who at the hospital ordered ministrations the poor doctors had not thought of—isn't that right, Véra? Almost right—Véra is a stickler for precision. But he was writing again, back to the old schedule. What was that schedule? (I knew, but knew he liked to tell it.) Up in the morning about six, read the papers and a few journals, then cook breakfast for Véra in the warren of little rooms where they had lived for seventeen years. After that he would begin writing and would write all morning long, usually standing, on the cards he had specially cut to a size that suited him (he wrote on both sides, and collated them finally into books). Then a light lunch, then a walk, then a nap and, in nimbler days, a little butterfly-chasing or tennis, then back to his writing until dinner time. Seven hours of writing, and he would produce 175 words. (What words!) Then dinner, and book-reading, perhaps a game of Scrabble in Russian. A very dull life, he said chortling with pleasure, and then asking questions about America, deploring the infelicitous Russian prose of Solzhenitsyn, assuring me that I was wrong in saying he had attended the inaugural meeting of the Congress for Cultural Freedom— he had never attended *any* organizational meeting of anything—isn't that right, Véra? This time she nods her head and tells him to get on with the business of ordering from the menu. He describes with a fluent synoptic virtuosity the literary scene, the political scene, inflation, bad French, cupiditious publishers, the exciting breakthrough in his son's operatic career, and what am I working on now?

A novel, and you're in it.

What was that?

You and Véra are in it. You have a daughter, and she becomes a Communist agent.

He is more amused by this than Véra, but not all *that* amused. Of course I'll send it to you, I beam. He laughs—much of the time he is laughing. How long will it take you to drive to the airport in Geneva?

My taxi told me it takes "un petit heure."

*Une petite heure* (he is the professor): that means fifty minutes. We shall have to eat quickly. He reminisces about his declination of my bid to go on *Firing Line*. It would have taken me *two weeks* of preparation, he says almost proudly, reminding me of his well-known rule against improvising. Every word he ever spoke before an audience had been written out and memorized, he assured me—isn't that right, Véra? Well no, he would answer questions in class extemporaneously. Well *obviously*! He laughed. He could hardly program his students to ask questions to which he had the answers prepared! I demur: his extemporaneous style is fine, just fine; ah, he says, but before an audience, or before one of those . . . television cameras . . . he would freeze. He ordered a brandy, and in a few minutes we rose and he and Véra and I walked ever so slowly to the door. "As long as Western civilization survives," Christopher Lehmann-Haupt wrote in the *Times* last Tuesday, "his reputation is safe. Indeed, he will probably emerge as one of the greatest artists our century has produced." I said goodbye warmly, embracing Véra, taking his hand, knowing that probably I would never see again—never mind the artist—this wonderful human being.

# Index

*Ada* (*The Texture of Time*), 98, 117, 141,
 155, 159, 162, 169, 175, 177, 185, 198,
 203, 207, 208, 212, 216, 224
Adams, J. Donald, 47
Adams, Robert M., 172
Albinus (character), 69
Aldonov, Mark, 35, 166
*Alice in Wonderland*, 30–31, 53, 108,
 111, 113
*American Mercury*, 166
American Museum of Natural History,
 96, 171
Amis, Kingsley, 6, 56
*Anchor Review*, 55
Andersen, Hans Christian, 136
Angelico, Fra, 173
Angry Young Men, 6
*Anna Karenina*, 4, 14, 73, 103, 141, 153,
 158, 177
*Annotated Lolita, The*, 187
*Ann Veronica*, 152
Appel, Alfred, Jr., 187
Aristophanes, 56
*Atlantic Monthly*, 167
Auden, W. H., 43, 159
*August, 1914*, 192
"Aurelian, The," 167
Austen, Jane, 103, 215

Baldwin, James, 211
Balzac, Honoré de, 45, 56, 57, 104, 203,
 216
Bardot, Brigitte, 41
Barry, John, 193
Barth, John, 130, 201
Beat Generation, 6
Beckett, Samuel, 163, 173
"Bells for John Whiteside's Daughter,"
 170
Bely, Andrei, 96, 121, 137, 138, 174
*Bend Sinister*, 6, 71, 72, 74, 122, 126, 133,
 134, 136, 141, 149, 164, 167, 168
Bennett, Arnold, 152
Berberova, Nina, 166, 176
Berlin, Isaiah, 106
Bishop, Morris, 167, 171, 191
Blok, Alexander, 87, 147
"Blood Bath of Kishinev, The," 162
Bloom, Leopold (character), 103, 127
Bobbs-Merrill Company, 135, 166
Bollingen Foundation, 57, 60
Borges, Jorge Luis, 88, 133, 134, 151
Brecht, Bertolt, 151, 163, 216
Brooke, Rupert, 87, 88
*Brothers Karamazov, The*, 138, 158
Brown, Clarence, 145
Browning, Robert, 87, 216
Bryusov, Valery, 122

*Bulletin of the Museum of Comparative Zoology*, 21, 54
Bunin, Ivan, 35, 84, 165, 166, 177, 195
*Burnt-Out Case, A*, 104
*Butterflies of Japan, The*, 173
Byron, George Gordon, 61, 63, 91, 208, 214

Camus, Albert, 151, 216
Capote, Truman, 211, 219
Carroll, Lewis, 56, 108, 134, 216
Carter, Jimmy, 216
Cash, Johnny, 202
*Castle, The*, 134
Castro, Fidel, 216
Cather, Willa, 219
*Chanson de Roland*, 57
Chaplin, Charles, 6, 174
Chekhov, Anton, 6, 45, 87, 121, 157, 176, 177, 216
Chekhov Press, 54
Chernyshevsky, Nikolay, 122, 176, 177, 181
Chevalier, Maurice, 41, 210
Cincinnatus C. (character), 130
*Circular Ruins, The*, 133
"Cloud, Castle, Lake," 167
*Colorado Butterflies*, 22
*Conclusive Evidence*, 4, 16, 42, 171
Conrad, Joseph, 35, 56, 57, 87, 136, 152, 215
Constitutional Democratic Party, 29, 52
Cornell Daily Sun, 7
*Country of the Blind, The*, 152
Coward, Noel, 184
*Crime and Punishment*, 158
Crossword puzzles, 113

*Daily Telegraph & Morning Post*, 56
Daniel, Yuli, 178
Darwin, Charles, 197

de Gaulle, Charles, 102
*Dead Souls*, 91, 96, 161
*Death in Venice*, 96, 137, 150, 176
*Death of Ivan Ilyich, The*, 103, 158
Dedalus, Stephen (character), 126, 127
*Deer Park, The*, 3
*Defense, The*, 135, 171, 176, 181
Delalande, Pierre, 126
Deledda, Grazia, 195
Derzhavin, Gavrila, 130
*Despair*, 97, 129, 135, 136, 140, 165, 181, 182–83
Dickens, Charles, 56, 133
*Doctor Zhivago*, 17, 19, 32, 96, 105
*Don Juan*, 93
*Don Quixote*, 151–52
Dostoyevsky, Fyodor, 56, 57, 59, 70, 78, 87, 91, 114, 122, 124, 136, 158
*Double, The*, 136
Doyle, Sir Arthur Conan, 88, 100
*Dr. Jekyll and Mr. Hyde*, 141
Dr. Zhivago (character), 11, 216
Dreiser, Theodore, 57, 96
Dupee, F. W., 55

Editions Victor, 147
Eichmann, Adolf, 188
Eliot, T. S., 88, 200, 216
Elliott, George D., 6
Emerson, Ralph Waldo, 121
Emmie (character), 50, 74, 136
*Encounter*, 192
Epstein, Jason, 55
*Esquire*, 166, 192, 203
*Eugene Onegin*, 32, 35–36, 57, 60, 65, 85, 93, 131, 149, 154, 162, 168, 175, 182, 201, 206
*Evergreen*, 149
*Exegi Monumentum*, 130
Existentialism, 7

*Exploit, The*, 139–40

*Eye, The*, 128, 133

Fadiman, Clifton, 50

Faulkner, William, 19, 92, 96, 151, 216

Fawcett Publications, 55

*Field Guide to the Butterflies, A*, 23

Fielding, Henry, 56

*Finnegans Wake*, 117, 127, 129, 151

*Firing Line*, 226

*First Love*, 51

Fischer, Bobby, 197–98

Fitzgerald, F. Scott, 56, 219

Flaubert, Gustave, 87, 131, 133, 189

Fogg, Phileas, 87

Fonteyn, Margot, 188

Ford Foundation, 54

*Forgetting Elena*, 211

Forster, E. M., 145, 216

*For Whom the Bell Tolls*, 92

Freud, Sigmund, 7, 32, 56, 69, 74, 94,
    114, 122–23, 150, 181, 196, 202, 216,
    218, 223

Frost, Robert, 92, 168

Galsworthy, John, 42, 96, 106, 216

Genet, Jean, 104

Gerhardi, William, 6

*Gift, The*, 59, 65, 71, 94, 116, 122, 125, 130,
    176, 181, 206

*Gigi*, 210

Gingold, Hermione, 210

Ginsburg, Ralph, 3

Girodias, Maurice, 149

*Glory*, 175

*Godbotherers, The*, 173

Godunov-Cherdyntsev, Fyodor (char-
    acter), 122

Gogol, Nikolai, 6, 56, 78, 91, 96, 115–16,
    121, 136, 150, 152, 161, 169, 208, 211

*Gone with the Wind*, 19

Gorky, Maxim, 42, 45, 96, 216

G. P. Putnam's Sons, 3, 55, 129, 208

*Gravity's Rainbow*, 207

Greene, Graham, 6, 104, 215

Grove Press, 137

*Guardian*, 213

Guggenheim Foundation, 60

Hamilton College, 164

*Hamlet*, 108

Harper & Brothers, 4

Harris, James B., 28, 57, 58

Harvard Crimson, 6

Hawthorne, Nathaniel, 121, 216

Haze, Dolores (character), 28, 75–76,
    107, 144

Hellman, Lillian, 218

Hemingway, Ernest, 57, 87, 92, 104, 133,
    134, 214, 215

Hoffmann, E. T. A., 136

Holmes, Sherlock, 87, 100

Homer, 201

"Hotel Room," 162–63

Housman, A. E., 87

*Hudson Review*, 6

Hugo, Victor, 203

Humbert, Humbert (character), 12, 44,
    66–67, 74, 75, 92, 101, 107, 108, 134,
    144, 145, 172, 184, 212, 216

Ilf, Ilya, 139

*In Cold Blood*, 211

*In Search of Lost Time*, 96, 205

"Inspiration," 196

*International Herald-Tribune*, 174, 185, 191

*Invisible Man, The*, 177

*Invitation to a Beheading*, 22, 50, 60, 71,
    74, 104, 122, 124, 126, 128, 130, 133,
    136, 142, 147, 164, 181, 185

Ionesco, Eugéne, 163

*Italics are Mine, The,* 176

Ivanov, Georgy, 86

James, Henry, 43, 121, 157, 200, 202

Jarrell, Randall, 6

Joyce, James, 6, 27, 56, 61, 73, 87, 96, 114, 117, 126–27, 130–31, 137, 138, 141, 151, 157, 163, 177, 200, 212, 215, 223, 224

Kafka, Franz, 6, 32, 56, 96, 103, 134, 137, 151, 177, 178, 181, 216

Karlovich, Hermann (character), 129

Karpovich, Mikhail, 164

Kaye, Nora, 188

Kazin, Alfred, 182

Keaton, Buster, 174

Keats, John, 32, 87, 216, 221

*Kenyon Review,* 170

Kerensky, Alexander, 53, 105

Kerouac, Jack, 44, 56, 70

*Killers, The,* 87, 134

*Killing, The,* 28

Kimbote, Charles (character), 118, 126, 128, 129, 131, 133, 142, 149

Kirkus, Virginia, 3

Klots, Alexander, 23

Knopf, Alfred A., 166

Krafft-Ebing, Richard Von, 56, 70

*Kreutzer Sonata, The,* 158

Kubrick, Stanley, 28, 57, 58, 72–73, 141, 153, 184

Kuprin, Aleksandr, 84

Lane, Franklin, 128

*L'Arc,* 134

*La Rue du Chat qui Peche,* 138

Laughlin, James, 183

*Laughter in the Dark,* 50, 69, 71, 108, 135, 136, 165, 166, 178, 181, 206

Laurel and Hardy, 174

Lawrence, D. H., 215

Leavis, F. R., 132

Lehmann-Haupt, Christopher, 226

*Le Monde,* 174

Lenin, Vladimir, 57

*Le Noeud de Viperes,* 219

Leon, Lucie, 138, 165

Leon, Paul, 138

*Lepidopterists' News,* 21

Lermontov, Mikhail, 121

Lerner, Alan Jay, 193, 212

*Les Misérables,* 4

Levin, Harry, 51, 170

Library of Congress, 61

*Listener, The,* 192

*Literary Gazette,* 25

*Lolita,* 3, 5, 8, 17, 18, 27–28, 59, 60, 66–67, 74, 91–92, 94, 101, 107, 110–11, 117, 123, 126, 128, 134, 142, 154, 162, 171, 182, 206, 224; banning of, 55, 56, 70, 108; film adaptation of, 28–29, 41, 57–58, 72–73, 117, 141, 153, 174, 184, 193; inspiration for, 12–13, 50–51, 66, 108; publication of, 31, 42, 54–55, 215; symbolism within, 9; translations of, 85, 95, 105, 129, 140, 183–84, 186; writing of, 19, 34, 37, 38–39, 49–50, 72, 109, 131, 153, 172–73, 185, 208

*Lolita, My Love* (musical), 193

*Look at the Harlequins!,* 203, 207, 209

*Lost World, The,* 152

Lorca, Federico, 216

*Lovat Dickson's Magazine,* 165

Lowell, Robert, 160

*Lyceum*, 129

Lyon, Sue, 72, 117

*Madame Bovary*, 131, 151

Mailer, Norman, 3, 201, 208

Malraux, André, 219

Mandelstam, Osip, 61, 147

Mann, Thomas, 45, 57, 96, 104, 114, 136,
    137, 163

Mansfield, Jayne, 29

*Mansfield Park*, 103

Manson, Charles, 190–91

Mao Tse-Tung, 218

Marcel, Gabriel, 138

*Mary*, 135, 181, 182, 214

Marx, Karl, 69, 196

Mason, James, 117, 184, 189

Maugham, W. Sommerset, 157

Maupassant, Guy de, 102, 157

Mauriac, François, 219

Maxwell, William, 149

McCarthy, Joseph, 218

McCarthy, Mary, 6, 117, 148–49, 201

McCartney, Paul, 173

McGraw-Hill Publishing, 208

Melville, Herman, 121, 136, 174, 216

*Memoirs of Hecate County*, 31

Mencken, H. L., 165

Metalious, Grace, 18, 29

*Metamorphosis, The (The Transforma-
    tion)*, 96, 103, 141, 151

Millstein, Gilbert, 56

Milton, John, 106, 157

Minton, Walter, 3, 55

Mizener, Arthur, 51

Monroe, Marilyn, 29

Montserrat, Nicholas, 10

Moravia, Alberto, 224

Morgan, Rex, M. D., 174

*Mozart and Salieri*, 149

Mrozovski, Peter, 151

Muromtsev, Sergey, 21

Museum of Comparative Zoology, 22,
    71, 93, 113, 167, 183, 205, 215

*Myron*, 207

Nabokov, Dmitri (Nabokov's son), 6,
    9, 32, 38, 48, 60, 83, 105, 114–15,
    139–40, 161, 165, 166, 173, 175, 182,
    207, 216, 225

Nabokov, Elena (Nabokov's mother),
    183

Nabokov, Olga (Nabokov's sister),
    187–88

Nabokov, Sergey (Nabokov's brother),
    115

Nabokov, Véra (Nabokov's wife), 5,
    9, 48, 49, 54, 102, 103–4, 106, 112,
    114–15, 153, 164, 169–70, 172, 177,
    185–86, 192, 193, 199, 201–2, 206–7,
    208, 209–10, 214, 225–26

Nabokov, Vladimir Dmitrievich (Nabo-
    kov's father), 5, 16, 53, 91, 112, 113, 115,
    146, 162, 163, 214

Nabokov, Vladimir Vladimirovich:
    background and early life, 4–5, 16,
    35, 52–53, 60, 94, 112, 162–63, 209,
    214; in Berlin, 30, 53–54, 70–71,
    95, 163–64, 182, 185, 214, 215; at
    Cambridge University, 5, 30, 53, 70,
    87–88, 126, 151, 163, 181, 213, 214;
    on censorship, 8, 29, 37, 61, 84; on
    chess, 98–99, 103; on coining the
    word "nymphet," 15, 37–38; at Cor-
    nell University, 5, 8, 19, 22, 31, 54, 60,
    71, 93, 110, 113, 167, 168–69, 170–72,

178–79, 215, 218; on education, 5, 9, 19, 29, 32, 46, 73, 152–53, 196; on God, 89, 218; at Harvard University, 6, 60; on humor, 59–60, 73–74, 107, 130–31, 196–97; on index cards, 61, 67, 79–80, 97, 189, 216; on language, 4–5, 9, 31–32, 35, 60, 65–66, 75–76, 83–84, 92–93, 154, 222; as lepidop-terist, 4, 21–26, 60, 62, 96, 111, 114, 132, 146, 149–50, 171, 183, 192–94, 205, 216, 223–24; on literary criti-cism, 82, 85–87, 123, 144–46, 157, 213; at Montreux Palace Hotel, 71, 90–91, 110, 143, 161–62, 173–74, 180, 184–85, 187, 189, 202; in Paris, 70–71, 95, 166; on poetry, 121; on politics, 82–83, 157–58, 159, 167–68, 190–91, 195, 213; on pornography, 28, 34–35, 37; on pronunciation of his name, 220; on reading, 45–46, 87–88, 223; on Russia, 5, 18, 39, 42, 53, 61, 62, 64–65, 93, 147; on Russian literature, 61; on science, 89, 132, 197; on the Soviet Union, 5, 84, 147–48, 158–59, 182, 210, 218; on speaking, 94, 175, 220–21; at Stanford University, 5, 18, 165, 215; on Switzerland, 77–78; on translating, 153, 203; at University of Salt Lake City, 170; on the United States, 16, 30–31, 42–43, 76–77, 91, 96, 113, 116, 148, 164, 204, 208, 213, 217; at Wellesley College, 31, 54, 60, 71, 93, 113, 165, 167, 183, 215; on writing, 6, 19, 43–44, 45, 63, 67, 68, 78, 81–82, 88–89, 97, 99, 120–21, 124–25, 142, 149, 156–57, 216, 221–22

*Nabokov's Dozen*, 51

Nabokov's Pug (moth), 183, 215

Nabokov's Wood Nymph (butterfly), 21, 22, 23, 24–26, 32, 96

*National Review*, 191, 225

New Directions Publishing, 165

*New Republic*, 149, 164

*New Statesman*, 6, 192

*Newsweek*, 185, 192

*New York Daily News*, 191

*New Yorker*, 17, 36, 60, 137, 149, 167, 170, 192

*New York Review of Books*, 191, 208

*New York Times*, 47, 56, 191, 226

*New York Times Book Review*, 42

Nicolson, Nigel, 56

*Nine Stories*, 167

Niven, David, 57

*Nose, The*, 136

*Nouvelle Revue Francaise*, 138

*Novyy Journal*, 142

Oakes, Philip, 173

Oates, Joyce Carol, 201

Odoevtsev, Irina, 86

Odoyevsky, Vladimir, 122

*Old Man and the Sea, The*, 87, 104, 134

Olesha, Yury, 139

Olivier, Laurence, 57

Olympia Press, 31, 36, 41, 54–55, 61, 110, 173, 215

O'Neill, Eugene, 59

Orczy, Emmuska, 88

*Original of Laura, The*, 216

Ostrovsky, Alexander, 104

*Pale Fire*, 59, 63, 68, 79, 92, 94, 107, 117, 118, 123, 125, 126, 127, 129, 131, 133, 134, 136, 137, 142, 162, 164, 166, 174, 175, 212, 224

*Paris-Soir*, 50, 108

Parry, Albert, 166

*Partisan Review*, 170

*Passionate Friends, The*, 152

Pasternak, Boris, 19, 32, 96, 105, 106, 112, 114, 212

*Paths of Glory*, 28

Perkins, Agnes, 165

*Petersburg*, 96, 137

Petrov, Yevgeny, 139

*Peyton Place*, 29

Picasso, Pablo, 173

Pirandello, Luigi, 129

Plato, 125, 131

*Playboy*, 189, 192

Pléiade editions, 223

*Pnin*, 6, 7, 36, 40, 60, 71, 117, 126, 136–37, 162, 167, 170, 182

Poe, Edgar Allan, 87, 88, 121, 136, 216

*Portrait of the Artist as a Young Man, A*, 126

"Potato Elf, The," 166

Pound, Ezra, 88, 151, 164, 216

*Prisoner of Chillon*, 214

Prokofiev, Sergei, 5

Proust, Marcel, 6, 56, 61, 87, 96, 114, 137, 177, 181, 205, 216

Pryce-Jones, Alan, 144

*Psyche*, 21, 171

*Punch*, 192

Pushkin, Alexander, 18, 60, 65, 87, 93, 106, 111, 117, 121, 129, 130, 138, 149, 152, 156, 157, 166, 168, 176, 177, 216, 221

Pynchon, Thomas, 130, 170, 207

*Quarter*, 166

Quilty, Clare (character), 13, 126, 134, 136, 172

Racine, Jean, 106

Rachmaninoff, Sergei, 215

Random House, 57

Ransom, John Crowe, 170

*Real Life of Sebastian Knight, The*, 57, 72, 128, 130, 140, 165, 166, 167, 168

*Republic of the Southern Cross, The*, 122

*Resurrection*, 158

*Return to Peyton Place*, 29

Richardson, Samuel, 45

Ridgewell, Rosemary, 55

Rimbaud, Arthur, 87, 223

Robbe-Grillet, Alain, 88, 133

*Robe, The*, 165

Rolland, Romain, 96

*Rolling Stone*, 208

Ronsard, Pierre de, 38

Roy, Winifried, 135, 165, 166

Rukavishnikov, Vasiliy (Nabokov's uncle), 53

*Rul'* (*The Rudder*), 164

*Russian Nights*, 122

Salinger, J. D., 19, 96, 211, 216

Sanders, George, 48

Sartre, Jean-Paul, 7, 19, 51–52, 97

*Saturday Review*, 192

*Saturday Review of the Arts*, 196

Sawyer, Buzz, 174

Scammell, Michael, 116

Scarlet Pimpernel, 87

Schiller, Friedrich, 203

Schweitzer, Albert, 7, 11, 151, 216

*Scoundrel Time*, 218

"Secret Life of Walter Mitty, The," 175

*Secret Miracle, The*, 133

Sellers, Peter, 161

Selvinsky, Ilya, 139

*Sex Life of Robinson Crusoe, The*, 215

Shade, John (character), 68, 69, 118, 126, 128, 142

Shakespeare, William, 32, 38, 105, 106, 121, 127, 140, 157, 162, 177, 201, 218

Shaw, George Bernard, 104

Shelley, Percy Bysshe, 32, 208

Sikorski, Elena (Nabokov's sister), 161

Sinyavsky, Andrei, 178

Sirin, V. (Nabokov's pseudonym), 113, 118, 164, 166, 176, 177, 215

Snow, C. P., 132

*Solus Rex,* 142

Solzhenitsyn, Aleksandr, 176, 192, 210, 212, 217, 226

*Song of Bernadette, The,* 165

*Song of Igor's Campaign, The,* 22, 57, 131

*Soviet Union Short Literary Encyclopedia, The,* 181–82

*Sovremennye zapiski,* 122, 142, 176

Spassky, Boris, 197–98

*Speak, Memory,* 30, 94, 100, 109, 113, 115, 123, 131, 136, 140, 141, 156, 162, 171–72, 212

*Spectator, The,* 6, 56, 192

Stegner, Wallace, 170

Steinbeck, John, 20

Steiner, George, 201

Stendhal, 104, 216

Sterne, Laurence, 45, 56, 129

Stevenson, Robert Louis, 136

"Stopping by Woods on a Snowy Evening," 92

*Strong Opinions,* 202, 204, 206

Struve, Gleb, 165

*Subterraneans, The,* 44

*Sun Also Rises, The,* 214

Suvorov, Alexander, 220

Swift, Jonathan, 129

Swinburne, Algernon Charles, 32

Tagore, Rabindranath, 96, 195

*Tempest, The,* 139

Temple, Shirley, 162

Tenishev School, 181

*This Quartet,* 165

Thurber, James, 56, 175

*Time* (magazine), 17, 182, 185, 191

*Time Machine, The,* 152, 177

*Times, The,* 174

Toffler, Alvin, 189

Toller, Ernst, 163

Tolstoy, Aleksey, 138, 139

Tolstoy, Leo, 4, 14, 32, 52, 61, 78, 87, 91, 96, 103, 121, 152, 157, 158, 160, 161, 177, 208, 216

*To the Finland Station,* 164, 168

*Transparent Things,* 173, 194, 207

Trilling, Diana, 6

Trilling, Lionel, 31

Turgenev, Ivan, 4, 152, 157

Turner, Joseph M. W., 38

*Twelve, The,* 147

*Ulysses,* 27, 73, 96, 103, 126, 127, 137, 141, 151, 223

*Unhurried View of Erotica, An,* 3

Updike, John, 96, 157, 201, 211, 212, 216

*Upstate,* 209

*V.,* 170

Veen, Aqua (character), 177

Veen, Van (character), 155

Vengerov, Zinaïda, 152

Verlaine, Paul, 87, 88

Verne, Jules, 88

Vidal, Gore, 201, 207

Voltaire, 56

*Waltz Invention, The,* 133

*War and Peace,* 158

*War of the Worlds, The,* 177

Waugh, Evelyn, 219

*We,* 122

*Webster's Dictionary*, 43, 105, 132, 173, 212

Weidenfeld & Nicolson, 56

Wells, H. G., 87, 152, 177, 216, 223

White, Edmund, 211

White, Katharine, 149

*White Thighs*, 215

Wilcox, Ella Wheeler, 104

Wilde, Oscar, 56, 82

Williams, Oscar, 170

Wilson, Edmund, 6, 31, 103, 106, 108, 117, 148–49, 157, 164, 168, 170, 201, 209, 211, 216

Wittgenstein, Ludwig, 126

Wodehouse, P. G., 59

Wolfe, Thomas, 57, 216

Zabolotski, Nikolay, 139

Zamyatin, Yevgeny, 122

Zhukovsky, Vasily, 78

Zola, Émile, 104

Zoshchenko, Mikhail, 139

www.ingramcontent.com/pod-product-compliance
Lightning Source LLC
Chambersburg PA
CBHW020652030726
47498CB00002B/476